THE COLLECTED WORKS OF
LORNA MOON

EDITED AND INTRODUCED BY
GLENDA NORQUAY

FOREWORD BY
RICHARD DE MILLE

BLACK & WHITE PUBLISHING

Doorways in Drumorty first published in the UK by Jonathan Cape 1926
Dark Star first published in the UK by Victor Gollancz Ltd 1929
'Broken' first published in Woman's Home Companion, 51, July 1924
All other poems except 'Bereft' first published in Richard de Mille's
My Secret Mother: Lorna Moon, Farrar Straus and Giroux, New York, 1998

This edition first published 2002
by Black & White Publishing Ltd,
Edinburgh
ISBN 1 902927 36 2

Foreword © Richard de Mille 2002
Introduction and notes © Glenda Norquay 2002

British Library Cataloguing Publication Data:
a CIP record for this book is available
from the British Library.

Photograph of Lorna Moon reproduced courtesy
of Richard de Mille

Cover design by Tim Byrne

The Publisher acknowledges subsidy from the Scottish Arts Council
towards the publication of this volume

Printed and bound by Bell & Bain Ltd, Glasgow

CONTENTS

ACKNOWLEDGEMENTS

This book would not have been possible without the support of Richard de Mille, who has done much to research his mother's life and who gave me access to a wide range of material. In addition to such material help, his enthusiasm, encouragement, and humour (a dry wit of which his mother would have been proud) made working on this project a pleasure. Sheila McLean of Strichen Library was extremely generous with her time and information, and Lynne Higham of Aberdeen Central Libraries also responded to my queries. Other helpful correspondences were with G.D. McLeman of Glasgow, and James S. Marshall, Fraserburgh. Richard de Mille and Aileen Christianson offered helpful comments on draft material, and Professor Isobel Murray and Marjorie Palmer McCulloch encouraged me with their own enthusiasms for Moon's work. I am also grateful to Siobhan Edwards, Susan Spalding and Campbell Brown at Black & White Publishing. Roger Webster and Jessie and Bob Norquay provided practical support of various kinds during the research process. The Institute for Advanced Studies in the Humanities, University of Edinburgh, provided a pleasant and stimulating research environment for the later stages of this project: my Research Fellowship there was supported by funding from the Carnegie Trust for the Universities of Scotland. I am also grateful to colleagues at Liverpool John Moores University for sabbatical support. I first came across the work of Lorna Moon in the editions published by David Toulmin: here as elsewhere he was an important force in publicising the work of writers from the north-east of Scotland.

G.N.

FOREWORD

RICHARD DE MILLE

While fleeing across Saskatchewan with a love-smitten young fellow named Moon, Mrs William Hebditch, lately a farmer's wife, became Lorna Moon, writer. There were three reasons. First, she did not want to be traced by the husband she was deserting. Second, custom required her to travel as a married woman. Third, and most telling, the heroine of her childhood had been Lorna Doone.

Born in 1886 in a lowland village in the north-east corner of north-east Scotland, Helen Nora Wilson Low went to school and came of age among 800 villagers and 1500 crofters. The land was poor, the work was hard and some days there was only gruel to eat. But there were treasured volumes filled with stories of adventure, vengeance, sacrifice and love, and she read them all.

Nora took an early chance to escape the village. She never saw her home again after she was 24, but Mormond braes and Buchan ways were ever in her heart. To the discomfort of some who had known her as a child, and the delight of others, a mysterious Scottish writer living far away in Hollywood, California, began to publish fiction in which her former neighbours found their own private habits, base deeds, noble acts and farcical pretences sharply drawn for all to see. Their surprise is our good fortune. Typical village days and nights unfold here as they were witnessed by a keen observer over a hundred years ago.

Lorna's colourful exploits and her bitter suffering in North America are not the subject of the present volume, but one event should be mentioned. In her reckless passionate way and against doctor's advice she bravely bore a secret son, who would over many years search out the hidden life of his long lost mother and write her biography. *My Secret Mother: Lorna Moon* rescued her from obscurity and now results in this collection of her best work, with a critical introduction by a scholar of Scottish fiction. Here are vivid portraits of the way things were in and around Strichen Parish, Aberdeenshire, in the nineteenth century. Here are gems of character, culture, and tradition found in kitchens and in kirks, in the fields and on the roads, at the travellers' hotel or in the tailor's shop, as residents and transients, honoured or despised, cherished or betrayed, knowing joy or sorrow, triumph or defeat. The authentic memories of a native daughter and natural storyteller take us to an otherwise irrecoverable time.

INTRODUCTION

GLENDA NORQUAY

Strichen, the birth place of Helen Nora Wilson Low, is a striking example of a planned Buchan village. Even today its streets run in symmetrical lines and neat intersections; the High Street is dominated by the tower and spire of the Parish Church, and the centre of the village is overlooked by the clock tower and spire of the Town Hall. In its layout, architecture and dull brown stone, it speaks of regulation, order and surveillance. And yet, on Mormond Hill above Strichen the outline of a huge white horse is laid out in stone. A few miles away on the coast of Aberdeenshire, the village of Pennan, which Nora would visit as a child, perches precariously around and under high cliffs that fall dramatically towards the sea. This contrast between romantic hill, extreme landscape and the tidy streets of Strichen stands as a metaphor of the oppositions shaping the life and the writing of the extraordinary 'Lorna Moon' – Nora Low's other self. Her life story – escape from Scotland, a series of romantic adventures, and a career as a script writer in the early days of Hollywood – presents the wildest challenge to our expectations for a woman in rural Scotland in the early twentieth century. Her writing, in equally dramatic manner, takes the conventional subject of Scottish small-town life and refashions it through a combination of satirical analysis and melodramatic romance that no other writer from the north-east has achieved.

Lorna Moon's fiction has, however, remained outside the mainstream of Scottish literature for a considerable time. The advocacy of David Toulmin, with his passionate support of north-east writing, and the republication of her collection of short stories, *Doorways in Drumorty*, and her novel, *Dark Star*, in the early 1980s by Gourdas House, together brought some local attention.[1] Since then growing interest in neglected Scottish women writers has given her name slightly wider circulation, but her work remains largely unknown, even in Scotland. Yet the story of Nora Low – recently revealed in greater detail through the research of her son and biographer, Richard de Mille, in *My Secret Mother: Lorna Moon* – merits retelling.[2] Equally, her writing deserves to find a wider audience.

This volume is a new edition of Moon's work, bringing together her novel, the short stories and a small selection of her poetry and letters, to offer a fresh perspective on this unusual woman: a woman who travelled a long distance from Scotland and yet, imaginatively, took Scotland with her and refashioned the experiences of her early years.

BIOGRAPHY

It is perhaps unsurprising that the facts of 'Lorna Moon's' life have been difficult to trace: not only did she travel extensively across tracts of Canada and America, establishing a complicated personal history as she went, but she was also inclined to invent suitably exotic biographies for herself. In an author's questionnaire completed for her publishers, she lists her father as Chas. Ewen Donald Cameron, Laird of Fassefern, and her mother as Margaret Helen Cameron of Erracht, at the same time taking ten years off her age.[3] For *Moving Picture World* she embellishes her upbringing even more remarkably:

. . . in a home which was built in the fourteenth century. She is 'pure Scotch' and until she was nine years old spoke nothing but Gaelic, learning English at a convent in Laon, France. She achieved considerable success on the Scottish stage.[4]

In fact, Helen Nora Wilson Low was born in Strichen, Aberdeenshire, on 16 June 1886, the second daughter of four daughters and a son. Charles Low, her father, was registered at birth as the illegitimate son of Mary-Ann Low and Charles May, the butler of a family for whom Mary-Ann had worked in Deeside. There was, however, some family speculation that his father may have been a more aristocratic member of the household. Brought up by his grandmother, he took up the family trade of plastering and stone-dressing, although he also worked abroad while Nora was growing up. On his return to Strichen he became landlord of the Temperance Hotel.

Charles Low was an unusual figure in the community, an atheist and socialist, eager for political discussion but also a man described as extremely intelligent, well-read and widely-experienced. His daughter was later to acknowledge the influence of both his ideas and his attitude: 'My Dad and I were "very thick" as the Scotch saying is.'[5] While local anecdote makes much of his supposed rejection of his daughter's success, close family members offer a different version of a man proud of Nora: certainly the dedication in her first book, *Doorways in Drumorty*, reads: 'To My Dad This, His Wee Nottie's First Book'.[6] Nora's mother, Margaret Benzies, a woman noted for her beauty and force of personality ('She'd 'a likit to be upper class'), appears to have gone through periods of considerable hardship in bringing up her family.[7]

With dark red hair, an intense beauty and a passion for reading, Nora Low gained an elementary education at the local Episcopal school. In 1907 William Hebditch, a 29-year-old commercial traveller from Yorkshire, was staying at the Temperance Hotel. He fell in love with Nora and they were married on Christmas Eve in Aberdeen, going to Selby in Yorkshire, where Nora gave birth to a son, Bill; shortly afterwards the family emigrated to Entwistle, in Alberta, Canada.

It is at this point that the details become somewhat blurred: as a result, all kinds of tales have been produced to explain the transformation from Nora Hebditch, née Low, into 'Lorna Moon'. Recent research by her son has, however, established that after a period of backwood pioneering she left Hebditch in 1913 for Walter Moon, another Yorkshireman, moving to Winnipeg then to Minneapolis with him in 1917. As her son wryly comments: 'after years of wishing to grow up as bewitching as the noble Lorna Doone, Nora couldn't refuse Walter's convenient offer of his rhyming name, or the provocative echo, "Lorna Moon".'[8] She worked on a number of newspapers in Winnipeg and had a child with Moon in 1914, but this daughter, Mary, was sent back to England and looked after by Moon's family. Lorna Moon's move to Hollywood is also mysterious but once there she appears to have left Moon and begun writing for Cecil B. DeMille on *The Affairs of Anatol* (1921). Hollywood at the time was an exciting and expanding world, eager to attract talent, and this lively writer with (by now) a range of experiences seems to have found a niche for herself. She worked on a number of screenplays, her greatest success being *Mr Wu* (1927), produced by MGM and starring Lon Chaney, although she wrote for screenwriting teams on a variety of silent films.

While achieving success as a scriptwriter she also became the mistress of Cecil's brother William de Mille (1878–1955), with whom she conceived another son, Richard, the 'foundling' whom Cecil adopted in 1922. Richard de Mille's biography gives some sense of the extraordinary family history which surrounded him. Conceding that there is a problem tracing Lorna's life because 'she told so many false stories', his book offers a remarkable account of the search for his mother.[9]

While pregnant Lorna was also diagnosed as having tuberculosis, apparently contracted when a young girl in Strichen, and she spent a considerable amount of time in a sanatorium, working on her fiction. *Doorways in Drumorty*, based on a number of stories which appeared in magazine form, mostly with *Century Magazine*, was published in America in 1925 (1926 in Britain), and her novel, *Dark Star*, appeared in 1929.

In its obituary the *Los Angeles Evening Herald* acknowledged Moon as one of the three best scenario writers in Hollywood.[10] In the final years of her life, however, tuberculosis made it difficult for her to realise her promise, although letters speak of plans for another novel. Her last film, *Min and Bill*, brought out in 1930, was the product of a plot hatched by her friend and fellow-screenwriter, Frances Marion, as a means of raising money to maintain her health care. Supposedly a comedy version of *Dark Star*, it presents a much-changed, Americanized version of her novel, which she had sold to MGM. With her health the subject of much media interest in America, she died from a fatal haemorrhage in Albuquerque, New Mexico, on 1 May 1930. In typical dramatic fashion her ashes were then brought back to Scotland by a friend, Everett Marcy, and scattered on Mormond Hill.

SHORT STORIES

Although the exotic quality of Moon's Hollywood career presents a striking contrast with her origins in rural Aberdeenshire, her fiction demonstrates the writing talent which won acclaim. Both Moon's collection of short stories and her novel draw on her experiences of growing up in a small and inward-looking community, presenting this world with a vividness and harshness which distinguishes her writing from the static and sentimental fiction known as 'Scottish Kailyard'.[11] Unsurprisingly, this parochial and nostalgic representation of Scottish life, produced by writers such as J. M. Barrie, Ian Maclaren and S. R. Crockett, proved highly popular both at home and with expatriate Scots. Moon's writing, however, although it works within the same kind of location, might be more closely aligned with the innovative work of Lewis Grassic Gibbon in the 1930s.

All the stories in *Doorways in Drumorty* explore similar themes: the particular codes and conventions created by such a closed community; the patterns of surveillance; the strictures of public morality and the evidence of private despair. They also engage with the margins of this world, presenting itinerants, outcasts and misfits with a distinct lack of sentimentality. Lorna Moon's work is also striking in its awareness of the position of women in the community: her stories deal with minutiae, with networks of power that operate in apparently insignificant areas of social and domestic life.

INTRODUCTION

It was, nevertheless, a Kailyard writer whose shadow fell most darkly over her writing in its early days. In a 1926 letter between her American publisher and the British publishers, D. L. Chambers comments that his author feels 'she might as well be buried as Barried' and the reputation and influence of J. M. Barrie does seem to hang over her fiction. Clearly her collection of short stories signals its relationship to what was, after all, a highly successful publishing phenomenon in America. 'Drumorty' inevitably carries echoes of 'Drumtochty', the village central to Ian Maclaren's highly successful recreation of rural community life in his volume *Beside the Bonnie Briar Bush* (1894), while Lorna herself acknowledged that the 'Doorways' of the title (suggested by Hewitt Hanson Howland, who left Bobbs-Merrill to edit *Century Magazine* in August 1925) contained useful resonances of 'A Window in Thrums'. Yet while she may have wished to profit by the generic associations, she certainly didn't want to be seen as producing exactly the same kind of fiction as Kailyard authors: 'I once said that I'd always wanted to write "as WELL as Barrie", and of course "well" became "like". I don't write at all like Barrie. Do I?'[12]

The differences and similarities between the authors are worth consideration. Lorna's publishers passed on to her the comments of the detective novelist Augustus Muir and they must have encouraged her:

> Lorna Moon quarries the same hard granite as Barrie, but her work has more rugged realism. Barrie stands alone when it comes to a touch of charm here and a wistful tear there. Realism, however, is not his forte; and it is here that Lorna Moon scores. She is a realist, and her book is a little storehouse of truth.[13]

Pleasing as the opposition of rugged realism with sentimental charm is, however, Muir's analysis polarises the writers in overly simplistic terms; rather it is in the narrative perspective that real differences emerge. As critics have noted, the Kailyard authors wrote with an increasing sense of the 'otherness' of their subjects – they wrote for those outside Scotland, and as if those inside the country were foreign. In the case of Barrie in particular it has been suggested that his voice became increasingly reductive and ridiculing. Lorna shares some of Barrie's bleak irony, but her stories more often offer a challenge to both community and the reader, thus avoiding the detached perspective of Barrie. A second characteristic of Kailyard fiction has been described as a tendency towards the anecdotal rather than the novelistic. As Roderick Watson comments, it becomes a series of vignettes that 'depend on a single moment of pathos, or comic discomfiture, and the result is static, knowing, patronising'.[14] In her stories Lorna Moon also creates social cameos but imbues them with a dramatic significance and emotion beyond the moment, which activates a wider range of interpretative possibilities and offers a powerful critique of local society, which is neither nostalgic nor patronising.

The differences between Moon and Barrie are evident if their treatment of small-town romance is considered: Barrie's 'The Courting of T'now-head's Bell' clearly differs from Moon's 'Silk Both Sides' and 'The Courtin' of Sally Ann'.[15] In Barrie's tale Bell is sought in marriage by the rivals Sanders and Sam'l, who circle each other, equals in pride, slyness and a canny reluctance to reveal their desires. The duplicity with which Sanders finally beats his rival (his superior both in speed and social standing) is presented by Barrie as evidence of the inadequate emotional economies of their community:

> Few Auld Lichts, as I have said, went the length of choosing a helpmate for themselves. One day a young man's friends would see him mending the washing tub of a maiden's mother. They kept the joke until Saturday night, and then he learned from them what he had been after. It dazed him for a time, but in a year or so he grew accustomed to the idea, and they were married. With a little help he fell in love just like other people.[16]

The rest of the village encourages rivalry between the men through sly comment and innuendo, but they also, like the narrator, watch the situation with a wry detached amusement. The woman in question, Bell, has little part to play, as the opening crudely indicates:

> For two years it had been notorious in the square that Sam'l Dickie was thinking of courting T'nowhead's Bell, and that if little Sanders Elshioner (which is the Thrums pronunciation of Alexander Alexander) went in for her he might prove a formidable rival.[17]

Much of the humour resides in the insignificance of the woman's preference: 'It was impossible to say which of her loves Bell preferred. The proper course in an Auld Licht lassie was to prefer the man who proposed to her.'[18] This lack of agency in the woman is manifested in the narrative by an almost complete absence of access to her thought processes.

The dynamics of this narration, in which the woman remains on the level of object and even those who desire her share a fear of emotional commitment, presents a fascinating contrast with Lorna Moon's version of the courting ritual, as explored in two very different stories. 'Silk Both Sides' is also concerned with apparent female powerlessness. The story opens with Jessie MacLean, aged 36, making the significant gesture of buying a ribbon with silk on both sides – in other words, a bonnet ribbon: to wear a bonnet is a sign both to herself and the community that she has resigned herself to spinsterhood. She has accepted, it would seem, that Jock Sclessor, who has been courting her for 15 years, will never make that equally significant gesture of wearing a white gowan, or daisy, in his buttonhole – the emblem indicating his intention to propose – when he comes to call for their Sunday morning walk to church. The irony of Jock appearing with the flower in his jacket the very day that Jessie emerges wearing her bonnet is bleak enough for Barrie, but the force with which the narrator attacks the communal pressure decreeing that neither gesture can be undone displays a fierce anger at the emotional denial demanded:

> Look your fill from behind the curtain, Mistress MacKenty! You can not see a heartache when it is hidden by a black alpaca gown and when the heart belongs to Jessie MacLean!
> Jock Sclessor, your one chance of happiness is now! Lead her back into the house and take the bonnet from her head! No, laggard and fool that you are, you are wondering if she has noticed the gowan! Has she not! She has watched for it for fifteen years! Speak, you fool! Don't keep staring at her bonnet!'[19]

Much of Nora Low's own sense of frustration at the regulations enforced by a community of watchers is articulated here. Yet the story not only voices a counter-discourse: in its conclusion it offers a more complex recognition that 15 years' delay may, after all, represent unspoken desires in each individual for their own space:

> At home, she brewed her tea, looking round at her rag rugs and white tidies with pleasure. . . . There was a certain contentment in knowing that it would never be; a certain exhilaration in knowing that next Sunday she could not be disappointed because next Sunday she would not hope. She sipped her tea peacefully and smiled at the bonnet sitting so restful-like on the dresser, and at the tidy on the big chair so spotless and smooth, and thought, 'Jock Sclessor would have been a mussy man to have about a house.'[20]

The story not only presents the characters with respect but also allows them an element of control. Apparently petty systems of signification are dissected with acuity but complexities of the characters' emotional lives – circumscribed as they may be – are restored to narrative attention.

A similar process can be seen in 'The Courtin' of Sally Ann', in which misinterpretation and the decoding of signals also feature. The worldly and determined bachelor, nicknamed 'the Gype', is determined to have some flirtatious fun with the sheltered Sally Ann, but misreads her tongue-tied and gentle submission to his charms as fear and innocence:

He had frightened her! Frightened her so that she was powerless to resist him. He had thought her free; had thought her willing for his kisses, and all the time the poor girl had been too mazed to cry out against him.[21]

Although Sally Ann perceives her own behaviour as wanton, her inability to articulate her feelings emerges as a desirable and respectable distancing – 'a lass that would take some reaching for'[22] – which produces an ironic conclusion: the offer of marriage:

Sally Ann could not speak. She was full of shame that she had ever doubted him. He had meant this from the first! He had been courting her for marriage, and she had thought he held her lightly. She had given her kisses while she doubted him. Oh, he must never know. He must never know what a wanton heart was in her breast. . . . she cried, 'How can ye want me for a wife, that none has ever sought before?'

And the Gype replied – for this answer had come to him many times as he wondered at his love for her: 'It takes a man o' taste t' appreciate ye, Sally Ann.'

And she was happy, not seeing that half the compliment was for himself.[23]

Again the narrator acknowledges an emotional complexity and explores a departure from courting conventions. Rather than Barrie's tales in which those emotions that matter most are trivialised because of the mute obduracy or emotional autism of the characters, and the reader remains amused and detached from such shallowness, Moon's stories demand our involvement and understanding.

Equally demanding is Moon's willingness to tackle subjects on the edges of respectability. Writing later than Barrie and other Kailyard authors may have allowed fewer restrictions, and her own experiences in

INTRODUCTION

Hollywood in the 1920s would have exposed her to moral codes very different from those of Strichen, but in a story such as 'Wantin' a Hand' she anticipates, even goes beyond, the use of grotesque realism to be found at times in the writings of Lewis Grassic Gibbon. 'Wantin' a Hand' shocks with the intensity of its opening, but soon switches to an emotional interiority as the rambling of drunken Jean is represented and her history narrated:

> But Jean was long past caring what Drumorty thought about her drinking, long past the time when she turned her head away so that they wouldn't catch her breath. She cared only for evening to come, and she worked through the day with a driving force which became a frenzy of haste as night-fall drew near, for she was going home to the kist under the stairs, home to dreams, home to love and revenge and despair, home to forgetfulness, home to the flat-sided bottle of whisky wrapped in a grey petticoat.[24]

Alongside such realism Moon is also capable of romance, as 'Feckless Maggie Ann', with its tale of a faithful and regretful husband who inadvertently crushed the very qualities he loved in his wife, demonstrates. The emotion involved, however, is not of a sentiment that comforts, but one that pushes us towards distinctions of value. The tale is also significant, as Moon herself noted, for occupying a different location. *Doorways in Drumorty* is, as Moon saw it, a book about 'land folk'; in other words, it operates within the confines of Strichen. 'Feckless Maggie Ann' and, by implication, *Dark Star*, are coastal works, and for Moon the coast is a world peopled by Celts – romantic and irrational: '. . . you see, the fishing people and the land people in Scotland don't mix, they are widely separated in their sympathies, even their blood isn't the same.'[25] Maggie Ann, whom Lorna describes as a 'blood sister', is part of the melodramatic world of the coast to which she was drawn as a means of escaping and challenging the constraints of Strichen.

In a letter of April 1925 Lorna Moon writes that 'The Courtin' of Sally Ann' was 'the last of the truly Drumortish tales of Drumorty'. She continues:

> Then look at 'Wantin' a Hand'; it was written in July after the land began to slide. I have nothing to say against it, except that it is a golf suit made of silver-cloth. The manner doesn't suit the matter. The style is fine, so is the story, but they don't belong to each other. The truth is I am through with Drumorty in that vein.[26]

While her judgement on 'Wantin' a Hand' may seem harsh in its assessment of an incongruity between style and content, Moon is prescient in seeing the story as a sign to move on. If there is a 'problem' with the tale it lies in the melodramatic intensity of the plot with its Hardyesque ironies, too powerful to be contained by the frame of a short story within a collection of 'anecdotes'. It is therefore unsurprising that the novel as a form called to her. And yet the novel she produced, *Dark Star*, while fascinating in itself, is a 'hybrid' piece of writing, not wholly at one in terms of style, genre or direction.

DARK STAR

Relatively well-received in both America and Britain, *Dark Star* again presents an uncompromising picture of rural life, drawing on Strichen but also nearby fishing villages such as Broadsea, Pennan, Rosehearty and Gardenstown. The novel dissects, with an odd mixture of realism and melodrama, the plight of Nancy, illegitimate and an outsider in her narrow world. Delineating her attempts to escape through romance, the text explores the precarious social structures, the sexual instabilities and the surface hypocrisies that shape its confines.

Overall the novel is a curious piece of writing: it begins with a brave and uncompromising first sentence – 'Nancy was glad when her grandmother died.'[27] – and in its first chapters paints an even harsher picture of the surface respectability and mean-minded codes by which small-town life is governed than *Doorways in Drumorty*. Tracing the adolescence of Nancy, it also offers a powerful analysis of developing female sexuality, as she deals with unwelcome and clumsy sexual overtures but also tries to understand the nature of her own aspirations and desires. Within this line of plot Nancy's search for the identity of her parents and her encounters with those on the edges of society serve as a convincing narrative quest for self. Her friendship with the 'Whistling Boy' – visitor from another class, another world – and her subsequent adult relationship with him, is less convincing, drawing as it does upon a mixture of conventional romance motifs – in which the small-town, lower-class girl realises fulfilment through an alien, upper-class and cultured masculinity – and concluding in the style of tragic melodrama.

It might be argued that it is the resultant hybridity, that uneasy mixing of forms, which has led to the critical neglect of *Dark Star*. For those expecting anecdotes in Kailyard style, it is strong meat: but for those seeking the psychological depths of the *bildungsroman*, it often seems too closely aligned to the parochial. Its proximity to romantic fiction, especially in the excesses of the later scenes, also sets it apart from more 'serious' twentieth-century women's writing, although it addresses questions of identity and issues of desire. Far from Scotland, forging a career on her own terms, Lorna Moon appears to have had a much less agonised sense of her own sexuality and a more developed awareness of the possibilities for its exploitation and control than most women of her time: 'It is revolting to me that in a civilized world a woman's virtue rests entirely upon her hymen. Excuse me I always get worked up over this.'[28] Although the novel offers a sharp representation of the sexual harassment to which a vulnerable girl in Nancy's dependent position might be subject, it also presents a striking image of the pain and pleasure of sexuality in the scene in which Nancy blows the bellows on the organ for the Whistling Boy until her hands bleed. In her correspondence Moon describes *Dark Star* as a 'sincere effort to show what the men in a woman's life bring to her, and take from her . . . It's the inside of a woman written from the inside.'[29] Within Scottish fiction, however, there is little precedent for having such issues addressed through romantic involvement with exotic musicians, illegitimate children who believe they possess aristocratic blood, and dark suicides off high cliffs. It therefore has an uneasy relationship not only to Kailyard fiction, but also to the realist novel and what might be termed the 'feminist novel of self-development'.

Indeed it is that 'coastal' quality of the novel which sets it apart from the short stories. In moving away from the architectural solidity of 'doorways' to the abstract dramatisation of *Dark Star*, it is no surprise that Moon peoples her novel with those who live on the edge, represented both by the novel's central character Nancy – with her aspirations for escape and emotional extremes – and by those on the margins of society – the tinkers, travellers, beggars and fairground folk who people the book. The novel uses those on the peripheries of the social – those associated with carnival and the itinerant life – to represent a dangerous sexuality and to contextualise Nancy's own sexual awakening: not only might her father be Willie Weams, the man who walks the stallion around the fairs, but her mother ran off with a medicine man. Sexuality is inevitably associated with outsiders, but it is also this world that offers the most life: dangerous, anarchic, vivacious, and most memorably represented in the novel by Divot Meg, the formidable woman who runs the local 'doss-house', and who presents a colourful alternative to the constraints of the community. Her's is indeed, a house of wonders:

> The yearly fair brought many strange guests. The man with the electric shock machine would come and bring his wife, who was fairly riddled with electricity, they said, and could stick her tongue on a forty-volt

current with the same ease that a kitten puts its tongue in milk. . . .

Even Ramos, the 'world-famous pin-cushion king,' had come to spend a night once when business was bad.

You could stick a pin in any part of him and never draw a drop of blood. . . . Divot Meg had a life-sized poster of him with pins sticking out of every muscle like spines on a porcupine.'[30]

As most critics agree, it is in its delineation of the clash between community and carnival that the novel is at its most successful. Later scenes in which the adult Nancy and Whistling Boy discuss art and creativity are generally felt to be less satisfactory.[31]

From her letters it emerges that the author originally wanted to bring Nancy to Hollywood, but 'She wouldn't budge.' Nor could she be sent to Paris or Vienna – 'Once more she turned into a wooden doll.'[32] This offers perhaps the most convincing explanation for the unevenness of the book: the scenes in which the hypocrisies of Strichen are portrayed are uncomfortably convincing, but the writer struggles to find an alternative to them which can be sustained throughout the novel. While the carnival space and the world of outsiders creates a powerful imaginative domain for the reader, it is not one which Strichen itself would view as escape for Nancy; rather it would be a predictable fall. In attacking Strichen values, Moon can also see and judge with Strichen eyes: she therefore has to find a means of escape for Nancy which contains an element of grandeur, which allows her to transcend the petty and mundane. Her hesitation in creating a narrative in which Nancy could follow Nora Low's own path suggests that Moon is still trapped in a double vision: one which has forced her out of Strichen but has also carried Strichen within her. She is left, therefore, with the unsatisfactory development of the Whistling Boy into an international artist, the unlikely conversations which follow, and Nancy's tragic end.

Further manifestations of the inconsistencies which are the product of her own unusual life are also evident in the attempts Lorna made to control the marketing of *Dark Star*. Melodramatic as the novel is, she didn't want it publicised on the grounds that its author was struggling with death – although she suffered a number of haemorrhages during its writing.[33] She also made a strong case for it to be marketed as a modern book with a message that transcends Scotland: she had deliberately avoided dialect in the texts, and opposed distinctively Scottish packaging: 'So, no plaid jackets please. No thistles, no heather, no Barrie blah.'[34] Considerable resistance was also expressed to the critical framing of her book within a Scottish tradition: 'I don't like the part which says she "belongs to the Scottish heroines of literature", and that Scott, Stevenson and Barrie would have understood her – because they *wouldn't*. (Thank God!).'[35] Yet she is forced to acknowledge that it is the very specific opposition between Nancy's aspirations and her environment which give the tale its dynamic. And in its fascination with moral and social outsiders, those Jessie Kesson, a later novelist from the north-east would describe as 'ootlins',[36] it is very much within a tradition of Scottish literature, manifest in the ballads, in Scott (most famously in the figures of Madge Wildfire, and Meg Merrilies), in Stevenson and, subsequent to Moon's death, in the work of Lewis Grassic Gibbon and Jessie Kesson. In her techniques too Moon herself remained determinedly an 'ootlin'. Her father told her 'Never learn rules, my lass. They're for dumbheads.'[37]

In its mixing of genres *Dark Star* breaks many rules, shifting from romance to tragedy, from comedy to social satire; as such it cannot be truthfully described as consistently successful. Nevertheless, it remains a revealing negotiation of the pressures involved in taking on the psyche of a small-town community, challenging it and moving away from it.

LETTERS AND POETRY

This volume also includes a small selection of Lorna Moon's letters and poetry. The letters, mostly to her publishers, are now either held in the Lilly Library, Indiana University, or owned by her son. Those selected indicate the ways in which Lorna viewed her own writing – not only presenting the seriousness with which she worked at fiction but also the acuity of her own perception of its value and the nature of critical responses to it. They serve to give a strong sense of the personality of the writer: her wit, bravado and willingness to challenge conventions. A small number of Lorna Moon's poems are also included, again indicative of her abilities as a writer. The poems appear highly personal but also reasonably proficient. In particular, in an unpublished and possibly unfinished poem, 'Bereft'[38] there is an uncanny anticipation of W. H. Auden's plea for 'clocks to be stopped' – or at least for time to stand still for the mourning lover.[39] Only 'Broken' was ever published, in the magazine *The Woman's Home Companion*, but the poetry displays the energy and emotional intensity characteristic of her fiction.

In this volume, therefore, a wide range of Lorna Moon's work is once again made available for public enjoyment and critical assessment. What the latter will be remains to be seen. The fascination of the story of Nora Low and Lorna Moon, however, and its reconfiguration in her uneven but powerful work is clearly evident in the material. If Strichen and Pennan, land and coast, Scotland and Hollywood, realism and melodrama remain unreconciled, the dynamic dialogue between them in itself contributes to our understanding of a particular conjunction of small-town life, constructions of femininity, and the desire to be different in early twentieth-century Scotland.

TEXTUAL EMENDATIONS

Some slight errors of punctuation, from the first editions and reprinted in subsequent ones, have been corrected. Attempts to moderate language, which Lorna herself excoriated, have also been restored to the original.

Lorna's letters to her publisher, especially to David Laurance Chambers, are informal in style and often inconsistent in spelling and in references to her own fiction. In order to maintain the sense of her rather breathless style, and the humour and intimacy of her exchanges with Chambers, the letters are presented as they were written. Minor changes have been made to punctuation only when crucial to the meaning of a sentence.

---

1. *Doorways in Drumorty*, with an Introduction by David Toulmin (Gourdas House Publishers, Aberdeen, 1981). First published by Bobbs-Merrill Co., Indianapolis, 1925 and Jonathan Cape, London, 1926. *Dark Star*, with an Introduction by David Toulmin (Gourdas House Publishers, Aberdeen, 1980); Bobbs-Merrill Co., Indianapolis, 1929, and Victor Gollancz, London, 1929.
2. Richard de Mille, *My Secret Mother: Lorna Moon* (Farrar, Straus and Giroux, New York, 1998).
3. A Bobbs-Merrill publicity questionnaire was sent to Lorna Moon in December 1928. She complains to Laurance Chambers that: 'your questionnaire has me wilted. I am really the press agent's curse because I am full of good news stories but none of them can be used.' (Letter of 24 December 1928.) In her response however she states:
   DATE OF BIRTH: ahem! 1896 [for 1886]
   NOTABLE ANCESTORS OR MEMBERS OF FAMILY: Adam
   FATHER: Chas. Ewen Donald Cameron, Laird of Fassefern
   MOTHER: Margaret Helen Cameron of Erracht.
4. *Moving Picture World*, 27 August 1921, p. 906. I am grateful to Richard de Mille for drawing this to my attention.
5. Letter to Anne Johnston of Bobbs-Merrill, February 1929, *see* p.267.
6. His granddaughter Evelyn and eldest daughter Annie are both quoted as disputing this account and claim that he was proud of her writing (*My Secret Mother*, p. 124).

INTRODUCTION

7. William Center, quoted in *Aberdeen Leopard Magazine,* February 1981, p. 15.
8. *My Secret Mother,* p. 122.
9. Ibid., p. 259.
10. *Los Angeles Evening Herald,* 2 May 1930.
11. This phrase refers to the work of a group of novelists in the late nineteenth century whose fiction portrayed Scottish life in predominantly rural terms, focusing on their own 'cabbage patch' – that is, backyard – to show the workings of cosy, close and enclosed communities.
12. Letter to Hewitt Hanson Howland, 9 May 1925, *see* p. 257.
13. Reported in a letter of 23 November 1925 from Laurance Chambers to Lorna Moon.
14. Roderick Watson, *The Literature of Scotland* (Macmillan, London, 1984), p. 316.
15. J. M. Barrie, *Auld Licht Idylls* (1888) (Hodder & Stoughton, London, 1895).
16. Ibid., p. 155.
17. Ibid., p. 145.
18. Ibid., p. 159.
19. *Doorways in Drumorty,* p. 11.
20. Ibid., p. 12.
21. Ibid., p. 51.
22. Ibid., p. 55.
23. Ibid., p. 58.
24. Ibid., p. 23.
25. Letter to Hewitt Hanson Howland, 9 May 1925, *see* p. 256.
26. Letter to Hewitt Hanson Howland, 30 April 1925, *see* p. 254.
27. *Dark Star,* p. 79.
28. Letter to David Laurance Chambers, 5/6 January 1929, *see* p. 266.
29. Letter to Hewitt Hanson Howland, 30 April 1925, *see* p. 255.
30. *Dark Star,* p. 130.
31. 'The young musician has his tiresome moments', V. S. Pritchett, *Spectator,* 3 August 1929, pp. 166–7; 'Nancy Pringle as an adult is terribly tiresome', *Times Literary Supplement,* 11 July 1929, p. 560; 'The book loses its grip when the heroine becomes adult and "arty"' St John Ervine, *Daily Express,* 11 July 1929.
32. Letter to David Laurance Chambers, 24 December 1928.
33. Letter to David Laurance Chambers, 2 May 1929, see pp. 269–70.
34. Letter to David Laurance Chambers, 20 August 1928, *see* p. 258; *see also* letters to him of 30 August 1928 and 5/6 January 1929.
35. Letter to David Laurance Chambers, 5/6 January 1929, *see* p. 265.
36. See 'The Sma' Perfect: Interview with Jessie Kesson', in *Scottish Writers Talking,* ed. Isobel Murray (Tuckwell Press, East Linton, 1995), pp. 55–84.
37. Quoted by Lorna in a letter to David Laurance Chambers, 22 March 1929.
38. *See* p. 252.
39. 'Stop all the clocks, cut off the telephone,/ Prevent the dog from barking with a juicy bone,/ Silence the piano and with muffled drum/Bring out the coffin, let the mourners come.' W. H. Auden, 'Twelve Songs, IX' *Collected Shorter Poems 1927 – 1957* (Faber and Faber, London, 1966), p. 92.

DOORWAYS IN DRUMORTY

TO MY DAD
THIS, HIS WEE NOTTIE'S FIRST BOOK

THE CORP'

By shutting the door to within three inches of the jamb, and moving her chair nearer the cat's hassock by the fire, old Kirsty could see Mistress MacNab's door and watch the mourners come and go.

She had been sitting there for three days, secretly watching, her dismay growing with every hour as she realised that it was possible that Mistress MacNab could carry her rage about the butter prize to the extent of not bidding her to see the corpse.

When Mistress MacKenty brought the startling news on Sunday evening that "Sandy MacNab had choked on a cold potato and hiccoughed himself to death," Kirsty had had a momentary qualm of doubt. She wished she hadn't openly scoffed at Mistress MacNab's butter and flaunted her own first prize on the way back from the show. It was "an unwise-like thing to do with death so sure and life so uncertain; but who would expect a braw man like Sandy MacNab to choke to death on a potato?"

"And besides," she reflected, "Mistress MacNab, be she as angry as she may, would never bury Sandy without all the honour that was due to him." And who in all Drumorty would think of being buried without Kirsty Fraser to cry as the lid was screwed down? Had she no' cried at every funeral for forty-five years? And was it no' part and parcel of the ceremony for her to have a fit when the body was carried out? And was it no' true that the laddies of the village hung round the house of sorrow waiting for the chance to run for the doctor to bring her round?

She recalled the first time. What a day that had been! Never would she forget looking in to the coffin of Maggie Sclessor and seeing her lying there so satisfied-like with the best-looking mutch[1] in Drumorty on her head. Never would she forget the rage that had filled her at the sight. For who would have expected Maggie Sclessor, poor as she was, to have a hand-made lace mutch laid away to be buried in and never to say a word about it? She had cried with envy, but the neighbours thought it was with grief, and they had turned their attention from Maggie and her braw mutch to Kirsty as her sobs grew louder; and when the doctor averred that Kirsty had been "on the very verge o' a fit," they screwed the lid down on Maggie without further to-do.

3

And as they carried the body out, Kirsty reflected with satisfaction, "Weel, she had a fine mutch, but wha will think o' that noo?"

And then, with each succeeding funeral, she had added to her laurels; having once tasted the joy of stealing the attention from the corpse, she could not forego the excitement and the commiseration and the secret gratitude of the mourners. Her "fits" grew more and more masterly, until the neighbours argued boastfully:

"I'm tellin' ye, when my man died, she had the worst fit she ever had." And the answer, as positive, would be:

"Mistress MacPherson, hae I no' got the use o' my sight, praise be to God? Did I no' see her eyes roll up to heaven and her legs stiffen when my Jeannie was carried oot?"

Certainly, Mistress MacNab would never think of burying her man without Kirsty's being there, butter prize or no butter prize. Thus reassured, Kirsty had resolved to outdo all her past efforts at the funeral of Sandy MacNab. Always in the back of her head she had had a notion that by biting the sides of her cheeks till they bled, and frothing the blood upon her lips, she could give a more convincing and gruesome fit than any she had ever given. She had saved this for some great day. And this was the day. The world would see that Kirsty Fraser scorned to bear a grudge in the face of death. She would treat Mistress MacNab better than if she had been a friend.

On Monday morning she felt so kindly toward Mistress MacNab that she was minded to step over and say a word of comfort to her. She even thought of offering to do the "biddin'," although she knew full that her legs would never stand it.

But Mistress MacKenty came in to say that Maggie Tate was to do the "biddin'," and that the funeral was on Wednesday, adding meaningly, "But there's no need to tell ye that; ye'll be the first to be bidden, nae doot."

Her tone made Kirsty uneasy.

At sundown, when Tammas, her son, came wearily in, she watched him wash his face in the tin basin, and as he spluttered and blew the water— he never thought he was clean unless he made a noise about it—she started to ask if he had heard anything, but stopped, mistrusting her voice. It would no' do to let Tammas know that she was anxious. And should it be that some were already bidden, Tammas would know that she had been slighted, being left to the last.

On Tuesday the coffin was brought home. Jimmy Tocher tripped on the step as they carried it in, and it banged against the door. Kirsty could hear Mistress MacNab raking them up-hill and down-dale for their fecklessness, and she wanted to join them and see for herself if they had dented the mountings, but she couldn't make the first advance.

At dusk she saw Maggie Tate on her rounds doing the bidding. She cried in at Jessie MacLean's and then went on to Mistress MacKenty's. "She'll be here inside ten minutes," Kirsty reflected, and rose to put the kettle on, so that she could make her a cup of tea. "It's unco thirsty work, biddin' to funerals."

It was getting too dark to see. The kettle boiled dry, and she pulled it forward on the crane. "Mistress MacKenty is talking her stone-blind. She'll never get here tonight," she decided, but she couldn't give up watching.

Tammas came home. He had heard something, and was uneasy in his mind. Kirsty could tell, because he was whistling *The Lass o' Ballochmyle* between his teeth, which was a sign. And forby that, he said the *long* grace before supper, and he said it slowly, as she always had begged him to. He was trying to be kind to her; he even blew the smoke from his pipe up the chimney instead of out across the room. It was unnatural-like, and Kirsty knew that his behaviour meant that he was sure that she would not be bidden to see the corpse. She resented his giving up hope before she did. He had never valued her fits. On occasions he had even advised her to bide away if funerals made her take on so. He was like his father, that he was. He was reliable-like, but he was dull. All the Frasers were dull. Why could he no' speak up and say, "Ye'll no' be bidden to see the corp', and I'm glad o' 't," if that was what he was thinking? She'd give him just a minute more; then she'd ask him outright.

"Mither." She looked at him as he spoke. To avoid her eyes, he bent down and used the heel of his boot to press the tobacco into the bowl of his pipe.

"Weel?" she prompted, and there was an edge on her voice.

"I'm thinkin' o' drivin' up to Skilly's the morn ti borrow their rake. Would ye like to go wi' me?"

So he believed she wouldn't be bidden, and he was trying to save her face. He little knew. *He* had never set store by her fits, but others had. Mistress MacNab might wait till the last to bid her, as was natural; she'd do the same herself, but bid her she would, as Kirsty knew well. So she answered tartly:

"I'm thinkin' yer losing the wee bit o' sense ye were born wi, Tammas. The morn's Sandy MacNab's funeral."

Tammas reddened guiltily.

"Oh, aye," he murmured. "I had forgotten, mither."

And now this was the day of the funeral. Through the small space between the jamb and the door Kirsty could see Mistress MacPherson knocking for admission to the house of sorrow. She had a small parcel in her hand, which she held gingerly upright.

"A jar o' calf's-foot jelly, nae doot," Kirsty informed Tammas as she called his attention to it. "That's the tenth parcel since ten o'clock. Mistress MacNab will no' need ti buy a bite o' food for a fortnight." She said this exultantly. Funerals were Kirsty's art, and she liked them to be successful. "Tammas, keep out from between me an' the door. I can no' see through ye."

Tammas had made another attempt to shut the door in a yearning desire to spare her. Manlike, he could not understand why she tortured herself by looking on. He had seen her put on her black mutch in readiness, and his heart was sick for her. He wondered why she could not give up hope. He paced the floor silently, stopping every now and then to do some kindly, useless thing; and she, knowing what prompted him, would snap at him furiously.

The minister came. Kirsty sat rigidly forward in her chair as he was admitted, and the door closed after him. Tammas stopped pacing. He didn't know what to do with his hands. He tried them in his pockets, and then took them out again, hanging them limply by his sides.

From over the street came the singing. Kirsty picked nervously at the crochet edging on her knitted wristlets. She half turned to look at Tammas, and her voice quavered:

"They're no' to bid me, Tammas." But as Mistress MacNab's door opened and Skilly's lad came running out, Kirsty rose to her feet, eager and joyous. "Aye, they're sendin' for me *noo*." She started toward the door. But the laddie ran past. Tammas helped her back to her chair. Then, for a Fraser, he rose to great heights.

"I'm sorry for them, mither," he said. "It will be a feckless[2]-like funeral without a fit at it."

She sat up at the thought, grasping at it eagerly.

"Aye, will it no', Tammas? Will it no'?" she cried gratefully.

Then, turning it over in her mind, she found it sweet with comfort, and she chuckled while the tears were still wet upon her face.

"They'll value my fits more than ever noo, Tammas. Puir Sandy Mac-Nab!"

She nursed the thought joyously. She was sorry that it had happened to Sandy MacNab, for he had been a good man, and deserving of honour; but she was glad that Mistress MacNab must share the humility.

"She's cutting off her nose ti spite her face, puir body! I could feel it in my heart ti pity her, Tammas."

Fully recovered in spirit, she got up lightsomely, and began to unfasten the strings of her mutch.

"We'll shut the door on the rest o' 't, Tammas," she said, and was moving toward it when Mistress MacKenty came breathlessly in. She was burning with news to tell, and greedy to see its effect.

"Mistress MacNab is havin' a fit, an' Skilly's laddie has gone for the doctor," she cried.

"A fit!" Kirsty screamed the words in a hysteria of unbelief. "What would *she* be knowing of a fit, she that has never had one?"

Gloating with the joy of telling it, for she had always envied Kirsty her fits, Mistress MacKenty's voice swelled with gratification as she answered:

"Such a fit as I have never seen. Her eyes are rollin' to heaven, and the blood is frothin' on her lips."

At that Kirsty's knees began to tremble beneath her. She put out a wavering hand and gripped Tammas by the sleeve, striving to keep upright and face Mistress MacKenty, who continued maliciously:

"Drumorty will never forget this fit. I'll mind on 't mysel' if I ever hae a corp.'"

And Kirsty Fraser knew that her glory was gone. Another had stolen the chief jewel of her crown. There would be none in all Drumorty who would do her homage again.

But not before Mistress MacKenty would she bow her head. She took her hand from Tammas's sleeve and stood alone, and nothing in her voice as she spoke told Mistress MacKenty that her pride lay stricken.

"Gie her the ammonia bottle to take over, Tammas. I hae had slight fits mysel', an' I ken ammonia's good."

And Mistress MacKenty wondered at this heroic thing that made Kirsty Fraser disclaim the glory of her fits and hand her laurels to another. She stood shamed before it, and she hung her head and crept away, unable longer to look Kirsty Fraser in the face.

Kirsty stood still till she had gone; then her hand went feeling blindly for her chair. She cupped one hand helplessly in the other as she sat. The string of her black mutch hung down like a weary pendulum that had wagged its hour. As Tammas knelt by her, dumbly anxious to comfort, she whispered:

"Think ye she knows I care, Tammas?"

"Niver, mither. I would no' have known it mysel'."

Assured of that, she let the tears steal down her wrinkled cheeks. Her hands trembled together helplessly in her lap. Tammas reached out and held them firmly in his, and they sat there silently together.

Her thoughts went seeking comfort everywhere, but found none. With every funeral her pride would die a little more; with every funeral Mistress MacNab would reap a greater triumph. None would think of Kirsty's fits except to say how poor they were, and how great were the fits of Mistress MacNab. And so until the end.

"O Tammas," she cried, "when I am dead and lying helpless, ye'll no' let that Mistress MacNab have fits at my funeral! Promise me that, Tammas!"

---

1 A close-frilled cap.
2 Without strength, worthless.

SILK BOTH SIDES

"And two and a half yards o' four-inch black satin ribbon."

Jessie MacLean added this last fatal item with an upward jerk of her head lest Mistress MacKenty, at the other side of the counter, should think she was ashamed of her purchase. But Mistress MacKenty had a nose for news rather than an instinct for tragedy, and by the suppressed eagerness in her voice as she asked, "And ye'll want it silk on both sides I'll warrant?" you could see that she was already half-way down the road to the smithy to spread the news that: "Jessie MacLean had lost heart and would be out in a bonnet in the morn, so help her Davey."

"Aye, silk both sides," Jessie answered, letting her eyes range the shelves carelessly to prove that there was nothing momentous in her buying bonnet strings.

Silk both sides proved it! A satin-faced ribbon might have many uses, but silk both sides was a bonnet string by all the laws of millinery known to Drumorty.

Telling about it five minutes later, Mistress MacKenty said, "I might hae been wrang when she bought the silk geraniums, and I may hae been over-hasty when she said 'half a yard o' black lace'—but silk both sides is as good as swearing it on the Bible."

In Drumorty, a bonnet with strings tied below the chin means that youth is over. About the time the second baby is born, the good wife abandons her hat—forever—and appears in a bonnet with ties. She may be any age from eighteen to twenty-five; for matrimony, and motherhood, and age, come early in Drumorty. The spinster clings longer to her hat, for while she wears it, any bachelor may take heart and "speer"[1] her; and if she be "keeping company" she may cling to her hat until she be thirty "and a bittock"; but after that—if she would hold the respect of her community, she must cease to "gallivant" about "wi' a hat" and dress like a decent woman, in a bonnet with ties.

And Jessie MacLean was six and thirty as Baldie Tocher could tell you, for did he no' have the pleasure of burying the exciseman the very morning that Jessie first saw the light of day, and was it no' the very next year that Nancy MacFarland's cow got mired in the moss?

Drumorty had been very lenient with her. Many a good wife thought it was high time that Jessie laid aside her hat, but always she held her peace, remembering her bridal gown and the care with which Jessie had made it, for Jessie was the village seamstress, and it was a secret, whispered, that she charged only half price for making wedding gowns, because she liked to make them so much.

Another reason for their lenience was Jock Sclessor. For fifteen years Jock had "kept company" with her; not one Sunday morning had he missed "crying by" for Jessie to go to morning service. He would come round the bend of the road from Skilly's farm just as the sexton gave the bell that first introductory ring which meant "bide a wee till I get her goin' full swing and then bide at hame frae the kirk if ye dare"; and Jessie would come out of her door and mince down the sanded walk between the rows of boxwood to the gate, and affect surprise at seeing Jock just as if she had not been watching for him behind her window curtain this past five minutes.

Jock was the cotter[2] on Skilly's farm. Every year he intended to "speer" Jessie when thrashing was over. Tammas, his dog, will tell you how many times he had been on the very point of asking her the very next day, but— always the question of adding another room came up and not for the life of him could he decide whether to level the rowan tree and build it on the east—or to move the peats and build it on the west; and by the time he had made up his mind to cart the peats down behind the byre and build it on the west, lambing was round again and he let it go by for another year.

And every year Jessie was in a flutter as thrashing was nearing the finish. One year she had been so sure that he would "speer" her that she bought a new scraper; for Jock could make your very heart stand still, he was that careless about scraping the mud off his boots. Often when she was alone, she would practise ways of telling Jock that he must clean his boots before he came in: "Good man, hae ye forgotten the scraper?" was abandoned because it wasn't strictly honest, for Jessie knew full well that he always forgot the scraper. "Gang back and clean your feet," was set aside also, because it was too commanding and "Dinna forget the scraper" was also discarded because it isn't good to nag a man before he has set foot in the door. But none of the expressions had been tried out yet—for when Jock dropped in with her, after service, Jessie hurried him by the scraper as if it might shout at him, "She expects you to speer her!" and so put her to shame.

But now thrashing had been over for weeks, and every Sunday since then, she had looked for the white gowan[3] in Jock's coat, for what swain "worth his ears full of cold water" ever asked the question without that emblem of courage in his button-hole? It is a signal to the world that he means to propose, that he is going in cold blood to do it—and forever after his good wife can remind him of that, should he suggest that he was inveigled into it by some female wile.

Last Sunday, on their way to church, Jessie cleared her throat nervously and grasped her new testament, bracing herself as she asked in a thin voice that was much too offhand: "Would your peats no' be better sheltered in the lea o' the byre?" and Jock replied: "Na, they are better where they are."

And so a hope, nourished fifteen years, died, and through the service she sat gazing straight ahead, with her eyes wide open, for the wider eyes are open, the more tears they can hold without spilling over. And next Saturday she bought black satin ribbon "silk both sides" and the world, meaning Drumorty, knew that Jessie's tombstone would not read "Beloved wife of—"

In Jessie's cottage the blinds were drawn on Saturday evening, and you who have suffered will not ask me to pull them aside and show you how a faded spinster looks when she weeps; nor how her fingers tremble when she sews upon bonnet strings; but let me tell you how bravely she stepped out next morning wearing her bonnet, with never a look through the curtain to see if Jock was on his way, nor a glance to see if the neighbours were watching. Her step was just as firm upon the sanded path, and her head just as high; perhaps she grasped her testament more tightly than usual, but what soul on the rack would not do that?

Jock came round the bend as she reached the gate. She clung to the latch to keep herself from tearing the bonnet from her head. Oh, Fate, that sits high and laughs, have you the heart to laugh now? Jock was wearing a white gowan. It was just a dozen steps or so back to the house, and a hat, and happiness; but the world knew that she had bought bonnet strings and was that not Mistress MacKenty watching from behind her curtain? Go forward, Jessie—there is no turning back, and go proudly! Open the latch and answer his "guid morning" and smile—and don't, don't, let your hands tremble so, or he will surely guess!

Look your fill from behind the curtain, Mistress MacKenty! You can not see a heartache when it is hidden by a black alpaca gown and when the heart belongs to Jessie MacLean!

Jock Sclessor, your one chance of happiness is now! Lead her back into the house and take the bonnet from her head! No, laggard and fool that you are, you are wondering if she has noticed the gowan! Has she not! She has watched for it for fifteen years! Speak, you fool! Don't keep staring at her bonnet! You dullard, Jessie must come to your rescue, and she does, "Is the sexton no' late this morning?" Jessie turned out of the gate as she spoke, snapping the latch with the right amount of care.

11

"Aye, later than usual," Jock agreed. (The sexton was never late in his life, and at that moment the bell rang out to give Jock the lie.) But Jock was so dazed, he would have agreed if she had said, "Let us choke the minister."

As they walked to the church, he meditated, "Evidently she never expected me to speer her, and she's never so much as glimpsed the gowan. I'll slip it out when we kneel in the kirk. But maybe I better sound her out first. It's gey⁴ and lonesome for a man biding by himself."

They were just turning round by the town hall where the rowan trees are red, when he said, "I had been thinkin' o' levellin' my rowan tree." Jessie's heart thumped. Here it came! (That was why he wouldn't move the peats.) But she wouldn't help him a foot of the road—she had waited too long—he must come every step himself.

"Oh, that would be a pity—it's a bonnie tree," she answered.

Not much help here, but he would try again. "I was thinking o' building."

"Building? My certies! What could ye be building so near the house?" this with some malice for all the fifteen long years. But you have gone too far, Jessie; he needs help.

"I—oh—I thought I'd build a shed for peats."

Thud! That was Jessie's heart you heard and that queer thin voice is Jessie's, saying, "I thought—ye were minded to leave the peats the other side o' the house."

"Aye, I am minded to leave them there—but a body canna hae too many peats."

And as they knelt in kirk, he slipped the gowan out—and Jessie did not need to widen her eyes to hold the tears this time. That sorrow was past, she would never weep over it again.

At home, she brewed her tea, looking round at her rag rugs and white tidies with pleasure. The tidy on the big chair was as white and smooth as when she pinned it there in the morning, and there was no mud to be carefully washed off the rug by the door. There was a certain contentment in knowing that it would never be; a certain exhilaration in knowing that next Sunday she could not be disappointed, because next Sunday she would not hope. She sipped her tea peacefully and smiled at the bonnet sitting so restful-like on the dresser, and at the tidy on the big chair so spotless and smooth, and thought, "Jock Sclessor would have been a mussy man to have about a house. I'm thinkin' his mother was over-lenient when she brought him up."

And Jock, at Skilly's, was thinking, "I wouldna had time to build it anyway. Lambing is here—and that is too bonnie a tree to be cut down."

1 Ask, particularly ask in marriage or propose.
2 A person renting a small portion of a farm from the farmer in exchange for his services. The cotter's wife also assists in the farm kitchen and in the fields at harvest time, so a cotter's wife must be strong.
3 A field daisy.
4 Very

THE SINNING OF
JESSIE MACLEAN

Jessie Maclean felt that their romance belonged also to her, for she had seen their first meeting. It was on a Sunday morning after service, and Jessie was returning from her walk along by Skilly's wood. She was wondering as she stepped daintily, rustling her Sunday-best alpaca gown, if the gold chain she wore had marked her neck; and whether the gimlet-eyed Mistress MacKenty had seen it as she sat behind her in kirk. (Well, it wasn't all gold, but, as Jessie protested defensively to herself: "Pure gold's that soft ye have ti mix it.")

On hot Sundays it was always a race between the sermon and the chain; about the time the minister got to the "thirdlies" and "lastlies" Jessie was in a fidget. She could wear the chain a bare hour and a half without it marking if the weather was cool; but this had been a very hot Sunday. Out of the sight of inquisitive eyes she stopped and spread her handkie between the chain and her neck. Then she turned along Skilly's burnside intending to cross it at the stepping-stones; and it was here she came upon them. So flustered was she, that she forgot the dangling handkie, but then she might have worn ram's horns and they would not have noticed it.

Gawky and shy, they were exchanging their first "It's waurm the day" and "What's yer hurry" which in Drumorty may mean: "Who is this gallant youth who stirs my bosom?" or, "Fair maid, eternity were too brief, could I but spend it gazing in your eyes."

Jessie understood, and seeing their embarrassment, blushed in sympathy and tilted her parasol between herself and them. She had meant to cross the burn at the stepping-stones, but, her heart pleasantly aflutter with a sense of being a sharer in a secret, she kept on down the burnside until she was out of sight; and there she sat down and removed her shoes and stockings before hitching her dress to her knees and wading the burn.

Jessie's own romance laid away in the lavender of memory, stirred again at the thought of the two. Walking home she pondered who the lad might be. He was a stranger in Drumorty. The lass was Bella Tocher, the kitchen wench at Skilly's farm; a well-favoured lass, and hard working, rosy and full-bosomed although barely sixteen.

So engrossed was she, that she went all the way home without remembering to remove the telltale handkie from her neck; and never gave it a thought, until, as she was turning in at her own door, Mistress MacKenty leaned over the gate and sweetly malicious, called, so that Jessie would know she had seen: "Ye do weel ti guard agin' blood-poisinin', Jessie lass."

Next Sunday Jessie did an unheard-of thing. She stayed at home from the morning service and watched the road to Skilly's farm to see if the lad would come back. She had fortified herself against disappointment by boiling dumplings in the broth. No matter how keen the edge of disappointment, Jessie had proved that dumplings in the broth could ease it a little.

And after spending all morning at the window watching, with a bandage bound about the neck to advertise to the curious that a sore throat had kept her at home from the kirk, she was just about to turn to the dumplings for solace, when he came by whistling and heading up the road to Skilly's.

"My certies!" she cried, pretending to herself that she was shocked at his ardour. "He's back *again*, doesna gie the lassie time to draw a lanely breath."

Feeling the need of some one to rejoice with her, she gave the cat a dumpling. It sniffed it, and showed its contempt for her frivolity by crossing to the other side of the fireplace and seating itself with its back to her. Jessie, taking this rebuff with unusual spirit, retorted: "You're a persnickety old maid, there's no' a romantic hair on yer head." And to show that she wouldn't be brow-beaten by the cat on this joyful day, she opened the glass-door of the what-not with a loud click; and later, ate her dumplings off the best willow-pattern china.

Through that winter Jessie didn't need the dumplings to fortify her. The lad was attentive enough. She would see the two by the hayricks, or wandering with fingers entwined by the burnside every Sunday evening. But in the spring he stopped coming. And Bella would stand for hours watching the empty road; while Jessie in an anguish of sympathy would watch both the girl and the road from her corner window.

Bella was listless and pale. There was something pathetic in the way she made no pretence of doing anything but watching. This was intolerable to Jessie who wanted the girl to save her pride, so when she would see a neighbour coming, she would whisper fiercely: "Walk along as if ye were looking for gowans, dinna let them see yer looking for the lad," but only the muslin curtains heard Jessie's advice. Bella, dazed with despair, was indifferent to gossip.

Then it was rumoured that, "Bella Tocher's lad had gone to Edinburgh to the soldierin'." And after that Bella watched the road no more.

It was Mistress MacKenty who said: "I'm thinkin' Skilly's will be needin' a new kitchen wench afore Whitsuntide; and there's them that will learn that nae guid ever came o' gallivantin' wi' a strange lad on the Sabbath day." And having delivered this darkly meaning speech she pursed withered lips with vindictive relish and refused to say more, adding only: "I hae lassies o' my ain, it ill becomes me to speak; but mark my words, there'll be an elders' meeting in Drumorty afore many weeks."

Jessie understood now the pale watching face of Bella; and understood, also, the despair that made her watch for him without pretence. "Puir wee lass," she whispered. "Watching for her man, and him awa' to no' come back."

When Mistress MacKenty came in that evening to say, that: "Skilly was sending the shameless limmer packin' the morn's mornin'," Jessie furtively hid something white and small upon which she had been sewing. She stood up while Mistress MacKenty spoke, and no line of her figure, nor any tone of her voice, could be taken to mean that she invited Mistress MacKenty to take a chair.

"It's a sore disgrace to the whole parish, and harder forby on Skilly himsel' and him an elder o' the kirk." Mistress MacKenty's voice was dulcet with sympathy for the poor elder. She was looking around for a seat in which to sink and continue her lamentations, when, in the chill silence of the usually sympathetic Jessie, she sensed something strange. Jessie was clasping and unclasping her hands in front of her thin waist, and her eyes were glinting. Could it be that the gentle Jessie MacLean was fighting to keep her hands from flying in the face of Mistress MacKenty? Mistress MacKenty must have shared that wild thought also, for, catching sight of Jessie, she paused and backed away, suddenly remembering that she had "a pot o' kale on the fire," and was gone without even closing the door as she went.

Jessie closed the door after her and bolted it, and drew down the blinds. The little bit of white sewing came out from its hiding-place. Mistress MacKenty vowed next day that Jessie's light had burned all night but added that she didn't know why, because; "Jessie MacLean is *that* secretive her window-blinds fit all the way round."

All next morning Jessie sat by the window watching Skilly's road, her head propped wearily on her palms, a bright red spot on the wrinkled apple of each cheek. All Drumorty was watching Skilly's road, but *not* with the tender purpose that was in the heart of Jessie MacLean. Drumorty was swollen with righteous wrath. The virtue of Drumorty was outraged; and it was waiting to visit its saintly indignation on the head of "the shameless limmer."[1] Jessie shut up alone knew nothing of this.

At noon she saw Bella coming along the road towards the village street, a bundle with all her belongings slung on her arm. She would proceed in little tumbling runs, then stop and sway, gather strength again and run a little more. Sometimes she would drop the bundle and have to get down laboriously on one knee to pick it up.

Then Jessie saw the thing that stilled her heart for a moment. As Bella turned into the street, the blinds of Mistress MacPherson's cottage snapped down and remained, like eyelids in death. Then, down with swift vindictiveness came the blinds of the next cottage; Bella heard, and looked about her, as blinds on either side of her hurried down to their righteous windowsills. She stopped and tottered feebly, then, as if blows were showering upon her, she flung her arm across her face, and lowered her head and ran.

"Click" went the blind of Mistress MacKenty's window as she passed; this brought Jessie to her feet with blazing eyes. Rushing out, she ran along the street after the fleeing girl, calling: "Bella—Bella Tocher."

Thinking she was being pursued only to be taunted, Bella gathered her strength anew and ran faster. Sobs rose in Jessie's throat as she saw her reel in her efforts to get away; and she called her name again, trying to make her voice both loud and coaxing. As Jessie caught up and touched her arm, the girl stopped and faced her panting, a driven thing, ready to fight if she must.

"Come back to my house, Bella," Jessie urged breathlessly.

"So ye can take yer ease while ye tell me I've disgraced the parish o' Drumorty?—So ye can tell me I am justly punished for my sins?" Bella's voice rose in hysterical gasps, her white face twitched piteously.

"Na, na," urged Jessie, speaking in soothing accents. "Come so I can show ye the wee shirts I've been makin'."

It was the tone of her voice and tear on Jessie's cheeks, not her words, that brought the answering sob in Bella's throat and softened the defensive lines of her form.

"Come back and stay wi' me." Jessie's tone was tender.

Responding to it, the tears streamed down Bella's face, but she shook her head: "I winna stay an' face the elders. I'll walk till I drop first."

"Ye'll no'—I'll face them for ye. Come awa'," Jessie coaxed, then in a warning whisper: "The blinds are down; but they are peekin' out below them." She put an arm round the girl and, reaching out a hand for the bundle, said tenderly: "Yer nathing but a bairn yersel'—come."

Bella relinquished the bundle to Jessie's urging hand, and, faltering like a tired child, turned back with her along the street of drawn blinds.

2

With what terror, or with what bravery, these two met the turmoil of that night we may not tell. Nor may we echo the brave words that a gentle spinster used, to hearten an erring child in her hour of sore trial. These things are written by the angels, and only mothers may read them.

But we may look in with dawn, and see the puckered pink velvet son of Bella Tocher as he lies on Jessie's lap screaming, for he can not see yet how near is Jessie's lap to the tender heaven of her heart. But we can see, and we are shamed to look unbidden upon the glory of a spinster's face, when mother-love has wakened in her breast.

3

There was defiance in Jessie's gait as she stepped up to the entrance of Mistress MacPherson's byre at milking time that evening. She rattled the two flagons she carried challengingly, and forestalled any comment from Mistress MacPherson about the extra flagon, by saying cheerily: "I'll need a quart extra ilka[2] day now."

Her boldness had the effect of completely winding Mistress MacPherson, who had been waiting all day for milking time so that she could "gie Jessie MacLean a piece o' her mind." "Let her come creepin' up here askin' for milk for that hussy—" Mistress MacPherson had finished the implication with a grim-faced nod, as she discussed the "goin's on" with Mistress MacKenty that morning.

But Jessie hadn't "come creepin'," and Mistress MacPherson, ready to attack, hesitated with that confusion which comes also to a dog, when it has got all ready to chase a cat that refuses to run. Jessie, palpitating with victory, airily handed over the two flagons; and Mistress MacPherson, unable to rally for the moment, took them murmuring only, "Oh, aye."

But if it was a victory for Jessie, it only added to the virtuous indignation Drumorty felt toward Bella. Had Bella been found dying in a ditch that morning, the good women of Drumorty would have found pity for her in their hearts. But that Bella should have faced her hour with a roof over her head and a bed beneath her, and a kindly hand to meet her needs; that, in the opinion of Drumorty was nothing short of "lauding the evil-doer."

"Revellin' in her sins," "Made o' and tended, as if she were an honest woman," these and other denunciations flew rife at mart and meeting as the weeks passed, and it was reported that "Jessie MacLean was sleepin' on a shake-down while that limmer was lying like a queen in Jessie's feather bed." But that was only hearsay, for not once did Jessie let one of them pass the door, though many were the pretexts devised by Mistress MacKenty to gain admission, from the borrowing of an egg which she returned the next day (the same egg, as Jessie could prove, for did she not mark it on purpose; for what use would Mistress MacKenty be having for an egg three days before Sunday?) to the bringing of a bottle of raspberry-vinegar to see if Jessie had a corkscrew that could get the cork out.

Bella sensed it all with sullen resentment which would show in her eyes when the baby's cries forced its existence more sharply upon her. She hated her motherhood. Motherhood, that was thrust cruelly upon her while she was still a child; motherhood, robbed of its honour and covered with shame; motherhood and its pains, stripped of the love which makes its agony a glory. This was the motherhood Bella knew, and her heart was bitter against it. She felt trapped. Perhaps the child, helpless in her arms, crying to her for food, might have saved her from this, and have roused in her girl-heart that compassion for the helpless which is mother-love. But Jessie, all eagerness to surround Bella with comfort, took the care of the baby upon herself; and as love for it fastened upon her heart, Jessie could not bear to let any hand touch it but her own. Its morning bath was a rite to be lingered over with exclamations of wonder and delight. If Jessie noticed at all that Bella did not share her ecstasy she didn't think it strange; for Jessie had quickly ceased to think of Bella as the baby's mother. Her feeling for Bella was in a smaller measure the same feeling she had for the baby. She felt herself mother to both of them. So while Jessie's heart was greatened and stirred by her care of these two, Bella, robbed of the saving outlet of service, became daily more morose. The memory of the drawn blinds seared her; and she knew that the day would come soon when she must face Drumorty again. She felt little gratitude towards Jessie, and just a cool wonder that a good woman could also be kind.

The baby was about six weeks old, when Jessie came in one day with heightened colour, and her step brisk with excitement. She opened her hand to disclose three gold sovereigns and a half-sovereign.

"Three pounds ten, Bella; the gentry at the big hoose hae paid their sewing bill." Then turning swiftly to the baby she cried crooningly: "Jessie's wee lamb will no' need ti sleep in the clothes-basket noo; it's a pram an' a cradle he'll be havin'."

Jessie dropped the money into the toby-mug on the mantel and was preparing to gather the baby up from the clothes-basket when she heard a step on the path outside. She glanced through the window, then dodged back with the warning whisper: "It's Skilly!"

Like a flash she clapped on her bonnet, and seized a basket and was stepping sedately out at the door just as Skilly raised his hand to knock upon it.

"My certies, Skilly," exclaimed Jessie, shutting the door carefully behind her as she stopped facing him on the step. "Wha wid expect *you* to be visitin' this time o' day?"

"I hae come ti see Bella Tocher," said Skilly, looking suggestively at the closed door before which Jessie stood like a sentinel.

"Weel, I'm vexed for ye;" cooed Jessie. "Bella's oot bye somewhere, an' I'm on my way ti the flesher's."

Skilly was not deceived, and indeed Jessie didn't expect him to be. She smiled grimly as she caught his eye glancing searchingly at the window as the muslin curtains moved under Bella's touch; but she continued to stand barring his way to the door, her arms folded militantly through the empty basket which posed like a shield upon her breast.

Skilly lengthened out his gangling inches to a greater assumption of dignity, and, ignoring Jessie's hostility with a lofty tolerance, said in the tone he usually kept for reading the first lesson:

"As an elder o' the kirk it is my duty to speak wi' Bella Tocher aboot her misbegotten bairn; and wha we may name as the father o' 't."

"An' it was yer godly duty as an elder, nae doot, that made ye turn her oot to die by the roadside?" Jessie's tone was the essence of sweetened venom.

But Skilly, not meaning to lose his unimpeachable superiority by bandying words with a woman, answered calmly:

"I hae no call to shelter a wanton and unrepentant woman; if Bella Tocher is minded to face the elders and make admission o' her sins—"

"Her sins!" Jessie broke in. "It's no' her sins Drumorty is punishin' her for; it's the evidence, Skilly. It's the bairn. There's them that sit on the elder's bench and gie judgment, that ken more o' sin than Bella Tocher, but they dinna get found out: their siller in the collection plate blinds the minister."

This was a home thrust, and Skilly reddened under it, but he clambered back to his official dignity by booming pontifically:

"It behooves us to deal kindly wi' the repentant. If Bella Tocher is humble of spirit and contrite of heart, I will see mysel' that her bairn is housed in the alms-house; an' I'll take her back—" Then, seeing the chance to make a bargain, Skilly dropped his oratorical tone, and added hastily: "But mind ye, no' at the old price; I'll gie her half o' 't."

At that Jessie laughed greyly, and two red lights flashed battle from her eyes.

"Yer a sainted and godlike man, Skilly, wi' a heart sweet wi' charity.

Now that the lass is able to work again, ye'll put her bairn in the alms-house at nae cost to yersel'; and ye'll let her carry swill to yer pigs at half the siller ye'd have to pay anither; it's a forgivin' an' tender heart ye have—"

Skilly bridled impatiently and turned away; the woman would try the patience of a saint!

"Aye! Run, run, Skilly," urged Jessie tauntingly. "If ye bide, I may let ye see yersel'; and the sight will make ye sick."

It was too much! An elder of the kirk couldn't be expected to stand it any longer. Skilly left her and stalked down the path, his back stiff as buckram.

Jessie turned back into the house all aflutter. Nature had not made her a fighter; she could not have lifted a whisper to defend herself; but accident had made her play mother and so she could fight like a tiger, although her knees might tremble for hours afterwards.

"Did ye hear, Bella?" she asked the girl who sat stolidly on the bench by the window, ignoring the whimperings from the clothes-basket.

"Aye." There was nothing in the girl's tone to indicate her thoughts. After a moment her eyes wandered up to the toby-jug on the mantel, and she said:

"How much will the pram an' the cradle cost?"

Jessie, with most of her attention centred on the commotion in the basket, answered:

"I can get the pram for thirty shillings; an' I've been promised the use o' Maggie Duncan's cradle for naething—but she kens fine I'll make her next gown on account o' 't."

4

In the straggling light next morning Jessie slipped a long thin leg out of bed, and her toes went searching with cat-like caution for a crocheted slipper; finding it, they wriggled into its woolly depth.

Jessie was making one of her countless trips to the clothes-basket by the fireside in the next room to see if all was well. She clutched her long pink flannelette night-gown to keep it from touching the floor; and was moving carefully past Bella's bed, when its unusual flatness made her look at it again.

It was empty! Jessie hastened into the next room with fussy concern, sure that whatever Bella was doing for the baby was wrong.

But Bella wasn't there! Her hat wasn't hanging on the back of the door where it had hung for six weeks. Her shoes weren't on the peat-basket[3] where she had put them last night.

The baby! Jessie gave a cry that ended in a strangled sound, half laugh, half sob, as she sprang to the clothes-basket and dropped down beside it. The baby was there. Jessie's heart resumed action again, she bent over the basket and tenderly touched the baby's warm sleeping face; then her thoughts returned to Bella. She looked about for fresh proof that she had really gone.

Against the toby-jug a sheet of writing-paper was propped. Jessie reached for it and carried it to the window. In the greying light she peered at the words written upon it until they formed into things of meaning. And she read:

"I am going to Edinburgh. I have taken two pounds from the toby-jug; that leaves enough for the pram. It is ill done of me, but I will no stay in Drumorty. If I get a place I'll send back the siller, and if Geordie will wed me I'll come back for the bairn. You have been kinder to me than I am deserving, and I will no forget. You can send the bairn to the alms-house; it will be better there than with me if Geordie will no have me."

Jessie trembled as she read. Bella had gone! And the baby was here— was hers to keep! Joy sent her heart racing heavenwards. She turned and sank to her knees beside the clothes-basket, stretching greedy arms about it and whispering passionately to the sleeping child:

"She'll no' come back. She'll no' come back—and ye'll be my ain, my ain wee lamb."

Then in the flush of her riches, kneeling there in the still grey morning, she thought of Bella and her poverty. Bella, stealing out loveless in the night. Bella who had borne the suffering and shame. Bella with empty arms. And a great remorse for the greed of her own rejoicing tore at her breast, and she clasped her hands and cried in anguish:

"God be merciful to her!—And forgie me, a covetous sinner."

---

1 A worthless, impudent girl.
2 Every.
3 A built-in box for holding peats.

WANTIN' A HAND

The moisture from the tub curled her hair into babyish ringlets that hung about her flushed face. Despite her form made broad with the daily travail of washing clothes, and her face pouchy with drink, suggestions of beauty still lingered about her as perfume might cling to a garment after it was soiled and torn.

There was no hint of age or decay in the square tower of her body, no thought of handicap in her actions as she squeezed and rubbed the clothes upon the board with her one powerful hand. The small stump of her missing arm jerked vigorously from the shoulder in time to the hand upon the board. She would stop at times to pin the empty sleeve more snugly to her side and then resume the crawling, gripping motion of her one hand in the tub. It was a great-jointed hand, corded along the back, and broad, and when it had squeezed the water from a garment she could defy any woman with *two* hands to wring one drop more from it. The clothes washed by Jean Sclessor were truly washed, and clear and fragrant when she took them from the line.

And so, although she tried them sorely by her frequent drinking spells, the good wives of Drumorty would rather wait for Jean than have some feckless two-handed woman wash in her stead. And the greatest church-goers among them would ignore the smell of whisky on her breath and would even comment sympathetically upon her bunions when her steps began to waver.

But Jean was long past caring what Drumorty thought about her drinking, long past the time when she turned her head away so that they wouldn't catch her breath. She cared only for evening to come, and she worked through the day with a driving force which became a frenzy of haste as night-fall drew near, for she was going home to the kist under the stairs, home to dreams, home to love and revenge and despair, home to forgetfulness, home to the flat-sided bottle of whisky wrapped in a grey petticoat.

And when at evening she groped her way toward the kist in the musty hole beneath the stairs filled with the odour of sprouting potatoes, she was already tearful with welling memories, melting with the vision of the lass that once was Jean Sclessor and the lad that had been Sandy Morrison. They came to her as always, bright with the sunlight of a harvest day and fragrant with the breath of reaping time. *He* stood by the reaper bareheaded in the high noon sun. Lesser lads had sought the shade panting and weary, but he, foreman of them all and master of them all by height and strength, stood stretching in the glare. And *she* came laden with the scones fresh from the griddle and the mulled ale cool in its great earthen bottle. There was a power in him that brought her eyes to his, and whether she would or no' she looked at him, and he looked back at her.

And then at milking time he came. She knew it was his shadow in the door as she sat milking there. But never a move made she, and never a turn of her head, although her heart was singing louder than the milk that struck the pail. And never a word she said about the singing of her heart, and never a word said he. But every night he came and watched, and every night he waited while she strained the milk.

Lightsome days they were, and work was easy in the doing. And she would sing and scrub the yard for Mary Tate, the second lass, and often she would do the work for both when Mary's cough confined her to her bed. Nor did she care about the extra tasks, but rather she welcomed them, knowing that Sandy loved her all the more that she was strong. And though at times he looked on Mary with admiring eyes, seeing her hair that lay like silken wheat against her head, Jean did not care; she knew the kindling of his heart was but for her, and the strength that lay in her round arms. And nearing thrashing time he said:

"Come Martinmas, I'll go a-cotterin'."

And Jean replied with hurrying heart, tossing her head to give the words a careless lilt:

"'Deed? An' wha will cotter wi' ye?"

"Yersel', I'm thinkin'," he made answer. And lingering by the stooked grain that stood like little tents beneath the moon, he told her of the fine bay mare he had his mind upon; and of the farm, come time, they'd rent together; and of the butter she would make for marketing, and of the long, long hours that they would work, he, with his back that had the strength of two, and she, with arms that had the strength of any man's. And by and by they'd own a farm, and *she* would go to kirk in taffetas and *he* would wear a tall gray hat on market days.

Down on her knees she fumbled for the bottle, pulling it with avid hand from its wrapper in the kist. Seizing the cork with yellowed teeth, she spat it out, and drank, gulping dryly in her haste. She settled back upon the piled potatoes in the fusty murk, her heavy throat racked with bitter sobbing. The thrashing machine sounded in her ears again. She stood in its sucking wind, feeding the yellow sheaves to its hungry mouth. Sandy swung by calling her above the roar, love glimmering in his face. She stopped to wave at him—to watch his glinting head go by—the crunching mouth reached for her fingers—drew them onwards with the wheat— seized them, pulled them in—the hand, the arm, up, up, the arm—Oh, God, stop it!—stop—

She jerked from side to side with the pain of sharp remembering, thumping the potatoes with the splashing bottle. And then she licked the whisky from her hand, and drank, whimpering as the glow stole round her heart.

Sandy came to the hospital, silent and down-looking, and every time he came his stay was shorter. The smell of medicine made him fit to spew, or the second man was away gallivanting with a lass, and he must hurry back to do his work. And then he got to bringing Mary Tate along, and she would sit and look at him and giggle when he looked at her as if they had a joke between the two of them. And Jean could never speak to him alone or ask a word about the cottering.

Long after thrashing she came back from hospital, and Martinmas was drawing near. Lads were speaking of feeing time and whether they would stay, or seek a better place. But Sandy never spoke a word, but had some business in the byre, or other work to do when she would question him. And Mary Tate would make his brose with extra butter, and mealy-mouth about him in the evening, and make as if she knew what she would never tell. When Jean could bear no more of that she asked:

"Is Sandy biding here or goin' cotterin'?"

And Mary laughed and said·

"If he's yer man ye've little need to ask."

And Jean could barely keep from riving her. "What mean ye by that taunt?" she cried.

But Mary laughed, smirked and simpered while she stepped about as if the kitchen were a dancing hall, and all the lads had come to look at her.

So she cornered Sandy in the stubble field at loosing-time. He bore the harness on his arms and round his neck, for he would sooner break his back than tire a horse for no good end. He saw her, and he tried to pass, making as if the horses needed him, but Jean put out her hand.

"A word wi' ye. What's come o' a' yer talk o' cotterin'?"

"Oh, nathin'," he replied. And cried: "Whoa, Bess, whoa!" as if the horses were astray.

"Nathin'?"

"No." And looked ahead, straining as if to see the horses reach the watering trough.

"Look at me, Sandy Morrison: Why will ye no' go cotterin'?" she cried, shaking his harness-laden arm with her one hand.

"I'll cotter come time, nae doot," he said, with more ease in his voice than in his face.

"Wi' *me*?" Her voice was shrill and cut him like a lash. The red rose up his throat. "Wi' me? Will ye go cotterin' wi' me? Answer me *that*, Sandy Morrison."

He could not look at her, and tried to turn away.

"Answer me!" She screamed and beat his breast, and as she struck her dangling stump jerked to the motion of the beating. Sandy's eyes were on it.

"I canna, Jean," he said. "I've nae use for a wife wantin' a hand."

And so he married Mary Tate and took her cottering, her that could never wet her feet, her with arms like matches, and legs like clay-pipe stems. He took her cottering for a year, and then the baby came, and Mary couldn't leave her bed for many a month, and when she *did* they said she'd creep about more like a ghost than anything that drew the breath of life.

Sandy left the cottering and hired out again. Soon there was another wean[1] to feed and tend; and every year or two another wean, another mouth for Sandy Morrison to feed, and Mary always lying in the bed. And he that had so proud a head left the farming to do what work he could about the town by nights, and tend the weans and make their porridge by day. He that spoke of fine bay mares, and cottering, and rented farms, and tall gray hats, was doing work that none would do—emptying garbage in the night. She lived again that first night of his shame, when he crept up the lane at dawn, his head hung low, hoping none would see. But *she* was there and screamed her scorn, as many a dawn since then she'd screamed her scorn:

"Nae use for a wife wantin' a hand, eh? Fine for ye emptying garbage, fine for ye." He never looked toward her, crying in the window there, nor raised his head. And all the years he never looked nor spoke, but moved about as if her jeering fell on ears that could not hear.

Why did he not cry back at her or lift his head? Oh, to make him give a sign, to get her hand upon his shrunken flesh and rive it with her nails. To tear him open that her eyes could see his bleeding. To make him scream his pain as *she* must scream—to make him cry her name—to *know* that he was suffering. She rocked, tortured, on the shifting pile of potatoes, breaking their white sprouts as her hand grabbed, anguished, for the bottle.

Oh, what was he to her? He was a dour, down-looking chiel,[2] thin he was, thin and withered, withered like a turnip at the winter's end. And his hair, his bonnie hair that shone like a Michaelmas penny, was grizzled and sparse and dry like dusty moss. And the shoulders of him that had filled the door from side to side as he stood watching her at the milking, were shrunk and bent, and bent and shrunken was his neck that had been straight and pink and moist with the sweat of the fields. And the eyes of him were bleared and wavering, and his gait was like a weary dog's.

Oh, what cared she? Why wait to shame a bleary dog—a bleary dog—a weary dog? Why sit and rock and wait, and cry at dawn? She'd stop her rocking and her crying. She'd stop her drinking and her wailing. She'd buy a dolman trimmed with bugle beads and go to kirk on Sunday. She'd cry in by to her that lay a-coughing in the bed, and him that pottered about wiping noses. She'd stop a while and sweep the floor, and wash the faces of the glowering weans. And all the time that image in the bed would hate her for her strength. And Sandy would be shamed and he would see what he had cast aside. She'd stop and bake and throw her dolman on the chair so that its beads would shine. She'd feed the weans and tend the image in the bed, and it would choke with rage and cough, and cough, and cough.

She'd stop her drinking, this would be the last. She'd be looked up to and respected, she'd go to kirk, she'd make red petticoats for naked heathens, she'd stop her drinking. The higher she was held the more would be his shame. She'd stop her drinking, break the bottle—break it on the wall—but first she'd drink—no use to waste good whisky—this would be the last—the very last—the last.

She started to sway pendulum-wise, settling deeper in the pile, rolling her head as if in time to some well-remembered chant. Her vacant eyes were bleared with tears that fell on this shoulder, and on that, with the rolling of her head. Her purple lips forming the silent words twisted in a half-forgotten pain, and then her voice meaningless as a wind in a hollow place took up the dirge: "Nae use for a wife wantin' a hand, wantin' a hand. . . ."

---

1 An infant.
2 A man.

THE TATTIE-DOOLIE [1]

His name was James MacDonald MacGregor, as you could prove by reading the newly-painted sign over his door, which told Drumorty in yellow and black that he was: "A high-class tailor: pressing and mending also done." But Jean MacFarlane had nicknamed him the "Tattie-Doolie" on the very first Sunday. But this was not until after the service, not until after he had outsung her, outsung her in time and outsung her in volume. Even in the final hymn, when she had held the last note until her ears buzzed and her face was like a harvest moon *he* had held it just a second longer.

Jean had always been proud of her breath. It lasted longer than any breath in the parish of Drumorty. She was proud too, that no voice in the parish could be heard above her own. Many had tried it, both man and woman!

Skilly's "Gype," [2] called that because he was daft-like and wore fancy waistcoats on week-days, had a roaring fine voice; and Mary Macrimmon, who had a wooden leg, "could make a braw noise when she put her mind to 't." But even they had lost heart at last and had left Jean to lead the singing. The Gype stayed away from the service altogether and spent his Sunday mornings "sellin' his soul to the devil on a dambrod." But Mary Macrimmon was a God-fearing woman, so she made up for her loss by coming late every Sunday, and the ring of the brass ferrule on her wooden leg announced her passage up the flagged aisle to her seat in the front pew. Each entrance was a dramatic triumph, for she changed the trimming on her hat every week, so that the congregation "wouldna crane their necks for naught." Jean MacFarlane was well content to let her have this triumph: there *should* be compensations for a wooden leg.

In four years none had ventured to dispute Jean's right to sing the last note of each line as a solo. The members of the congregation accepted it with the same placidity that they accepted the fact that the varnish had never really hardened on the pews; and if you sat too long or too solidly on one place, you left the nap of your suit embedded on the seat.

In time they came to be proud of Jean, and they waited for her to finish with their mouths agape, as much out of admiration as out of a desire to be ready to start the next line when her breath finally gave out.

The organist, who was blind, knew better, and longed for the courage to terminate Jean's stentorian solos. But she dared not, for the congregation believed that she couldn't be so good as an organist that could see, and this made her timid; so she would humbly hold the last note until Jean's final gasp signalled that she could start a new measure. But in return for this, Jean defended her when some young snip would suggest that she wasn't much of an organist. "No," Jean would admit. "She's no' a great musician, but she's a gran' accompanist, an' that's what's needed in a kirk like ours."

Until that first Sunday Jean had held no grudge against James MacDonald MacGregor, although it would have been natural, and even dutiful, for her to have sniffed a little in affected disdain when she heard his name mentioned, for his arrival was a source of much distress to her father, Perney MacFarlane, who had been the only tailor in Drumorty for twenty-five years, as had been his father before him. Indeed, old Perney had given Jean the rough side of his tongue for her undaughterly lack of resentment over the new tailor. But Jean, while realizing that his advent would end her father's sartorial monarchy, was none the less conscious of a pleased flutter when Mistress MacKenty stepped in by to say: "The puir man's single dootless, for I hae seen neither hide nor hair o' a wife, nor her belongings."

"That's a consideration," Jean had answered; and, giving her father an accusing look, added: "to them that never sees a man frae one day's end to the other."

Jean was a little irritated with her father on this score, and blamed him that she hadn't been married long since. For, although his trade should have supplied her with more suitors than any other lass in Drumorty, it was a fact that, while the grocer's daughter by making smirking pretence of helping, could meet young men on Saturday evenings in her father's shop; and even the druggist's boarding-school daughter could "happen" to come in to kiss her father good-night when a prosperous young farmer was in, Jean could never meet a man that way, because Perney insisted that it wasn't seemly for a single woman to come in, when a man *might* be having his trousers fitted. To Jean's protest: "Father, ye canna always be fittin' the crotch," he merely answered, "I *might* be."

On the way to kirk that first Sunday, Jean was in a twitter. She had even gone the length of putting Jockey Club on the front of her bodice as well as on her handkerchief. This made her feel akin to Jezebel, and for a moment she liked the feeling. She wished that a woman could be "wanton in her ways" and yet seem respectable. Then, appalled at her own wickedness, she made a hasty prayer for her soul's salvation, and decided that scent was a handmaiden of the devil and that she would never use it again.

But the next moment she was glad that she *had* used it, and sorry that she hadn't used more, as the new tailor passed her on the road and remarked to his neighbour something about "a fine smell."

He was grand beyond Jean's expectations. He wore a frock coat and a "tile,"[3] and she gasped in admiration of his "venture-someness" in wearing them when there was neither a marriage nor a funeral in the neighbourhood to justify such splendour.

For in Drumorty the laird is the only man entitled by common opinion to wear such grandeur on ordinary Sundays. Many a tattie-doolie in the fields around Drumorty flapped in solitary dignity with the scarcely worn frock coat and "tile" of some deceased farmer, who had been too modest to wear them.

Jean had even been pleased when he came boldly up to the choir and took a seat in the front row of the men's pew directly facing her. It was a bit forward of him to sit in the choir without a public invitation from the minister, but Jean thrilled. "It's all of a piece wi' his wearin' a tile, he's a man that kens his mind and does it." She was glad also that he was where he could see her, and know at once who it was that sang so long and so loud.

She settled herself in her seat with the dignity that a duck acquires upon water. Debating the relative effectiveness of a lace handkerchief emerging from her sleeve or thrust daintily into the front of her bodice, she decided in favour of the former, because if she wore it on her breast the book would hide it when she stood up to sing.

Satisfied that she was at her best, she glanced across the aisle. She was disappointed to find that he was not watching her. He was reading the hymn numbers on the announcement slate and looking them up in his hymn-book.

"A singer himsel', nae doot," she reflected. "All the better; it takes a singer t' appreciate a singer." She looked him over carefully and decided that he was "over thin for good looks, and over white in the face. But he had a grand moustache. A manly-like, an' full-growin' moustache. A careful wife that tended him like a chicken on a brod,[4] could make a fine strappin' chiel out o' him."

A yearning tenderness toward him, the passion of a brood hen, stirred in her breast. She wanted to envelop him in her care; already he seemed to belong to her. Feeling the need to emphasize this to herself by speaking of him, she whispered to Mary Macrimmon:

"What think ye o' the new tailor?"

When Mary answered: "He's unco chilpet[5] and hungry-like aboot the jawbones," she answered tartly:

"He's no' hog-fat. For *mysel'*, I like a man on the thin side."

Indeed, Jean had even found herself thinking with satisfaction of the twenty-four hand-made and feather-stitched night-gowns that lay at the bottom of her kist.[6] Not that she was ready to jump down the throat of the first man that asked her. Indeed not! She wouldn't fash[7] herself if she never married! But twenty-four nightgowns made a body feel prepared for anything.

When the organist began the prelude to the first hymn, Jean took a deep breath, and set her head like a filly fighting the snaffle.

Now he would see! Now he would take notice! She charged the first note with a vociferation that made Mary Macrimmon drop her hymn-book. Never had her voice been so loud. Never had she felt more exultant in its power. He would be looking at her now! But wait! Wait until the end of the verse when she could show him the length of her breath. *That* would make him take stock and wonder. *That* was where breath could show to advantage.

As she reached the last phrase, she filled her lungs. Now he would see. This would be the best that she had ever done.

Her voice rose powerfully above the others. They were falling away. As the last note was reached, Jean's voice took hold of the ragged edges of sound and knit them up. Soon she would be singing alone.

But what was this? A voice full and strong was keeping pace with her. *He* was still singing. Was he trying to compete with her? It couldn't be! She glanced across at him, her face red with the strain of holding the note. Yes! He was wilfully trying to outsing her. In his eyes was the insolent look of a duellist who is sure of victory. Outraged, Jean lost her hold upon the note, and James MacDonald MacGregor's voice boomed out in triumphant solo for two beats more.

Affronted! Affronted she was and shamed before the whole congregation! Shamed and affronted in her own kirk. And by *this*; this whippersnapper. Made mock of and be-meaned by a half-starved bantam-cock, with a tile on his brainless head.

There was a spluttering and sizzling of suppressed mirth from the body of the kirk. The new verse started, and staggered along in gusts like a drunken man. The McKenzie lassie with the fat legs was giggling and nudging her neighbour. The minister was hiding behind his prayer-book, but the redness of his ears told that even *he* was laughing. Mary Macrimmon was making no pretence of singing, but was frankly laughing under cover of the organ. The new tailor was looking about him, smirkingly appreciative of his victory, although he did not yet know its magnitude.

Jean's heart was fit to fly out of its cage, so angry was she. For little more she would have thrown her hymn-book in his face. He would come up here, would he? Come here and set up opposition to her father. Horning his nose in on a man that had worked in Drumorty all his life. But that wasn't enough. He must dare to outsing *her*, that had led the singing for years. He must make a byword of *her* that had defended him against her own father. Oh, but she was well punished that she hadn't hated him from the first, the swaggering dandyprat, the fribble popinjay, all dressed up like a tattie-doolie! In that moment she hated him as only a heart that might have loved *can* hate.

It had been a bitter Sunday morning; and a bitter, bitter walk back from the kirk with whisperings and laughter all about her, and handkies held up to hide wide grins of amusement. It had been hard to bear with Mistress MacKenty when she said with ill-disguised glee: "Weel, weel, he's goin' t' lead the singin' as well as the tailorin'."

But there had been comfort in seeing the pleasure it gave old Perney to hear her flay the new tailor. So delighted was he with her nickname for his rival that he pressed her to take the neck of the boiled fowl, a delicacy which he only relinquished in moments of great emotion. For Perney was troubled in his heart, deeply troubled and anxious, and he dare not speak of it. He had a secret which he believed was shared by no one. It was this. He didn't know how the collar of a coat should be cut! For, although he had been fully thirty-five when his father had died and left him the tailoring business, he had never up to that moment either cut or fitted a collar. It had been the elder MacFarlane's belief that his son was a witless warlock[8] who was by nature bound to ruin any piece of cloth into which he put a pair of shears.

In time he begrudgingly and with loud-voiced distrust, allowed Perney to cut and fit trousers, and at a pinch, when his eyes began to trouble him, he would prayerfully let him work on a portion of a coat. But never to his last day would he let him touch a collar.

So Perney inherited the business with a perfect knowledge of trousers, a partial knowledge of waist-coats, and a complete ignorance of collars. For so jealous was old MacFarlane of this knowledge that he had always retired behind a screen for the cutting and fitting of this mystic portion of the garment.

On the first day he was alone, Perney had embarked on a series of experiments. From then on, every suit he cut was a hazard, an adventure. This much he suspected about collars. Something had to be cut on the crosswise, and something had to be stretched. But which had to be stretched, which had to be cut crosswise, he never was able to find out. Sometimes he did it one way, and sometimes the other, but little satisfaction resulted.

When, occasionally, the miracle happened, and he would produce a collar that did neither stick out at the back like a spout, nor shy away from the neck in a coy semi-circle, he had always forgotten how he had cut that particular collar, and try as he would he couldn't duplicate it.

Perney had never told this to a soul, not even to his wife; nay, *least* of all his wife. But sometimes he wondered uneasily if she knew. There was something too impassioned in the way she defended him when a customer complained that the collar didn't fit. It looked like something more than chance that brought her hurrying down the stairs just in the nick of time, and there was something more than affability in her voice when she exclaimed to the customer upon her entrance: "My certies, but that jacket brings out the breadth o' yer shoulders." If, in the face of her evident admiration, the customer still murmured that the collar didn't set to his neck, her voice became a shade scornful as she replied: "Think ye the collar's human? How would *it* know where yer neck is? Hae patience and wear it a while, and come time, it will grow to the set o' yer body." And if he still complained, she would deride him playfully, crying: "Certies, man, expect ye the collar to grip yer neck like yer lass's arm?" If this didn't send him away with his face red and the suit under his arm, she could go even further.

It was not so easy with the young ones who had been to Aberdeen to take the agricultural course at the university. *They* were "very notional," and would bring a suit back again and again for alterations. But smart though they were, they hated to encounter Mistress MacFarlane, and would peep in at the window first to see that she was out of the way. But in the end she would always vanquish them. And it is a tribute to her eloquence that they sometimes came to agree with her that "a collar couldna be expected to fit, until you had worn it for six months."

In all the twenty-five years, Perney had never had a suit left on his hands; but he knew well where the credit lay for that.

He spent long hours turning it over in his mind. Did she truly believe that his collars were perfect, and his customers sorely wanting in sense? Or did she know all the time that he couldn't cut a collar? But no—that thought smarted too keenly. She would never be able to keep from telling him if she knew. He knew women, with their tongues always wag-wagging. She'd cast it in his face in one of her tempers. She'd never be able to hold it back. No, she didn't know. Of course she didn't know. But why, then, did she never mention collars when they were alone? Because she thinks I can cut them. Because she knows I can't. It was plausible either way. She knows. She doesn't. She knows. She doesn't. For hours his needle would flash out and in to this torturous refrain. Overhead he would hear her, heavy-footed, going back and forth about her work. Many times he had risen from his bench, determined to go up and have it out. Or sitting by her in the evenings, he had often been tempted to break the long silence by shouting the one word "Collars!" just to see what she would do. But he never dared carry out his resolve, because he couldn't bear to learn that she knew.

Most of the time he was comforted by the thought that she didn't know, and he loved her fiercely for her blind faith in him. But on occasions when she would defend him too loudly, he was convinced that she knew. And he tortured himself by the thought that she despised him in her heart. At such times he almost hated her, not only for the knowledge she had, but that she was strong enough never to give it voice.

One thing made it bearable. He could laugh at her. She had a notion about the making of broth. Nay, more than a notion, it was a belief as dear to her heart as her religion. And he knew it to be founded on folly.

Mistress MacFarlane was a Fraser, and the Frasers had always held the reputation of making the best Sunday broth-with-dumplings in the parish. It was their crown. How to make it was their secret. It necessitated the constant attention, for the whole forenoon, of a member of the family. This meant that some one must stay away from the kirk during the morning service; and as this mortification seemed to be borne more cheerfully by the male portion of the family, it came to be a tradition that the Fraser men were a godless ilk that would rather tend broth than praise the Lord. Indeed, one minister had even preached a sermon on setting up graven images, and it was clear that he exhorted the Fraser family to choose between their broth and the Kingdom of Heaven. But it was useless.

So, the Sunday morning after his marriage Perney learned the secret of the Fraser broth. His wife told him every detail, as indeed she had continued to tell him every detail every Sunday morning since, for somehow she could never believe that he could retain all its intricacies; and never once did she fail to come back from the door-step to repeat: "Mind ye now, quarter of an hour apart."

That was the secret! Other benighted Drumortians put everything into the pot at once. But the Frasers first boiled a shin bone in the water for half an hour, then added the turnips. A quarter of an hour later the carrots went in, and so on, until finally the dumplings.

Before leaving for the kirk, Mistress MacFarlane would arrange the different vegetables in bowls and set them in a row leading away from the fire. Just before tying her bonnet strings, she would drop the bone into the water and remind him: "The bowl next the fire goes in first."

It was a ritual gone through with much gusto on her part and great patience on the part of Perney.

At first he had blundered, forgetting this or that, or he would go down to the shop to play a solitary game of chess and forget the broth altogether, and bowls of raw vegetables would betray him to his wrathful wife upon her return.

One Sunday, in a flush of rebellion, he had dumped the contents of all the bowls into the pot the moment she was off the doorstep, and thumped defiantly downstairs to play chess. But he had little peace that morning, for, in spite of himself, he believed in the superiority of the Fraser broth. He was apprehensive about its flavour, and in two minds whether to confess or not, until they sat down to the table, and Mistress MacFarlane, taking the first spoonful exclaimed just as she always did, just as every Fraser always did: "My, that's fine broth." And he agreed, just as the spouse of every Fraser always agreed. He never let a hint of what he had done cross his lips; after that, his Sunday mornings were tranquil.

But now Perney was troubled. The arrival of the new tailor sharpened his anxiety about the collars, for not only might his wife discover the truth, but soon all Drumorty might know. He tortured himself by attributing to his rival great skill in collar-making, and by magnifying his own lack of skill. Soon the sight of a new suit, with the collar snugly fitting the neck, justified his fears. And with every day came discouraging news of another customer gone over to the enemy. Fear was added to fear, as orders came in more and more slowly. Even the report that the "Tattie-Doolie" couldn't hang trousers didn't bring the consolation it should have. He began to lean on Jean, seeking comfort in the increasing scorn she expressed for the "Tattie-Doolie," for Jean's emotion was growing more keen with each Sunday. She existed from week to week in a fever of anticipation. She lived only for those moments when they faced each other across the aisle in combat. One morning he was late and she was beside herself for fear he would not come. At his sudden appearance her heart raced in an intoxication of *something*, she called it hatred.

After the services, when she reached home, she would deride him with a wit that delighted Perney, and a venom that surprised herself. But sometimes, following these outbursts, she would go to her room and cry helplessly, and she knew that she wasn't crying because he had outsung her.

There is no knowing how it might have ended, had not the organist died suddenly, making it necessary to send hurriedly to Aberdeen for another to take her place. Five minutes after the train came in with the new one, Mistress MacKenty was spreading the news that it was a man this time, with most extraordinarily thin legs. By noon the next day she was able to tell that he demanded no less than two eggs for his breakfast, and that he was bound and determined to conduct the choir practice himself without interference from the minister. So it was clear that he was a feckful man in spite of his legs.

And his hands on the organ proved this to be true. Jean was filled with a new excitement as the organ woke clamorously and shook itself at his commanding touch. This was playing! This was music worth singing to! The "Tattie-Doolie" would never outsing her again. Here was music that would give her strength to conquer him. The new organist would see who had the longest breath. He would judge who was best fitted to lead the singing.

Her voice rose with clarion strength. The tailor was doing his best also. Jean was reluctantly obliged to admit that there were worse voices than the tailor's. They were nearing the end of the line. *Now* for the struggle! But something was amiss. The last note slipped away from her like an eel, and the next line was in progress before she knew it. She tried to hold on at the end of the next line; but again the organist didn't wait.

Of course he didn't know any better. *That* was it, Jean reasoned. She would have to wait till the end of the verse to show him. *Then* he would be glad to hold the note for such a voice. An organist had to be trained to a singer's ways. Nearing the end she raised her voice so that he couldn't help but hear her. But with a loud blast from the quaking pipes he drowned her out and briskly started the next verse.

Dumbfounded, she looked across the aisle to see what the "Tattie-Doolie" thought of this. He was glaring furiously at the organist's head. Presently his glance met Jean's, and they gazed at each other in a common bond of indignation. He signalled to her not to sing, and closed his hymn-book emphatically, to show that he meant to be silent. Jean did the same, and he nodded his approval. Exchanging knowing smirks they waited for the collapse of the singing.

But it was not the hopeless failure they expected it to be. Their revenge was *no* revenge. Nobody missed their singing. The organ sped its multisonous way with the abandon of a calliope at a circus. It cared not a penny who sang or who didn't. Its very abandon was inviting, and they fain would have joined in the singing, but pride forbade them.

The tailor became more and more crestfallen as the service progressed. He fingered his hymn-book longingly, but he could not bring himself to start again.

Seeing his dejection, Jean forgot her own disappointment and yearned over him. She understood only too keenly how he was missing the exaltation of singing to the full capacity of his lungs. She knew only too well the sense of loss he felt, and the bitter hurt to his pride. His emotions found a dual echo in her breast; she was heartsick for herself, but she was doubly heartsick for him. Her one thought was to save his pride for him at any cost.

At the close of the service she eluded her mother, and caught up with him as he walked, with slackened step and drooping shoulders, along the road. It was a thing she could not have done for herself. But she was doing this for *him*. Nothing else could have given her courage to make that advance under the critical, watching eyes of the congregation. She reached his side gasping, and a little hesitant, but the sight of his despondent face spurred her afresh, and she cried with well simulated derision: "Heard ye ever such singin'! A lot o' women squeakin' like mice in a trap, an' no' a man's voice among the lot!"

He braced up at her approach and the gloom lifted from his face at her words, but settled back again as he answered doubtfully: "Skilly an' the minister were singin'."

"Singin', were they!" Jean cried with a chuckle. "Man, yer over-generous to call it *singin'*."

"They're no' so bad," he said, inviting her to fresh protest.

She laughed shrilly. "Ye ken fine, we never had a proper man's voice till ye came."

The swing was coming back to his shoulders again, and he was taking bigger strides.

"Think ye that?" he questioned anxiously. "I had a notion ye didna like my singing."

He would never know what her next words cost her. For a moment the old rivalry came to life and pride strove with love. In that swift space she was a singer again, proud of her voice and contemptuous of his, but *only* for a moment. Then came her admission from quiet lips: "I was jealous o' yer voice; jealous o' yer breath bein' longer than mine." With those words she retired forever, leaving the stage to him. She would never compete with him again.

His step was jaunty now, and his face beamed with gratification.

"Aye, my breath is a *lot* longer than yours," he replied.

Jean's heart faltered a little at his reply. It was true that his breath was longer than hers; it was true that his voice was louder, but he might have said something kind about her voice, even if he didn't believe it. *She* could tell any lie to make him feel better, it hurt that he didn't care to lie for her. Now that his spirits were restored and he no longer needed her, Jean lost her courage. A dull ache assailed her heart and sharp tears forced their way into her eyes. She continued to walk beside him only because she could not do otherwise with all Drumorty looking on. Her brimming tears were about to fall in spite of her struggle to keep them back, but the tailor saved her this humiliation. His momentary exhilaration was passing away, and shadows were gathering over him again.

"I missed the singin'," he sighed dolefully. "I like to sing. It seems like as if I had to sing something out o' me on the Sabbath, to get a fresh start for the next week."

"I ken what ye mean," Jean cried with ready sympathy, blinking away her unseen tears. "That's the way *I* feel—bottled up like."

"Aye," he agreed.

A daring thought came to Jean, a very daring thought. Quivering with excitement at her own temerity, she said: "I hae a harmonium. Would ye like to step in by wi' me for an hour an' sing the hymns?"

He looked full at her for the first, and there was admiration in his eyes. "Ye can *play*," he questioned eagerly. "I'd like it fine, if—if—"

Jean knew what he meant.

"My father likes music," she answered.

She was fluttering inside like a nest of young birds, half with joy, and half with fear of her father. But she would go through with it if the heavens were to fall.

As they reached the door, Mistress MacFarlane caught up with them. Being a true woman, she had already decided that Jean's wedding veil would be at least half a yard longer than the veil of that high-handed lassie of the druggist's had been.

"I'm goin' to play the hymns for Mr. MacGregor," Jean explained.

"Aye, aye," said Mistress MacFarlane, with a comfortable, round, pink smile, as if it were the most natural thing in the world. "Aye, aye, that will be fine." With an elaborate wink to Jean, she slipped in and up the stairs. Understanding her manoeuvre, Jean lingered below until she heard the kitchen door shut quickly, then, knowing that her father was safely imprisoned, she followed, leading the tailor into the heavy-curtained, musk-scented parlour.

It was well that Mistress MacFarlane went first and pushed the enraged Perney backward into the kitchen, for he had seen Jean approaching with the "Tattie-Doolie" and was seething at her treachery.

"What means this?" he demanded when he regained his balance after his wife's unexpected violence.

"Whist!" she commanded. "Dinna make an uproar. It's the new tailor come to sing the hymns wi' our lassie."

"In *my* hoose?"

"Why should he no'?" questioned his wife with irritating calmness, pulling at the tips of her black kid gloves the while, but carefully keeping between Perney and the door.

"Nae in *my* hoose! Step aside, woman."

"Sit doon, man, an' stop yer haverin',"[9] she answered with easy contempt. "Do ye expect yer bairn to go to her grave a maiden?"

"What's that?" cried Perney, with fresh fury. "He wants to *marry* Jean. He would *dare?*"

Mistress MacFarlane snorted and elbowed him out of the way with a pitying superiority.

"No," was her cryptic reply. "He has no' dared *yet*, but he'll dare come time."

Perney was bewildered. It was hard to maintain his indignation in the face of his wife's dispassionate assurance. She was his rock of strength. He followed in the course she steered, for her steering was always for his betterment. But now she seemed to have turned traitor and he felt lost. If she would only speak up and tell him her mind; he could always bear her lectures better than her silences. She was stepping about the room quietly, as if it were no concern of hers that his rival was here, under his roof.

The tailor's voice rose lustily singing. "Oh, come all ye faithful."

It was more than Perney could bear in silence.

"What mean ye, woman?"

"Man, hae a little sense," she urged, as if speaking to an unreasoning but lovable child. "It's high time that Jean was married—an' there's no room for *twa* tailors in Drumorty."

So *that* was it! It was a staggering thought. He sat down in his chair the better to support it. He might have known that she had some bee in her bonnet. She was not a woman to act without a purpose. And she was right. She was quite right. It would be a blessing to have a partner instead of a competitor. He would give him the collars to do! That would be a great relief. The thought made him light-hearted, and he was just about to show her that he saw some reason in her plans, when she said: "Ye can give him the collars to do."

At that he straightened in his chair, on the defensive again. So she knew! She had known all the time! She had lain beside him for thirty years with that secret knowledge in her heart. Despising him, perhaps! Yes, despising him. It wasn't for Jean she wanted the new tailor; it was because she knew that *he* could make better collars. She put her trust in the "Tattie-Doolie," in a stranger, an enemy, and she had turned against *him*, that had sheltered and loved her for thirty years.

She despised him, did she? Laughed at him? Well, he'd let her know that there were *others* that could laugh. He would tell her about the Fraser broth. He would lay *her* pride in the dust. There would be more than *one* humble heart in the house this day!

He turned toward her to launch his arrow of revenge.

All innocent of her blunder, she was lifting the lid of the broth pot and sniffing ecstatically: a Fraser worshipping at the shrine of the Fraser broth. He couldn't do it. Never, if she trod him in the dust, never could he hurt her like that. He turned away, his heart sick and lonely, his soul bereft and bitter. She was no longer his. No longer the woman who believed in him.

But there would be no more hiding behind a wall. He would speak to her about the collars. He would have it out with her. He turned back and asked in a voice sharp-edged, because it was so near to breaking: "Why say ye I can give him the collars to do?"

A flicker of alarm came into her eyes, but she finished the sip of broth she had in the spoon before answering, and then her voice came with easy assurance:

"Weel, ye'll never be able to trust him wi' trousers; so ye can give him the coats and waistcoats to do."

"An' the *collars*," he said, bitingly.

"Aye, an' the collars, an' other easy bits," she answered with lazy ease.

Collars and other easy bits! So she *didn't* know. The foolish woman didn't know! She thought a collar was an "easy bit." She had always believed in him. In face of everything, she still believed that he was right. Oh, she was a foolish, feckless woman, with her blindness about collars, and her folly about broth. But he loved her. The very pattern of his soul was woven with the threads of hers, dear, blind, trusting woman that she was. She didn't know. And now she would *never* know.

Her feet as she stepped about setting the table made a happy homelike music in his heart. How he loved her!

She paused at the table with an extra plate and spoon, and looked toward him questioningly. He had been so silent, she was not sure that she had won him over yet, so her voice was timorous and a little pleading: "Could I ask him, Perney?"

"Aye, lass, ask him," he agreed. Then, searching in his flowing heart for words to tell her how he loved her, he said: "An' I'm thinkin', he has never tasted the like o' the broth he'll taste this day."

1 A scarecrow.
2 A corruption of "geck", a derisive term applied especially to anyone putting on airs.
3 A high hat.
4 Something requiring careful attention, like a newly hatched chicken under which a board is placed to keep its feet off the damp ground.
5 Pinched, thin.
6 A chest.
7 Worry.
8 Witch-body, applied to anything that doesn't use human reasoning.
9 Nonsense, flattery.

THE COURTIN' OF SALLY ANN

Mistress MacIntosh was firmly upholstered back and front in black satin of a thick, dull quality. In front she was tightly encased and well pushed up. On the resulting ledge, there rested a locket containing on one side a picture of the deceased Sandy MacIntosh, "a saint on earth if there ever was one," and on the other, a portrait of "my poor blind girl when a child."

Everything about Mistress MacIntosh seemed to be pressed backward by determined though invisible fingers. It was as if she were forever breasting a gale. Her shoulders were thrown back so far that there was an indenture between her shoulder-blades. Even her thin, gray hair seemed to be striving to leave her face; the marks left by the comb divided it into little railways that went hurrying to the back of her head, and the scalp between was pink with the exertion.

The small black lace cap on her head, coming to a point neatly on the front parting, carried out the illusion. At either side of the point, three baroque pearl beads were sewed into the lace half an inch apart. For some reason they suggested hidden artillery. She resembled nothing so much as a battle-ship steaming out to the field of action.

Mistress MacIntosh had dealt fairly with life, as she was wont to point out, but life had been far from dealing fairly with her. First there was Sandy MacIntosh, a hard man to catch he had been, and no such great catch at that, when all was done. But this she wouldn't admit now, for it is ill-done and unwise-like to belittle the dead. So she loudly proclaimed his saintliness to the neighbours, but in her heart she admitted that he had been a sore disappointment.

When, after thirty years of constant persuasion, she had got him at last convinced that it was his clay pipe that made his tongue sore and bleeding, and got him to give up smoking, a saving of eighteen pence a week, he had gone out one Sunday morning for a walk along the railway tracks, "and him as deaf as a door nail."

They gathered him up piecemeal and brought him back in a gunny-sack, and there had been nothing to dress up and show the neighbours. All the expense and work of a funeral and none of the pleasure.

And then there was young Sandy, sure to be dead by spring with that cough he had that was like to split him in two; but nothing would do but he must get up and put on his braw new boots and walk with them in the backyard, scratching the soles up so that the shoemaker would never take them back in this world. And *this*, after she had watched him every day for three months to prevent it, for what was the sense of letting him put the boots on at all when he'd never live to wear them out? But he was just as contrary as his father. He *would* have the boots bought, and he *would* put them on. And now the best she would get for them would be four or five shillings, if she would get *that*; for there were them that thought that you could get consumption by barely touching something a consumptive had worn.

And the blind girl! A body might think there would come an end to trouble *sometime*. But no! She was just as unreasonable as the father of her. Without giving a thought to anybody's comfort except her own, and with no provocation whatsoever, she had died the week after they had laid her father away, and *this*, mind you, at the very time that the elders had finally consented to raise her salary for playing the organ, from ten shillings a week to ten shillings and sixpence.

It was just another instance of the perversity of life, that the daughter who had the musical education should die, and Sally Ann, who had nothing, not even enough get-up-and-go to catch a man, should be left.

Goodness knows it wasn't for the want of help that Sally Ann was single! Fowl after fowl had been killed, even the speckled hen that laid the brown eggs that were so tasty; and pot after pot of broth had been thrown away on lads that never came to the scratch. Worse-looking lasses than Sally Ann, with nobody to help them, had landed good husbands. It was Sally Ann's own fault, as she had told her time and time again, when some lad that might just as well have married *her*, stepped up the aisle with another.

But it was useless to speak to her, useless to instruct her in the ways to inveigle a man. If you left her alone with one purposely, instead of edging him into a dark corner to give him courage to kiss her, she would hand him the family album to look at, and flutter back and forth like a hen before rain, until somebody came to keep them company. It seemed that the more you threw a man at Sally Ann, the more she drew back and let her chances slip by.

She had no more sense than the father of her, and *he* had little enough. Many a time when a customer had called to take out an insurance policy, she had waited just out of earshot till Sandy would call her to witness the document, but when, after an hour had passed, she would hear the front door shut on the customer's departing heels, she would find him carefully putting away his lustre china, with never a thought of insurance policy in his head, and his only excuse would be: "It's unpleasant-like, woman, t'keep harpin' on death when a man comes t' see ye."

She was a sorely tried woman, Mistress MacIntosh; sorely tried and ill-done by.

But after all, the way things had turned out now, it was a mercy that no man would batter down the door to get Sally Ann. With nobody else to bring in a penny, it was just as well that Sally Ann was free footed and not tied to some man who might not so much as give her mother a pail of skimmed milk on Saturday night. For you can never tell about a man; there was Mistress MacKenty's Nellie that married Bransbog's laddie, you would think that she'd get all the butter she needed, and him with a byre full of Jersey cows, but no, she was down at the grocer's every Saturday night as usual buying her pound, just as if she had never had a daughter in this world.

It was a blessing too, although it had looked like a wilful waste of siller at the time, that Sally Ann had spent her grandmother's legacy of three pounds ten shillings to go to Fraserburg and learn candy-making. And it seemed like a special consideration from the Lord, that at the very time Sally Ann started in business, Sweetie-Annie's asthma took a turn for the worse, and she was obliged to give up her shop and go to live with her daughter, so that Sally Ann was able to buy her bottles and pans for next to nothing, and get all her trade forby.

Not that Sally Ann would ever make a success of the business if it were left to her. Indeed no; it was a case of constant watching to see that she didn't give the candy away to any red-cheeked bairn that pushed his nose against the window. Things had come to such a pass one day that she had even caught her putting her thumb on the weight side of the scales right under her very eyes, and she had barely prevented her from giving the Fraser bairn three half-penny's worth of butterscotch for his half-penny.

It was the like of *this* which proved that Sally Ann was not fit to serve the public, and that finally persuaded her to don her black satin gown and serve the candy herself. It was a sorry down-come that the widow of an insurance man, with a brass plate on his door, should be serving candy to any wet-nosed bairn that had a half-penny to spend; but the black satin gown made it bearable. And even the like of Skilly's Gype, that carried a high head and an impudent tongue in it, had been impressed by the gold locket, and remarked that it "dootless had cost a bonnie penny"; and when he ordered a pair of knitted gloves, he asked if she would *mind* knitting them in a heather mixture colour; so it wasn't as if they didn't *know* that she was above such doings.

It had been a bitter privation to give up the front parlour and turn it into a shop where all and sundry could come to geek and glower; and harder still to take the lace curtains off the window and fill it with pans of candy. She didn't want to do it, but Sally Ann had been determined about this; she had even gone the length of saying: "It's no secret that we're sellin' candy, mither." That wasn't like Sally Ann, she was unreasonable and feckless like the father of her, but it was seldom that she was impudent.

Sally Ann turned out to be very notional about the window. She thought it was a tasty-like arrangement to have the woollen gloves knitted the same colour as the candy, and hang the pink gloves above the pink candy, and the red above the red. But everybody kept crying for navy blue and heather mixture gloves, and try as she would, Sally Ann couldn't make heather mixture candy, and when she *did* manage to make *something* like it, it was so queasy-looking that the bairns wouldn't buy it.

So there hung the pink gloves and the red, and the green and white ones that matched the peppermint rock, and nobody would buy them. But Sally Ann didn't care. They charmed her eye, and she excused them to herself and to her mother by saying: "We have t'look on 't as necessary oot-lay t' decorate the winda. It lets them ken we sell gloves as weel as candy."

She banked the back of the window up with pink and red geraniums, and sometimes in the quiet of the morning, she would steal out to the middle of the street and take a sly look at it, coming back to say guilelessly: "It's unco bonnie, mither, I hae the real knack o' trimmin' a winda."

But Mistress MacIntosh would only sigh, and her sigh would mean: "T' think that I hae come t' *this*!" It made Sally Ann feel guilty, as if somehow in selling candy, she were also selling her mother's pride, bit by bit in paper bags; and she would take tenti[1] steps on the edges of her feet the rest of the morning, and speak to her mother only in compassionate whispers.

There was something gleyed[2] about Sally Ann. She had started to be a perfect copy of her mother, and then lost heart. Her prominent brows were made to be heavily marked with dark eyebrows, but instead, each hovered naked as an unstroked T above a timid, vague blue eye. Her shoulders had the challenging set of her mother's, and her dominant cheekbones were moulded by the same firm hand, but her hair was the yellow of a mavis' breast, and her ways were shy and tender, as if some essence of her gentle father had crept by mistake into the wrong casket.

In the shelter of her room as she braided her hair by the candle-light, Sally Ann would dream rash and glowing dreams of flashing lovers who would not be denied. Or walking alone in the bracken-scented gloaming, she would thrill in sweet enchantment at the thought of some bold gallant, riding down the lane to clasp her wildly to his breast.

But it was only in her dreams that she was brave enough to lift eyes to them; for the very approach of a man made her wits fly two ways at once in a frenzy of embarrassment. Before her sister died, leaving her to provide for the family, she had been steeped to the lips in mortification at her mother's constant angling after a man for her. She liked it better the way it was now, with her mother on the watch to prevent her seeing any man who might want to marry her. There was more room for self-respect in that; although in truth, as she told herself ruefully, her mother had no need to watch; the gallants of Drumorty took little heed of *her*, they hankered after quick-eyed saucy lasses that were loud in their laughing, and free at tossing gibe for gibe.

Sally Ann also hated the "church socials" at which she would perch nervously on the edge of a chair, with a strained smile to show that she was enjoying herself. As she sat hour after hour watching the lads petitioning smiles from other lasses, but with never an eye for *her*, she would seem to herself to get smaller and smaller and quieter and more grey with every passing hour, until she would think that she had become invisible, and would relax her effort to smile; but then her mother would nudge her, whispering impatiently: "Dinna sit there wi' a face that would sour milk; there's nae lad likes a dour-faced lass." And she would pick up her smile again and wear it dutifully the rest of the evening.

Each time she would plead to stay at home, saying that sitting so long gave her a stiff neck, as indeed it did; but her mother insisted, and somehow managed to prove that it was some unnatural ingratitude in Sally Ann that made her not want to go.

But all that was changed now. Far from urging her to go, Mistress MacIntosh even contrived to have "a sinkin' aboot her heart" every time there were any social doings, so that Sally Ann had to stay at home and tend her. She even kept her from going to serve the customers in the front parlour, except on those rare occasions when the water on her knee made her a cripple. And she believed that Sally Ann was content, and would never give marrying a thought unless some man came troubling her with his haverings.

It was a Monday morning when Sally Ann made all the treacle candy for the week. She always pulled it on a big hook in the front parlour, and because customers might come in, she wore her sky-blue print gown fresh from the ironing.

"Here's Skilly's Gype ridin' doon the brae, the dirt flyin' o'er his head as if auld Nick were at his heels," commented Mistress MacIntosh. "He'll be after his gloves, an' them barely cast on yet. Tak' the candy ben the hoose, Sally Ann; ye'll no' be wantin' t' hae speech wi' the like o' him."

"I canna, mither," Sally Ann protested. "I hae t' pull it when it's at *this* heat, or I'll hae t' heat it o'er again."

"Weel then, turn yer back on him, and dinna let on ye ken he's here."

"He'll think I'm deaf," said Sally Ann with a flustered giggle. Her heart was capering queerly at the nearing clatter of hoof.

"Better think ye deaf than think ye wanton," warned her mother, bracing herself against the Gype's arrival by feeling if her lace cap was straight.

He came in like a hurricane and was filling the parlour to the ceiling before Sally Ann had time to catch up with her heart. Everything about him, from his checked yellow waistcoat to his crinkling red hair bespoke achievement and the poise and pride that comes of it.

Ten years ago they had called him daft-like, and nicknamed him "Skilly's Gype," and had cried down scorn upon him at market and meeting-place because he had come back from Aberdeen University with new-fangled notions about farming. And the worthies had held their sides when he put a roller over his newly sprouted oats; and loud had been their clamour over the "tiled bathrooms for his Jersey cows." This was when he put a tiled gutter and running water in byre. But the derision had died out when his oats and Jerseys robbed them of the best county prizes; and though they called him "the Gype" still, and cracked their jokes about his waistcoats, there was not one of them above stepping up to Skilly Farm on a dark evening to ask him for a little advice. And now that "Auld Skilly" was dead, and the Gype owned the farm, the lassies were fairly on tiptoe at his approach and angling to catch him with every wile, as much for the fine figure of a man he was, as for the grand farmhouse and byre full of Jerseys.

But he had a high-handed way with them, and never went so far forward that he couldn't step back, for he was not minded to be married for his Jersey cows, and indeed, he was not minded to be married at all while there were willing red lips to be kissed and new waists to be circled in Drumorty.

He included Sally Ann in his hearty "Guid day t' ye," but minding her mother's warning, she didn't turn round. Indeed, she *couldn't* have turned round, in such a flurry was she. The sound of his horse's hoofs had made her heart float out of her, and for the moment he was strangely mixed up with the lover of her dreams, whose horse's hoofs also sprayed the sod behind him in his haste to reach her side.

"Yer gloves are no' but just cast on yet," Mistress MacIntosh was saying discouragingly.

But the Gype was leaning far over the counter to attract Sally Ann.

"How long will I hae t' wait t' get some o' the candy ye're pullin', Miss

MacIntosh?"

Her mother made answer, cutting off his view of Sally Ann. "We hae lots o' treacle candy all ready in the winda. How much wad ye be wantin'?"

"But I'm minded t' hae some o' the fresh," he answered, stepping round the short counter to Sally Ann's side. Seeing him, she missed the hook, and the candy would have fallen had he not deftly grabbed it and tossed it upon the hook again.

"It's sticky stuff, that," he laughed, taking out his handkerchief to wipe his fingers. Sally Ann smiled shyly up at him.

"It's the verra colour o' yer hair," he said, contemplating her. "Only it's no' so bonnie as yer hair."

"Yer horse is scarin' at something," said Mistress MacIntosh with a clinking chill in her voice. "Better tend t' yer ain business and let the lassie tend t' hers. She wants none o' yer haverin', keep that for Bransbog's lassies that hae nothing better t' do than listen t' the like o' ye."

"Mither!" cried Sally Ann reproachfully.

"Dinna 'Mither' me," snapped Mistress MacIntosh. "Gae ben the hoose as I tel't ye in the first place."

"Mither—" began Sally again.

"Na, noo," remonstrated the Gype. "I'll no' tak' a bite oot o' the lass." He put out a hand to detain Sally Ann, but, obeying a commanding signal from her mother, she had the candy from the hook and was through the door like a frightened squirrel.

"Be steppin' yer way, my mannie," said Mistress MacIntosh with withering patronage.

The Gype loitered. "I'll tak' a pound o' candy first." He was not minded to go at Mistress MacIntosh's bidding; it pleased him to make her drop her triumphant air and reach down groaningly to the shelf under the counter for a bag of candy.

"Noo," he said, with the devil dancing in his face, "present it t' Miss MacIntosh wi' my compliments an' tell her frae me that I'd tak' her walkin' if she didna hae such an ill-natured mither."

"Awa', ye impudent bletherskate, an' tak' yer candy wi' ye. I'll break her twa legs afore I let her tak' a step wi' the like o' ye."

"We'll see aboot that," he mocked. "Tell her I'll be in by on my way home t' kiss her guid night."

"Awa'!" Mistress MacIntosh was too angry for further speech. "Na, ye'll no leave it here," she cried as he pushed the candy back at her, and hurried laughing from the shop, banging the door so hard that the glass bell that covered the wax flowers on the mantel, jarred loose and crashed to the floor. She hurried round the counter as fast as her stiff knee would let her, intending to throw his candy after him, but as she heard the thud of departing hoofs, she stopped to consider it. After all, it was a shilling's worth of candy and it had been paid for; and she could sell it again and never let on to Sally Ann; and forby that, she would charge him for the broken bell the next time he came in.

The Gype went thudding down the street, scattering the sod along the gutterside as he went, and laughing in appreciation of his own wit. Then he bethought him of Sally Ann and his threat to kiss her good night. He hadn't meant it at the time. But why should he not? He was surprised that he hadn't noticed before how bonnie her hair was. And she had a soft-like look in her eyes that was unco becoming in a young lass. He recalled the rustling cleanness of her starched blue gown. He liked that in a lass. His mother had always said it was an ill sign when a woman could bear to be aught but spotless. She was wont to say: "Dirt on the sark³ is a sign o' dirt on the soul" And he believed her words to be true, although he had often found her too clean for comfort when she would follow him through the house with a besom⁴ and a duster, crying out upon him for a worthless clout that kept her cleaning from morning to night. Nevertheless he felt it was a failing that brought her all the nearer to the kingdom of Heaven; and somehow his heart could never centre for long on a lass who was not "persnickety" about dirt. There had been a chorus-girl in Aberdeen who could keep him waiting by the hour, and who had even made him miss a class or two to humour her; but a glimpse of her grimy chemise showing at the neck of her dress had cured him of that.

You could tell that Sally Ann was clean right to her skin; and how white her skin was, almost blue white, like milk that had been skimmed. It would not be a very sore trial to have to kiss Sally Ann! He grinned at that. How would she take it? She would like it, of course. She would pretend that she didn't, but she *would*. He knew his worth too well to doubt that. Doubtless she would be proud and brag about it. He must watch, though. No use letting a lass think fun was more than fun. Lasses had a way of seeing wedding rings and the like—queer how the least thing could set them thinking that way. It would be wise to make it clear to begin with— that was the best way.

Then he wondered who came courting Sally Ann. There was sure to be somebody, for all her quietness. His mother had often said that the quiet ones were the worst. She had been a wise woman, his mother. Maybe Sally Ann knew a lot more than she was minded to let people see. She had given him a look, shy-like, up out of the corner of her eyes. There had been encouragement in it, for all it was shy and soft-like. Oh, she was no guileless lamb, blush though she may. It might well be that she was as free with her kisses as Bransbog's lasses, for all her mousey ways. Doubtless she was expecting him this very minute, and thinking him blate[5] that he hadn't ridden round to the back of the house as soon as he left the shop. And why hadn't he? Dullard that he was, to keep a lass waiting! He wheeled his horse about, his mouth widening roguishly. "All right, Sally Ann. I'm no' one t' keep a lass waitin' for a kiss. My mither always tel't me I must be obligin' wi' the women-folk."

Sally Ann dumped the candy back in the pan, and took her flushed cheeks out to the back yard. Her heart needed more room to beat. She was dismayed by the pother it was making, and looked round for some sane thing to do with her hands. Something to steady her.

A bag of oats for the chickens stood near. She noticed for the first time that rust had made little holes in the tin basin, and she found herself trying to push a kernel of oats through one of the holes. "Fine nonsense," she scolded, stopping herself. "Fine nonsense, this," and with reproving haste she filled the basin and took it down to the henhouse, although it was unheard of and witless to give chickens their evening meal at ten in the morning. She stood scattering the oats before the lackadaisical hens and wondering at herself that she could be so mazed by the Gype.

"It's no' as if I thought he meant a word o' 't." she reasoned. "And what did he say, but that my hair is the colour o' the candy, which is nothing but the bare truth. Fine nonsense, this, to fash mysel' o'er a bare civility."

She barely heard the Gype ride up to the hedge when he vaulted over it, high-headed, thinking she was waiting there for him. He swaggered approaching her, his cap far back upon his head, his lip lifted in amusement over his glistening teeth.

Expecting some coquettish resistance, he lunged toward her and circled her tightly with his arms. The pan slipped from her hands and rolled away.

Sally Ann, crushed against his breast, lay quiet. This was her dream as she had dreamed it. This was love. This was her lover come to claim her. A tide of sweetness welled up to her eyes.

Her quietness surprised the Gype, who would have understood better if she had given him a clout on the ear.

He looked down at her quince-coloured head lying bright against the rough grey of his coat.

"She's a bonnie lass," he jested to himself. "It would be ill-done to disappoint her." He felt for her chin and raised her scarcely resisting face. She looked up at him timidly; tears darkened her yellow lashes. In alarm the Gype relaxed his hold. "This is a bonnie business," he reflected irritably. "Devil take me for a witless lout to meddle wi' her. She'll hae me walkin' down the aisle to the altar afore I've time t' draw my breath."

He would have taken his arms away, but Sally Ann leaned helplessly against him. He was thinking of escape when a smile flickered across her tear-wet face. This reassured him. So she wasn't blaming him. Maybe she wasn't taking him as seriously as he had feared. Some women cried for nothing, and meant nothing by it.

His arms closed about her again and his arrogant lips covered her warm mouth. Its willingness bewildered and conquered him. His emotions took a new colour, his arms about her were more gentle and his lips sought her kisses with greater tenderness. He thought how soft and small she was against his breast, and how foolish she was to trust him so. He must warn her of that. A man might well think her wanton to be so free.

Sally Ann turned her face against his shoulder, a gentle sobbing fluttered in her throat, her small round body drooping in his arms. Seeing her so helpless, he thought he understood, and a bitter shame smote his heart. He had frightened her! Frightened her so that she was powerless to resist him. He had thought her free; had thought her willing for his kisses, and all the time the poor lass had been too mazed to cry out against him. Oh, prideful popinjay that he was, he had frightened the lass out of her wits, and now she was crying as if the heart of her would break in two.

"Oh, Sally Ann," he cried, "I didna mean t' fright ye so. Dinna greet,[6] dinna greet, my wee lamb. I'm a lout that's no' worth the hangin', but I'd bake on a griddle afore I'd do aught t' harm ye, Sally Ann."

She stopped sobbing, wondering at the trouble in his broad, flushed face.

"Yer no' a lout," she said, ignoring all his protestations save that one. Eager to drive away the signs of weeping, he was daubing awkwardly at her face with his red-spotted handkerchief. But more tears kept falling, for Sally Ann was so full of happiness it *had* to overflow.

"Sally Ann," came shrilly from the house.

"My mither," cried Sally Ann, and her eyes became alert. "She'll flay me alive."

"Wait," begged the Gype, staying her as she started toward the house. "Will ye meet me at gloamin'? Come along the Bracken Lane. I'll be waitin', Sally Ann."

"I canna."

"Ye can. I'll be waitin'," he urged, releasing her struggling hand as the cry from the house rang again more insistent.

"I canna," and she darted away.

He watched her as she ran unsteadily along the cobble path between the rows of boxwood, and when the last pale blue glimmer of her was lost in the shadow of the doorway he went soberly out by the gate and found his horse.

It was a day of mazement past all telling. What pans of candy were left to burn. What pails of water left to overflow. What questions left without answer. Well might Mistress MacIntosh cry out upon her for a heedless limmer. No warlock upon the moors at evening ever went its way with less direction than did Sally Ann. At gloaming she sought her room beneath the thatch, brushing her hair with hands that flew aimlessly and got tangled. And when at last she was ready, dressed in her Sunday best taken by stealth from the kist on the stair landing, she found that no feet of hers could take her one step from the shelter of her room.

Could *she* go boldly down the lane to meet a lad at evening time? Could *she* walk up to him with lightsome words upon her lips as he stood waiting there? Oh, no, she could not. Lasses there were that could go with high heads and light laughing, and go, and go again. But *she* could not. Trysts in the gloaming were not for her.

She sat down upon her chair again, contemplating herself in the blistered glass between the candle-sticks. Oh, to be broad-hipped and glib-tongued like Bransbog's lasses; to toss a lightsome head when lads were havering; to swing by in rustling petticoats, confident that they were admiring. Oh, to be *anybody* but Sally Ann MacIntosh, so that the Gype might love her. Oh, to *know* that he loved her, so that she might be bold enough to go to him!

And what had made her believe that the like of the Gype, proud footed as he was, could love Sally Ann MacIntosh? What folly was it that made her think that he was waiting for her now? Why would the Gype, sought as he was by every lass in Drumorty, why would the Gype love her?

Oh, it was well she had come to her senses! Fine food for laughter it would be if she walked down the lane to meet the Gype; fine food for laughter if she found him there with Bransbog's lassie, waiting to see her come; or with the MacKenty lass that had so sharp a tongue. Well was it that her feet were wiser than her head and kept her home where none could see her folly. She began to undo the black ribbon at her neck, which was clasped by the brooch of twisted gold.

By sunset the Gype had reasoned with himself that no lass could cry over a kiss of his. The little limmer had tricked him, had made him go further than he meant. Oh, well, he was not unwilling to make her happy for a time. She was a bonnie wee lass. He turned his horse into the Bracken Lane with a sense that he was being very kind to Sally Ann. He had come early, for he knew that in her eagerness to see him again she would think gloaming had come when the sun had barely set and it would not be the gallant thing to keep her waiting. He was pleased with himself. He liked to make a lass happy.

Dismounting, he found a place to tie his horse, not so near that every passer-by could see it from the road, for he was not minded to be explaining to Bransbog's lass, nor to Janet MacKenty whose tongue was keen, nor even to Mary MacIntyre, though *she* would never reproach him; but it was hard to bear with her when she sat with tight lips and looked past him as if seeing warlocks. A lass had many ways of making a man itch to slap her. He sat where he could see Sally Ann approaching, and measured with his eye just where her head would come as she turned the corner by the sweetbrier rose-bush. It got darker and he had to change his seat in order to see the road. He had been wrong to think that she would come early. Of course she would come late. They always did for the first tryst. Lasses were so retiring to begin with, and so demanding at the finish. He wished that they worked the other way, it would save him many a weary hour. It was getting murky and thick and well past gloaming. Sally Ann could come now without any blame of being hasty at a tryst.

Doubtless she was on her way. Little limmer to keep him waiting so. But clever little limmer!

The moon was coming up. This was past a joke, past clever wiles. The lass must be blate to think he'd wait for her till moonrise. She must set high store by herself to think he'd cool his heels for two hours waiting for a kiss of hers. Did she think that James Minty of Skillymarnoc was sore put-to to get a lass to meet him at gloaming? Thought she that? What had she to command her that she set such value on herself? Little that *he* could see. Nothing for looks, and never a penny to her name. Was he going to sit till he took root waiting for such a lass?

No, he was but waiting to let her see how little store he set on any kiss of hers. He'd make her rue this high-handed work. He had set down higher-headed wenches than Sally Ann MacIntosh. When she came, he would kiss her light-like, and he'd talk a while cheerily, then he'd say canty[7] and smiling at her, "Weel, my lass, it's gettin' late. I maun be gaun' back to Skilly." And he would be forgetful to kiss her good-night, but very friendly with it all for fear she thought that he was vexed. And when next he saw her he would call her "Miss MacIntosh" as if naught had been between them.

But she wasn't coming, that was clear. How could he lower her pride for her if she didn't come near him? He'd go after her. Just at first it would give her more reason for her pridefulness, but the higher he made her think of herself, the greater would be her downcome when he passed her by.

Sally Ann was braiding her hair with troubled fingers when she heard a light tap upon the small window that opened upon the roof of the peat-shed. Her heart told her who it was, and she hurriedly snuffed out the candles, fearing that he could see her as she sat there in her nainsook night-gown with the frilled cuffs.

But how could he come without a sound? How climb the roof without her brother hearing?

The tapping again! How dare he knock so loudly? How could he be so bold? Her fingers danced about the dressing table in a frenzy. She was afraid, but wildly happy. "Fairly batterin' down the hoose t' get me," her heart sang. Oh, that this should happen to *her*. And then she saw his face against the window-pane, a white wedge in the moonlight. He was raising the sash. Her heart broke into panic. What should she do? Should she call her mother?

The Gype was propping the sash with his shoulder. There was just room for his arm and face in the narrow opening of the window.

"Sally Ann," he whispered, searching for her in the dark room. "Come here."

"I canna," she whispered back at him, but left the chair and came a little way toward him.

"Come here," he said again as she paused timidly.

"I canna," she answered, coming nearer as she spoke.

"Come and kneel by me," he commanded.

"I canna," she said softly, but came and knelt by the window so that her face was level with his.

"Noo ye'll gie me a kiss, Sally Ann MacIntosh," he said, catching hold of her.

"I canna," she gasped. How sweet was the tumult in her heart!

"Ye *will*."

"No, I canna," she faltered, praying that he would insist.

"It would be a sore pity t' wake yer puir sick brother," he whispered mockingly. "A sore pity, but there's a loose slate by my foot, and down it goes unless ye kiss me this minute."

"Oh!"

"It would be ill done t' wake him, puir lad," sighed the Gype.

"No, dinna," she begged.

"Weel, I'm waitin'." He thrust his gleaming face through the opening.

"Then I maun do it," said Sally Ann, more to assure herself than him.

"First put yer arms about my neck," he ordered.

"I canna." But her arms trembled to obey.

"Down goes the slate then," he threatened.

Her arms flew up in obedience. Oh, how bold she was. How bold, but how happy.

"Kiss me!"

"I canna," she said, and kissed him eagerly.

"Again an' longer," he ordered.

"I canna," kissing him as she spoke.

"Na, dinna stop," he said, as she drew back. "Ye'll hae t'keep on wi' the kissin', for I'm sorely tempted t'kick down the slate."

"Oh!" Surely this was Paradise.

"I'm sorry for ye, Sally Ann," he commiserated. "It's a sore trial t' hae t' kiss me."

"It's n' a trial," she whispered shyly.

"Is it no'?" His voice was eager, and then he was vexed at his eagerness. He was there to lay low her pride. This was the time that he should go away and leave her. Leave her lightsomely, and then, when next they met, greet her as if naught had ever been between them.

But it would be well, and nothing more than just, to let her tell why she had broken the tryst. So he'd sound her out on that.

"I'm thinkin' ye hate me for my impudence," he ventured.

"I dinna hate ye," she said softly, a timid hand reaching up to his crinkling hair.

"Then why did ye no' meet me?"

"I couldna."

"Fine story, *that*," he cried scornfully. "Nae lass ever missed a tryst t' please her mither."

Sally Ann could not answer. How could she say all that was in her breast? How tell him that her feet were not brave enough to go to him? Go to him? Oh, no, her heart was too faint with her unworthiness. Sally Ann had no words to tell him this.

The Gype brooded upon her silence. "She didna wish t' cheapen hersel' by meeting me at the first askin'," he told himself. Here was a lass who was not minded to melt in his mouth like a ripe berry at the first tasting. Here was a lass that would take some reaching for. And she was right. His mother had always said: "A worthy bride's no' easy won." She had been a wise woman, his mother.

But he was thinking of Sally Ann as a bride? Oh, no, but there was no harm admiring a lass that held herself high. He wondered what she thought of him, and longed for some reassurance, some word to show that she did not quite despise him.

"Ye dinna hate me, Sally Ann?"

She shook her head.

"Yer no' angry that I made ye kiss me?"

She shook her head again.

"Will ye let me kiss ye, Sally Ann?"

She nodded shyly and turned her face to his. And then he knew that there was nothing sweeter than to lie there on the slated roof in the moonlight with Sally Ann's timorous arms about his neck, and her breath, fragrant as the air from new milk, upon his face. He knew that there was nothing dearer than the warmth of her lips upon his, and the gentle flutter of her breast.

And so throughout the months of sweet-brier roses, and well into berry-picking time, he sought Sally Ann by stealth upon the roof or in the gloaming along the Bracken Lane. And on market days, when Mistress MacIntosh was well occupied, he would venture into the kitchen for a hasty kiss. But he had never said a word of marriage to Sally Ann, and though at times she saw herself riding to the kirk in Skillymarnoc's phæton behind the dappled greys, she would push the picture away from her, not daring to look upon its brightness. Nor did she grieve at the thought that it might never be, but rather she held her happiness breathlessly, as one might hold a gleaming bubble with spread fingers.

It was the evening of "Stookie Sunday" and the Gype had been to the kirk to pray for drought to dry the grain, for this was the only occasion when he put any faith in the Lord. He had hoped to overtake Sally Ann in the Bracken Lane, but she was *not* at the kirk, and neither was Mistress MacIntosh. This was more than unusual, it came nigh to being alarming, and the Gype made sure that some mishap had come to young Sandy. So it was with little caution that he sought Sally Ann in the kitchen.

"Yer brother?" he asked as he entered the door.

"Na," said Sally Ann, understanding him. "It was the hens."

"The hens?"

"Aye. They're crop-bound. We fed them wi' the oats left frae decoratin' the kirk. My mither thinks it's a visitation frae the Lord for stintin' Him. We hae operated on sax o' them wi' Sandy's razor. Five are doin' fine, but this ane's like t' pass awa'!"

She put the basket with the drooping Black Minorca hen upon the table. The Gype inspected it, fingering its faded comb soberly.

"Tell yer mither t' put a drop o' oil t' keep the feathers frae stickin',"

"Aye, she's done that. Ye'd better awa'," Sally Ann advised. "My mither's only at the hen hoose."

"Come down the lane, then."

"Na, I couldna an' leave the hens."

"Hens or no hens, I'll no' leave without a kiss." He pressed her close, and held her all the closer as she struggled, begging him to mind her mother.

And then it was too late. Mistress MacIntosh stood in the doorway, a wilting hen under either arm, her face as red as the combs upon their heads.

"Fine work this on a Sabbath day! Fine wanton's work! Standin' there haverin' wi' the scum o' the earth while a hen worth eighteen pence is like 't pass awa'. Lord pity me that I brought the like o' ye into the world, ye wanton limmer."

"Nae more o' that!" cried the Gype. "Ye'll no' call wife o' mine a wanton limmer."

"Wife o' *yours*," screamed Mistress MacIntosh derisively.

"Aye, just that," said the Gype with furious calm. "Sally Ann, come wi' me."

"No' a foot," cried her mother. "Oot o' my hoose, ye worthless prodigal, afore I hae my sick laddie rise frae his bed t' throw ye oot."

"Sally Ann," said the Gype, "I maun go for Sandy's sake. Meet me in the lane."

"Niver!" cried Mistress MacIntosh.

"The lass has a tongue o' her ain," the Gype reminded her scathingly as he went.

Sally Ann faced her mother, trembling, but there was something of new strength in her blue eyes.

"Dinna glower at me," cried her mother. "Tak' yer sinful face oot o' my sight. Up t' yer room, ye worthless besom!"

"I canna, mither, I maun meet him," said Sally Ann, in a voice so quiet with certainty that Mistress MacIntosh floundered, incredulous.

"Ye defy yer ain mither? Oh, that I should live t' see this day!" She set the hens down hurriedly, not caring how they flopped helplessly on the floor, and clutched the front of her bodice, gasping as she did when her sinking spells were upon her.

Sally Ann regarded her with troubled eyes, but made no move toward her.

"Dinna hae a sinkin' spell, mither," she advised, "for I maun leave ye."

"Devil tak' my glib tongue," thought the Gype as he went striding down the lane. "What call had I t' go proposin' marriage? I'm no' hankerin' t' be tied faster than a ram at shearin' time. Forby that the lass never looked for it. Never so much as said, 'It maun be lonesome for ye at Skilly-marnoc.' Never so much as mentioned that a hoose is na a hame without a woman in it. Never even tried t' sew a button or mend a sock for me."

No, he couldn't blame the lass. She was not one to snare a lad with wiles and glances. But it was not too late. He could pull in his horns again, blame his hasty speech upon her mother, and keep away from Sally Ann. Never see her again, that would be best.

Never see Sally Ann again? What havering was this? How could he live without seeing Sally Ann? What would he do without her kisses at gloaming? What could he do without her gentle glances? It was for Sally Ann he hurried through the day with lightsome singing. It was for Sally Ann he had painted the barn. How could he live without Sally Ann?

He looked yearningly along the lane. Why didn't she come? He could not bear this waiting. His heart was harried with the need to hold her. How could she loiter so?

And then he saw her coming, her feet falling daintily upon the moss-dappled path. How could she take such care in coming? How dally so? He could not bear the space between them any longer, and so he ran to meet her, stumbling in his eagerness, his face strained with the pain of his need.

"Oh, Sally Ann," he cried, sweeping her within his grasp. "I canna wait. Say ye'll have me. I ken I should hae asked ye afore. I ken I should hae asked ye different—Sally Ann!"

Sally Ann could not speak. She was full of shame that she had ever doubted him. He had meant this from the first! He had been courting her for marriage, and she had thought he held her lightly. She had given her kisses while she had doubted him. Oh, he must never know. He must never know what a wanton heart was in her breast. She was so poor a thing, how could he love her so? And from the full tide of her humility, she cried, "How can ye want me for a wife, that none has ever sought before?"

And the Gype replied—for this answer had come to him many times as he wondered at his love for her: "It takes a man o' taste t'appreciate ye, Sally Ann."

And she was happy, not seeing that half the compliment was for himself.

---

1 Careful, cautious, quiet.
2 Off the straight, wrong, oblique.
3 A shirt, vest.
4 A broom made of heather.
5 Dull-witted.
6 Cry.
7 Cheery.

THE FUNERAL

"I'm no' urgin' you against your will, O Lord, I'm but just asking you. If it be your will let the siller come to-day, for I begrudge, and *more* than begrudge, to ask help o' Mistress MacKenty; and I'm loath, and *more* than loath, to let them know that Tammas is walking the streets o' America wanting work."

Mistress MacBride raised her head at the end of her silent prayer and looked toward the box-bed near the ingle-nook. From where she sat on the window bench she could see wee Jimmy's knees, thin and pointed, drawn up beneath the quilt. He lay still, as he had lain for hours. Round the room her eyes ranged looking for something to do. But the board-floor was scrubbed and sprinkled fair with fine sand, the hearthstone and the window sills were pipeclayed white, upon the dresser the tin and pewter shone, and the kettle on the crane glistened black. Nothing to do but clasp her hands and wait. Nothing to do but watch the distant hedge for the uneven bobbing of the postman's head.

Across the cobbled street the thatched cottages in a row stood white-washed and spotless like placid faces looking back at her. She turned her eyes away. Her hands ran nervously up and down the smooth round buttons on her bodice front. They were feverish, jerking hands, driven by hunger to a ceaseless unrest, and the eyes in her thin young face were harried and glinting. The last penny in the Toby-jug was gone, and Jimmy must have broth. In all these bitter weeks with the money ever dwindling, she had fed him on the best, but for herself only turnips, turnips, turnips. But now there was not the colour of a penny in the jug upon the shelf, and the last of the broth stood in the rosy-bowl covered with a plate. But the siller *would* come to-day; Tammas had said that he had work in sight. Her eyes strained painfully towards the hedge again. She tried not to see the tight-lipped little houses, but her eyes would keep ranging them, saying:

"Which one shall I ask for help? Mistress MacKenty? No; *she* would tell it to the town to prove that her opinion of Tammas MacBride was justified. To Mistress Fraser? Mistress Fraser would whisper it, pitying her, believing all that Mistress MacKenty believed, though she would not give it voice.

59

Jean MacFarlane? No! No!"

Her wasted cheeks burned. She could see them whispering behind doors, telling their opinion of her man, and everything they did for her would be recounted as a proof that he was all the wastrel they had said he was. They would be kind, nay, more than kind. They would forgive the lies she had told about the weekly money order; they would forgive her false bragging about his success; they would heap her with gifts and laud her for a good wife that had protected her man's name to the point of starvation, but oh!—how their tongues would rend Tammas MacBride, and what joy they would find in doing it. For all Drumorty had told her on her wedding day and long before it, that the lass that married Tammas MacBride had need of a stout heart. Aye, and need of more than a stout heart; need of two blind eyes as well, if all they heard was true. And true it *was*, for hadn't Mistress MacKenty herself told them about the graven images? And hadn't she sworn it on the Bible when they doubted her? And why would Mistress MacKenty be throwing away her chance of heaven, and her with three laddies there already, and their father forby, though she wouldn't be breaking her neck to see *him* again, and the bad temper he had. Still she had nothing to gain by lying about Tammas MacBride, and it was no hearsay about the box of dirt he had sent from Aberdeen. What Christian in his sane mind would pay cartage on a box of mud? And would he have it left in the back yard, think you? Oh, no! He must have it up the stairs in his bedroom and right underneath his bed. As Mistress MacKenty said, it was like having a grave-yard in the house, and she couldn't think but that he got it to bury something in. But after keeping a watchful eye on him for weeks without so much as getting a foot inside the door, she caught him one night, when the latch was off, and was inside before he had time to hide the evidences. She was out again in a second with her apron over her head, and screaming like a banshoe crying for death. It took three glasses of Skillymarnoc's best whiskey to quiet her, and all she would say that day was "Graven images!"

The minister agreed with her that it was not a Christian thing to have such goings-on in the same house with her two innocent lassies, so he spoke to the sinner, but in a roundabout way, for, as Mistress MacKenty said, he was a quiet boarder and a small eater, and it would be ill-done to put him from the door if they could persuade him to part with the box of dirt and stop his evil ways. But he moved anyway, taking the dirt with him, and then Mistress MacKenty told in confidence, that it was figures of women he had been making, without a stitch of clothes on that *she* could see, but standing as brazen as brass for all that. It made a body's blood chill to think where he got his knowledge. Though she *did* say that they were like no women *she* had ever seen, but were long and thin as if they'd been fair famished for a six-months.

It wasn't as if he hadn't a good trade. Them that knew, said he was the equal of any plasterer in all the parish. But even about *that* he was full of notions. For did he not finish the schoolhouse ceiling with fancy cornices, although the Elders had warned him that he wouldn't get an extra penny for doing it? But what was that to him? As Mistress MacKenty could prove, he spent days cutting zinc to shape the mouldings with, whistling all the while as if he were making his fortune at it.

Drumorty had told her all of this the first day he stopped by at the schoolhouse with a handful of marigolds by way of introduction. It had added warning to warning as the rumour went out that: "the young pupil-teacher and that worthless Tammas MacBride had been seen walking by Skilly's barn on Sunday afternoon, and him holding her hand and swinging it as they walked along." Even the Elders had given her a careful word of advice. But what did it profit them, or her? Come Martinmas that year, she handed in her resignation and was married to Tammas MacBride before the snow flew. Drumorty sat back to wait!

Five years! And never a word of fancy cornices or graven images. Nothing but plastering and staying with his job. It was even said that he had several pounds in the bank, and some thought the school teacher had made a man of him. But what's in the blood will come out, and no sooner did they hear that he was itching to go to America to work at the World's Fair than they knew that their first judgment of Tammas MacBride was sound. Running away from his wife and child! Well, they had warned her. Fine nonsense about making a fortune and sending for them. She'd never see hide nor hair of him again, nor the colour of his siller! That was Drumorty's verdict at his leaving.

It was six months since Tammas went away, and every week the money in the Toby-jug grew less, and every week his letter came, saying: "Have faith in me, my lass, times will be better soon," or in the hopeless words: "I've tramped the streets for days," she read the sharpness of his suffering. But to Drumorty's avid ear she said only that her man was "doing fine."

If the money didn't come to-day she would have to tell. But it WOULD come. A swift prayer left her lips as she scanned the hedge-top again, a prayer that was half an apology, as if she would say: "I know you will not fail me, Lord, but I fear you may forget that there is only one more helping of broth for Jimmy in the bowl."

The postman's cap appeared and disappeared beyond the hedge; soon he came, trailing his crooked foot along the road. As he neared the gate she stiffened; when his hand touched the latch she sprang to meet him. Closing the door she gripped the letter at either end, staring at its face as if it might speak to her. In this grey envelope was the Will of God, whether she must tell, or whether her man was to be spared the shame. Her fingers began to tear feverish scallops along its edge, nicking the corner from a pink slip within. A money order! She hurried to the window light and read:

"Salvation Army—Soup and bread for one."

And on the back, in Tammas's writing, "I've had to come to this, but I'm promised work to-morrow." Her fingers sought the envelope again, disbelieving, begging it to give up something more. It rustled thin and relentless, gaping wide to show its emptiness.

Her God had spoken! She would have to tell. Submissive tears came pitifully upon her eyes, and through their glaze the tidy little houses rocked crazily. Which one? Mistress MacKenty? And then she saw her coming, her hands rolled tightly in her apron and resting on the ample dome of her belly. Here was the one that she must tell, sent to her at the very hour? Oh, that it had been another; one with less barbed a tongue. She would have chosen otherwise.

A knock, and Mistress MacKenty was in, for she was never doubtful of her welcome.

"A letter frae yer man, an' another money order!" she cried, with the frost of envy on her voice as Mistress MacBride held the Salvation Army slip toward her. "My certies, with all the money he sends you, I'd think ye'd be away to America. But maybe he's no' pressing ye to make the trip—on account o' yer sick laddie, I mean," she added, with an elaborate pause to convey beyond doubt that she meant nothing of the kind.

Mistress MacBride stuffed the slip back into the envelope, and answered steadily:

"I'm leaving for America as soon as Jimmy's better; my man is fairly wearied for the sight of him."

"Weel, weel," Mistress MacKenty purred, with oily disbelief. "Yer laddie sleeps sound."

"It's on account of the medicine the doctor gave him."

"Aye, aye,—I'm thinkin' a little chicken broth would revive him. I'm sellin' my cockrels this week for eighteen pence. Would ye no' like to buy one?"

"He's no' so fond of chicken broth."

"Hmm! Ye'll no' be wantin' to leave him. I'm goin' in bye to the post office. If yon's a money order I'll cash it for ye."

"I'll no' put you to that trouble, thank you kindly. I've money and to spare on hand."

"Weel, weel, I suppose yer no' wantin' us to ken how rich yer getting!" Mistress MacKenty made her way towards the door. On the threshold she paused: "For mysel' I'd rather have my man where I could watch him." And she was off the doorstep without waiting for an answer.

When the latch clicked after her, Mistress MacBride sat weakly down wondering at herself. With the truth ready on her lips and submission in her heart she had told the lie again. God had given her a sign and she had turned from it. She fell upon her knees; but what use to pray? She knew His will; yet deeper than all she knew that she could never tell, something stronger than herself would hold her back.

. . . But Jimmy must have broth . . . to-morrow was market day. . . . Her thoughts flew up to Skillymarnoe, to the long table in the milkshed that would be filled with butter and eggs, to the grey stone slab in the corner and on it the rows of dressed fowls ready for the market in the morning. It was a late rising moon, and early dark. They'd never miss a fowl or two and a dozen eggs. . . . What was this she was thinking? Kneeling silent for a long time she turned from this blank wall to that, and then she spoke that God might know her heart and strike her dead upon her knees there if such was His will: "I canna ask them, O Lord, I canna ask. . . . I'll turn thief afore I turn beggar and shame my man."

When the light in Mistress MacKenty's house had been out for an hour, Mistress MacBride pinned a shawl about her head and kilted up her skirt about her wincey petticoat. With a final look at the still little hillock in the bed, and a glance at the lamp to see that its low-turned wick wasn't smoking, she lifted the latch and slid out carefully. For a little she stood irresolute upon the step. A flutter of terror shook her knees. A cold damp broke out upon her palms. The night was full of hostile things that knew her mission and hissed in little gusts about her head. She crossed the road, stumbling on its cobbles; along the hedge she crept, keeping well within its cover, screening the white of her face with the dark woollen shawl. Past the town hall shrouded with rowan trees; their fallen berries crunching wetly as she walked. A dog yelped from its kennel, rattling its chain. Her mouth was dry with fear. Past the doctor's door, its dim blue light glimmering above the bell; past the church hung in shadow, the big nails upon its door looked darkly down. She ran, but the shadow of the church ran with her, its steeple bent and followed her. She reached the turnpike leading out to Skillymarnoe. It opened like a toothless mouth empty and black before her, and behind the cold, angry finger of God pointed at her back.

But Jimmy turned his face away, and neither broth nor eggs could still the fretful rolling of his head. Still-lipped she watched by day and in the night she waited prayerless for the dawn; and every dawn came damply in to show the little face grown thinner and more pale. The need to pray harried her; she wished to scream a supplication that would shake the Lord upon His throne, but her voice lay fainting in her breast, and her heart, sick with its sin, sat waiting for its certain punishment.

Then, on a chill dawn it came. She made no outcry. To the neighbours gathered about in sympathy she said not a word, but went about walled off from understanding. Their words rattled without meaning about her head. Mistress MacKenty was busying herself at the bed. Haggerty, the undertaker, sat on a stool, thumbing a catalogue, the tails of his frock-coat hung like a split fan behind him.

"An oaken casket wi' silver mountings," he droned, with the right balance between sorrow and salesmanship.

"But for a wee laddie," Mistress MacKenty remonstrated, "a plain deal box wi' a lick o' white paint is tasty-like and no' expensive."

"Aye, but there's dignity about an oaken casket," he urged.

"But expensive—I've always said it's ill-done to spend siller on the dead that might better be feeding the living, so as I said, Mr. Haggerty, a plain deal box—Mistress MacBride will no' want extravagance wi' her man at the other side of the water, and only God in His wisdom knows if she'll ever see a penny o' his siller."

Mistress MacBride heard that last with all its meaning. Instinctively she rose to her feet to cry out upon them, to deny, but she stood stricken and silent before them. Not even the plainest casket could she buy, and they must know it soon.

"I've been tellin' him the plain deal box," Mistress MacKenty urged helpfully.

Mistress MacBride tried to speak. The postman's sudden knock cracked out like a command, and she was still. Sharp eyes watched her tear the letter open, and as her fingers found what she had sought for weeks, she turned away to hide her tortured face. Wild laughter dashed about her like a mad thing, striving to vent itself. She held it prisoner, and turned to them with high held head:

"I'll take the casket with the silver mountings," she said. "Tammas MacBride would no' want his laddie buried skimpy."

And Drumorty never saw the like of Jimmy MacBride's funeral. The laird himself had gone to rest with humbler trappings. Plumed and flower-laden it wound, stately with chant, along the road, choir boys singing plaintively, and pall-bearers with mournful tread. And with its passing passed also the last misdoubt of Tammas MacBride.

Mistress MacKenty declared at kirk and market that she had always known he sent his money home, and some remembered this or that upright thing that he had done, and all agreed that Tammas MacBride was a worthy man, little deserving this grief, though it was not for them to question the Almighty and His ways. But in her darkened room, Mistress MacBride sat alone, bowed beneath the sharp justice of her God. Black had been her sin of theft, and still more black her pride. Just was the weight of His hand upon her. Not to make complaint, nor yet to ask forgiveness for her sins, but only to make Him turn His ear and break the isolation of her soul, she cried: "I know I wasna fit to keep him, and me a thief; but I couldna tell them, Lord."

FECKLESS MAGGIE ANN

"I'm sure it's Shiny Dan. I can see the glint o' his flagon, and forby that, the *Bonnie Maggie Ann* came round the Windy Scaup five hours back. Even wi' a big catch he'd be through by this time." Jeannie's Sally flung this back over her shoulder into the darkening room without any suggestion of expecting an answer, and continued to watch through the cottage window, carefully sheltering behind the geraniums lest the neighbours should even suspect that Shiny Dan's movements were of any interest to her. At her remark the click of steel needles from the arm-chair in the shadows stopped for a second and then went on again.

"Aye, it's him, and he's heading this way. Get out the griddle, mither. I'll be makin' scones when he comes. There's nothing makes a lone man hanker for a woman like the sight o' her makin' scones."

The needles stopped, and a thin, bent figure hoisted itself and hobbled obediently toward the griddle without a word.

It was Jeannie, the mother of Jeannie's Sally. The neighbours held it against Jeannie's Sally that her mother spoke so little. They whispered the words "domineering limmer," and sometimes they called Jeannie "puir auld Jeannie," but not when Jeannie's Sally was around. They had to admit, though grudgingly, that no daughter in the whole fishing village of Rosarty kept her mother wearing better goffered mutches or brawer wincey petticoats than did Jeannie's Sally.

"Mither!"

It was a sharp cry of reproof. Jeannie, bracing herself with her head against the mantel to lift the griddle up to the crane, almost dropped the griddle into the glowing peats beneath as she guiltily drew back her head, with its snowy starched mutch, from the soot-stained mantel. She looked across at her angry daughter and faltered apologetically:

"I dinna think I've spoiled it, lass. I aye forget." Then, justifying her carelessness in soiling her mutch, she added, "It's no' easy to lift the griddle without leanin' a'gin' the mantel."

"Easier than to stand for hours gofferin' mutches, I'm thinkin'."

Jeannie's Sally slammed the chimney on the oil-lamp she had been lighting as she tossed this taunt. The light steadied down, showing her round, high-cheek-boned, rosy face and smooth black hair sedately parted in the middle. Her black eyes, glinting with anger, gave colour to the neighbours' whispered "domineering." She was a bonnie enough lass, however, and buxom, and could mend nets better than any guidwife in Rosarty. And for gutting herring she was paid sixpence a day more than any other lass during herring season. But for all that she had turned six-and-thirty and hadn't landed her man yet, although she'd been setting her cap at Shiny Dan ever since his wife Maggie Ann died, twelve years back.

Before Shiny Dan had married her, they had called her "feckless Maggie Ann" in the herring yard, because she hadn't the strength to wheel her barrel of herring aside when it was full, and had needed to call upon some man to help her. Jeannie's Sally had pointed out this failing of Maggie Ann's to Shiny Dan one day when showing off her own prowess with a full barrel. She expected him to laugh at "feckless Maggie Ann," as the other men did, and was sore puzzled to see him cross the yard and wheel Maggie Ann's barrel aside for her, and more than puzzled when day after day Dan made a point of moving Maggie Ann's barrels. Exasperated, Jeannie's Sally confided to her mother: "And he never knew the little snippet was on earth till I pointed out her fecklessness ti him; noo he's dancin' round, waitin' on her hand and foot. He'd be the laughing-stock o' the yard were it not that he's over-broad in the shoulders to be laughed at."

And Jeannie's Sally wasn't the only one who gasped, amazed, that winter when Danny, braw, strong fisherman that he was, owning his own boat, chose to "wed wi' white-faced bit slip o' a lass like feckless Maggie Ann." Maggie Ann herself was astonished when Danny, wheeling her barrel aside at the end of the day, said with grave concern:

"Ye're over-light for work like this, Maggie Ann, and I'd be easier in my mind if ye'd wed me. I'm no' exactin'; I'd mend the nets mysel'."

And Maggie Ann, wise with woman's wisdom, knew that this was love, and she raised her brown eyes, moist with the wonder of it, and cried:

"But how can ye love me, Danny? I'm sae useless-like and dependent!"

"Maybe that's why, lass," said Danny, speaking with more truth than he knew. "There are whiles ye mind me o' a birdie wi' its wing broken."

And the next herring season the gossips, prompted by Jeannie's Sally, told with shrugs and headshakes how Dan was up at four of a morning mending his nets, when any bairn could tell you that a man that stood his watch by the nets for forty-eight hours had sore need o' his sleepin' time. And what was a fisherman's wife for, they would like to know, if no' to mend the nets while her guidman was sleeping?

But, for all their tongue-wagging, Danny and Maggie Ann were foolishly happy. In the evenings she would sit on his knee, run caressing fingers over his ruddy, long-lipped face and through his upstanding thatch of wavy, black hair, and croon adoring nonsense into his ear at a time when any right-thinking guidwife would have had her needles clicking their way through a new jersey for her man.

Danny never abandoned himself to this love-making; a shamefaced reticence kept him pretending that he only tolerated it because such foolishness seemed to make her happy. But he never reproached her for the things she neglected while doing this. Sometimes, to try him, she would sit off in the chair at the opposite side of the fire, and fall to mending a shirt with great industry, watching him slyly the while.

He would glance at her from time to time, surprised at this new aloofness; then he would noisily tap the ashes from his pipe to indicate that he had finished his smoke. Maggie Ann would continue to sew diligently, quite deaf, apparently, to the tapped invitation. Thinking she didn't hear, he would reach up groaningly to the mantel to put the pipe away, and settle back in his chair again with a loud "Ho hum!" But the needle would still flash back and forth in Maggie Ann's slim fingers. He would be forced to speech, and after deliberation he would say:

"The light's kind o' dim to sew by, lass," but not for the life of him would he say, "Come and sit on my knee," which was what he was longing to say and what she was aching to hear.

And she would answer:

"It's no' so dim, Danny," and go on sewing, although every nerve of her was urging to throw the sewing away and hurl herself into his arms.

"Are ye no well, Maggie Ann?" he would add, after fifteen minutes had passed. It was his next clumsy move to bring her to him.

"Aye, I'm well, Danny," she would answer indifferently, but her heart was crying, "Ask me, ask me to come Danny!"

Hearing only the indifference of her answer and not the cry of her soul, he sighed, and his rough-hewn face darkened unhappily. Her heart smote her. What did it matter that he was too proud to ask her? He wanted her in his arms, and she knew it. So, with all the sweet generosity of her nature, she would forbear to try him further. She would look across at him and say hesitatingly, as if she dare not ask it:

"Danny, could ye bear to have me on your knee?"

And, consummate actress that she was, she would pretend not to see the sudden glow that lighted his eyes at her request, and would continue to look at him tremulously as if fearing a refusal. Nor would she smile at the assumed coolness of his answer as he settled back to make a seat for her on his knee, saying:

"Aye, for a little while; but ye must na set store by sitting on my knee, lass. It's no dignified in a married woman."

But after she had buried her face in his blue-jerseyed shoulder she would smile that tender, amused maternal smile that wives smile only in secret.

His first and last words of reproach to her were over the flagon. They had been married six months when a tinker came up the Windy Scaup to Danny's cottage peddling in tin flagons and Turkey-red twill. Danny was still at sea, and Maggie Ann had twelve shillings in the corner of her kist, for Danny was more generous with her than fishermen are wont to be. The red twill and the tin flagons were no temptation to Maggie Ann. She had seen both all her life, and owned flagons and to spare for all the milk Danny and she needed. But wrapped in oil-cloth and dangling from the end of the peddler's pole was the flagon that proved Maggie Ann's undoing. Such a flagon she had never seen, a fancy, ribbon flagon plated with copper.

"Is it no' bonnie?" she gasped as the wily peddler undid it temptingly.

"It's the brawest flagon in the countryside," asserted the peddler, holding it up to let the sun glint on it, "an' it's only five shillings." He placed it in Maggie Ann's hands, like a high priest conferring a blessing.

"Five shillings!"

Maggie Ann handed it back. She never could pay five shillings for a flagon. Danny would think her daft.

"There's no anither like it," wheedled the peddler, using the age-old weapon against which no woman can fight. It is the mirage which tempts her when she buys a gem, it is her Waterloo when she buys a bonnet; and it works just as surely with a fisherman's wife when she buys a flagon. Satan used it in the garden when he showed Eve the apple. "There's not another like it," he whispered, and Eve fell. And so Maggie Ann, true daughter of Eve, paid five shillings for the flagon for the same reason.

She spent hours placing it first on the mantel, then on the window-ledge, then on a nail by the fireside. It had a dozen settings before dusk, and in each one it seemed more desirable. By evening she was convinced that money had never been better spent, and when Danny came home, she showed him the flagon with pride.

It was the wrong time to show him the flagon; he was weary and spent with lack of sleep, and that night the *Bonnie Maggie Ann* had come home with empty nets. To her eager, "Is it no' bonnie, Danny?" he answered soberly:

"How came ye by that, lass?"

"I bought it for five shillings frae Sandy the Peddler," she answered, her voice scarcely faltering on the price. Danny didn't answer. He turned away and, seating himself, pulled off his deep-sea boots and set them inside the fender to dry. Not yet understanding the quality of his silence, Maggie Ann approached him, the flagon in her hand; her delight in the ownership of it could not reach its full unless he shared it. So she urged, "Say ye think it's bonnie, Danny."

He turned deliberately from her and sat looking into the fire.

"Danny!" It was a hurt cry of reproach, tinged with surprise that he could treat her so. He stirred unhappily in his chair. He was loath to hurt her, but remembering snatches of old rumours that Maggie Ann's mother had been "sorely extravagant wi' her man's siller," he knew that he must be firm with Maggie Ann; so there was a distant deliberation in his voice as he said:

"It takes a hantle o' herrin' to bring five shillings, Maggie Ann."

Had he lifted his deep-sea boot and struck her to the earth she could not have been more outraged. Criticism from him! Nay, all the world might call her feckless, all the world laugh and slight her, but he had made her his queen, and now he had torn the crown from her head, and stood ranged with the world to find fault in her. She stood staring at him as he sat with averted face, condemnation in every line of him. Then rose a blind agony of desire to hurt him as he had hurt her. Quivering with a passion that was too strong to be held in her frail body, she cried:

"I'll never spend anither penny o' yer siller. And *this*"—she held the flagon out at arm's-length—"I'll throw over the Scaup—and mysel' I'll throw after it." She whipped round and dashed out of the door.

Danny sat dazed. She was all too quick in speech and action for his slow-thinking mind. But as she passed the window, heading swiftly up the cliff-side, he sprang to his stockinged feet and rushed after her.

She reached the summit and swayed, wind-swept, at its perilous edge. As her arms went up to make the plunge, he caught and held her fiercely, his weather-beaten face pale and furrowed with new lines. Over her struggling, panting head he looked down at the seething death-trap of the Rumbling Gulch fifty feet below, and there was a new ferocity in the tightening of his arms as he turned back and silently carried her down the cliff. There was a new sternness in his face as he set her down on her feet at the fireside. He took the flagon from her hand and put it on the mantel. The colour was returning to his face, but a forbidding wall of silence was settling about him.

Her anger spent, Maggie Ann's heart grew cold with fear that he loved her no more. She watched him set the flagon down, and hoped that he would turn and scold her, that he would beat her, anything just so long as he would touch her. She felt miles away from him. She *must* have his arms about her, but she dared not go to him while he looked like that. If she were to make another dash for the door, he would seize her and hold her, and she would be able to feel the rough wool of his jersey against her face and inhale all the dear odours that were Danny. And she would feel his heart beat, even though it were beating angrily; still, she would be near it. If his arms were round her, she could make him come to her. But, no, she remembered the agony of his face on the Scaup. Better far that she should humble herself and crawl every bit of the way back to his heart than that she should bring that look back to his face again.

Almost like an old man he let himself down into the chair and sat looking into the fire, his hands still resting on the arms of the chair as if the effort of moving them were too much for him.

Maggie Ann, regarding him with growing remorse, fell on her knees by his side and laid her cheek supplicatingly upon his arm.

"Danny," she whispered—"Danny, I'm sorry I bought the flagon."

"It's no' that that's hurtin' me, Maggie Ann."

She didn't need him to tell her that; she knew what was hurting him. But she liked to know that she could hurt him, and she liked more than all to know that she could hurt him most by saying that she would never spend money of his earning again. And she liked to hurt him still a little more by pretending that she did not know that this was what was hurting him now. Oh, she could be as compassionate as an angel and as tender as a dove; but she loved, and so she could be as cruel as any fiend in hell if by being cruel she could prove the depth of his love for her. So she let him suffer a little longer, and knelt by him, staring into the fire also and ticking off the minutes of his suffering, while he, in inarticulate agony, tried to understand why it hurt him so when Maggie Ann refused to spend his money.

She shifted the position of her cheek upon his arm a little, so that she could see his face; its heavy, dumb misery filmed her eyes.

"Danny"—her voice was faint and penitent—"I'll spend yer siller, Danny."

Dan was silent, but the quality of the silence was changed. He brought his other hand up across his eyes as if shielding them from the fire, and his throat worked as if jerked from within.

"And ye'll no'"—he paused, struggling for words—"ye'll niver—run up the Scaup again, Maggie Ann?"

Something wet and warm fell on Maggie Ann's face; another drop followed it. Maggie Ann buried her face on his knees and cried: "Niver! niver, Danny! Oh, Danny! Danny!"

His arms went round her shoulders protectively. She felt him feel for

71

his kerchief and wipe his eyes, and heard him struggling to make his voice natural as he said:

"It's queer how peat smoke makes my eyes water whiles."

"Aye, it's queer," Maggie Ann agreed hysterically between laughter and tears. She crept into his arms and sobbed against his breast, while he told her that it was all right about the flagon, and wondered, as he tried to comfort her, why she took the scolding about the flagon so hard.

But she was weeping over Danny, over the poor dumb love that could not express itself, and over the strange pride that made him unwilling to admit his tears even to her.

And that should have ended the quarrel about the flagon; but next day there was the flagon, and there was Maggie Ann, and being a woman, she would never rest until Danny had said that it was a wise purchase and a most desirable and bonnie flagon. And Danny, being a lowland Scot and having a long upper lip, would never own it while he lived. So when he was leaving at sundown to go to sea, she ran a coaxing arm about his neck and said:

"Say it's a bonnie flagon! Say ye like it, Danny!"

He stiffened in her embrace and answered:

"I think o' 't as I thought o' 't yesterday; it's a useless geegaw and a senseless waste o' siller."

So she let him go to sea without a good-bye kiss, and she wouldn't even lift her eyes from the ironing-table to watch him through the window as he went down the cliff to the harbour, and she told herself that if it killed her, she wouldn't go to the top of the Scaup to wave good-bye as his boat went round the point.

Dan watched for her as his boat went slowly by, sure that she would relent and come to signal him good luck. He strained back to see as the distance widened, but no waving little form broke the outline of the cliff. Soon he was too far away to see, and as he gave up hope, he thought bitterly, "All this over a flagon!"

Maggie Ann, unable to hold out a moment longer, raced hot from her ironing up the wind-swept Scaup, and reached the point as the boat dipped out of sight. Too late! She screamed "Danny!" and the wind whipped the words from her lips and struck like a knife through her thin breast. She sank down, and beat the earth with futile hands, crying, "Why could he no' say it was bonnie?"

And in the night a thousand searing knives of pain darted through Maggie Ann's lungs. She gasped and strove to cry his name, but by daybreak she was still and cold. And still and cold was Danny in his sorrow when he looked upon her face, and silent as had been his love, so silent was his grief. He sat by her coffined form for hours, holding the flagon on his knees. By moonlight, when there was none to gape and wonder, he dug her grave at the top of the Windy Scaup, and he lowered her in his arms as the sun rose, and laid the first earth upon her gently, handful by handful, lest it hurt her. He dressed her grave with the shells she loved, and raised a cairn of stones, gathered by hand one by one, each one chosen for its beauty.

In the long, lonely evenings he would polish the flagon to keep it bright; then he got to taking it with him when he went out. The flash of the sun on its shiny surface would signal his approach when he came along the turnpike. When questioned why he carried it he answered, "The glint o' 't's company," and closed his silent mouth so forbiddingly that gossip forebore to question him further. But from then they nicknamed him "Shiny Dan."

Twelve years, and every night he was ashore Shiny Dan would sit on the cairn and smoke his evening pipe. He told himself that he sat there because it was a fine place to see the boats go round the Scaup. Twelve lonely years coming back to a bleak fireside; cheerless home-comings, with no waiting form on the door-step; silent leave-takings, fastening the latch, with no looking back to say good-bye; nothing on the Windy Scaup as his boat went by but the quiet cairn of stones: and all the while Jeannie's Sally waiting and anxious to change it.

He would ask her to-night. She was a bonnie lass, and buxom, and her house had a warm and cheery air. True, his arms didn't hanker to hold her as they hankered for Maggie Ann, but Jeannie's Sally had a "wee mither that was feckless and dependent; he'd like to see her sitting cosy-like when he came in frae sea."

The light of Sally's cottage blinked in the distance. He strode toward it with quickening step, the flagon clinking against him cheerily as he walked.

In the cottage Jeannie's Sally was baking scones, while old Jeannie's needles clicked with new excitement. Shiny Dan was a heroic and romantic figure to old Jeannie. She hoped Sally would land him, but she secretly thought he was too good for her. Forgetting discretion, she spoke some part of her thoughts aloud.

"It's a bonnie notion o' Shiny Dan's to carry the flagon."

"It's a daft-like notion," snapped Jeannie's Sally, "and one I'll wean him o' the day I face the minister wi' him."

Rushing on to her destruction, Jeannie chuckled:

"He's no' over-anxious to face the minister, I'm thinkin'."

Jeannie's Sally paused, amazed at such temerity from her mother; then ruthlessly she hurled her answer.

"He'd be more anxious were it no' that the day he weds me he'll have to house you."

It was a cruel lie, and Jeannie knew it was a lie, but it hurt, and she wilted in her chair. The needles stopped like the slow ebbing of a breath. Even Shiny Dan's brisk step on the threshold didn't liven them up again, and as soon as she had greeted him she crept brokenly to bed.

Jeannie's Sally, in a feigned fluster, apologised over being caught baking, and, wiping the flour from her rosy arms, begged Dan to be seated. He sighed appreciatively as he took the chair. The cheery blink of the peats under the fragrant griddle, the cosy red-and-white rag rugs on the floor, the glint of china and polished tinware on the dresser, and Jeannie's Sally flushed in her starched gown—Dan sighed again in blissful contemplation and said admiringly:

"It's hame-like. A woman looks bonniest when she's bakin'. It's what I miss."

Jeannie's Sally, sensing the coming declaration, said nothing, but smiled across at Dan. Already her thoughts were on the Paisley shawl that Dan had given Maggie Ann as a wedding present; she wondered if the moths had got into it.

Dan sat wondering how to proceed. Perhaps it would be best to let her know that the season had been extra profitable, and then lead on from that and say that he would like to help her make a home for her mother. Or maybe he had better tell her that he was lonesome. No, she might wonder why it took him twelve years to find that out. In his dilemma of indecision Dan was moving the flagon nervously from one knee to the other. Jeannie's Sally saw this and was barely able to keep from seizing it from his hands. The flagon had been a constant irritation to her for twelve years. Without *knowing* anything about it, she sensed everything about it.

Dan cleared his throat loudly and began:

"I've bought a half-share in the Mackenzie's boat, an' I'm goin' to repaint the *Bonnie Maggie Ann.*"

"An' rename her, maybe?" asked Jeannie's Sally, unwisely.

"Na"—a cold decision took the place of the uncertainty in Dan's voice— "I'll no rename her. She was named for my wife, as you'll mind."

"We'd mind that better if ye'd named her the *Feckless Maggie Ann.*" Jeannie's Sally could have bitten her own tongue before the words were well out of her mouth. The look on Dan's face told her that she had made a mistake, but it also added fire to her raging jealousy of Maggie Ann, and stole the last shred of caution she had left. So when Dan answered soberly:

"Maggie was feckless, Sally; but she was unco bonnie forby," she sneered:

"There was nane thought her bonnie but yersel'—and nane but think ye daft that ye carry her flagon."

"I carry the flagon because it's company," Dan answered stolidly, "and I'm no' mindin' wha thinks me daft."

"Ye carry it because Maggie Ann set store by it, and ye sit on the cairn because she lies beside it." Jeannie's Sally was drunk with jealous rage that had fermented for years; too drunk to count the havoc she was making of her own hopes. Her voice rose in a strident torrent. "If it's no' that, then throw her flagon in the peats and make an end o' 't."

Shiny Dan rose to his feet, the flagon in his hand, and said quietly:

"I'll be steppin' up the Scaup, Sally; it's gettin' late, and I hae nets to mend."

Jeannie's Sally watched him go and knew that she was powerless to change his love for Maggie Ann. As his footsteps died away, she cried in helpless anger:

"The white-faced, feckless little snippet!"

There was a fixed purpose in the tread of Shiny Dan as he headed past his own cottage up to the cairn on the Windy Scaup. He seated himself as a man that had come home safely and was glad. Setting the flagon between his feet, he took out his pipe and began to fill it slowly.

The starless dark night wrapped about him. No sight of passing boat broke the current of his thoughts. The light of his pipe glowed and ebbed with the rhythm of a heart-beat.

He felt again the slender fingers of Maggie Ann steal caressingly over his face and pause to outline his eyebrows before they crept up to twine themselves in his hair. He heard her croon adoringly over the curve of his ear and chuckle over the solemnity of his face. He felt again the coaxing circle of her arm about his neck and saw her eyes look up entreatingly in his as she urged, "Say ye think it's bonnie, Danny!"

And in a voice husky and tender he whispered to the soul of Maggie Ann:

"It's a bonnie flagon, lass."

DARK STAR

TO FRANCES MARION

BOOK I

Nancy was glad when her grandmother died. Glad, but a little afraid, like some wild thing, long caged, suddenly let loose. She cried a little because the neighbours seemed to expect it and because it gave them pleasure to tell her that it was "all for the best and you must be brave." There was also a secret elation in being suddenly the object of their sympathy, surrounded by their jars of calf's-foot jelly and healing potions, after having been a nobody all the fourteen years of her life.

Grandma Pringle had "slipped away in her sleep." This was characteristic of her contrary nature. Her heart attacks, attendant upon eating hot bread or cabbage, had brought her to the point of death fifty times in the preceding two years, and only Nancy's quick administration of the prescribed hypodermic had snatched her back. At such times Nancy would act with a sportsmanlike determination to give her every chance, but with a grim dispassionate speculation whether *this* was the time. But Grandma Pringle, with her usual contrariness, had not died after a supper of cabbage, but had gone peacefully over the border after eating a bowl of toasted bread and milk.

When Nancy took in her morning cup of tea, she found her, her thin withered hand under her cheek, its fingers curled over her hawklike nose.

Granny was convinced that the night air was poisonous, and would exclude it with the quilt held firmly against her nose on those occasions when Nancy insisted that she must have the window open a few inches.

There had never been any exchange of "Good morning" between them. Nancy would come in with the tea and say, "All right," and Granny would sit up alert, and almost before her eyes were open would voice her incessant complaint that the cup was barely half full. And Nancy would say:

"I can't carry it without spilling if it is brimming full—and anyway the doctor says you're not to have tea at all."

Or Granny would lie playing dead, watching her through scrubby grey lashes until Nancy would impatiently exclaim:

"If you're going to lie there and squint at me until your tea's cold, don't expect me to make fresh!"

79

Balked in her desire to cause a sensation, Granny would come to life reluctantly before her tea was cold. But she would chant tearfully as Nancy retreated to the kitchen:

"I'm just so much dirt—if I died this night she'd sweep me out with the besom in the morning. O-o-oh, the heartlessness, o-o-oh, the ingratitude!"

And Nancy would shrug indifferently as the chant reached her.

This morning she came in and said: "All right."

But the figure on the bed lay without even a quiver of squinting eyelashes. Nancy watched the eyeballs under their wrinkled lids to see if they rolled. They did not move. She said "All right" a little louder and watched the eyeballs again. But no result. She was not easily going to be trapped into showing emotion or alarm. Granny had played dead too often; so she made a strategic move. Shuffling her feet as if about to go, she said:

"I'll take your tea back if you don't want it."

And her lip curled amusedly as she looked, expecting to see the old woman make startled movements of just coming awake. But the smile faded as the figure lay still. She set the cup on the table and reached out a hand to touch the clawlike fingers upon Granny's nose. They were cold, icy cold. Nancy drew back, amazed that it had happened at last. She murmured, "That's funny," but it was not clear even to herself what she meant by the words.

When Granny had had her first attack, Nancy was told that the next one would doubtless be the end, and the red-faced country doctor had shown her how to give a hypodermic if Granny should get grey in the face and start gasping in the night.

It had been an eye-widening horror to the child the first time she stood shivering in her striped shirting nightgown, and, with teeth chattering, had tried to press the needle into the shrivelled flesh of Granny's arm. She never would have managed it but for the threatening gleam in the old woman's eyes as she gasped orders to "hurry, hurry." Then Nancy had closed her eyes and pushed. As the needle crunched home, she became faint and swayed in a nauseous nightmare. But in the months that followed she acquired a detached, almost careless expertness, and would wonder at the old woman's terror of death as she pinched a fold of the aged flesh between her firm fingers before inserting the needle. This expertness annoyed Granny. To cause alarm was the very breath of life to her, and the only compensation she had for the discomfort of her attacks. When she would recover sufficiently, she would begin to upbraid the girl for a "heartless young hussy."

But now the need of hypodermics was over, and over too was the morning wrangle about tea and the evening wrangle about fresh air, and over and done with was the smell of clothes from an old withered skin that dreaded soap and water, and Nancy was glad. Her first untrammelled act was to open the window wide, and next she pulled her hair loosely over her ears as other girls did who had no grandmother to nag them. Then she went and told the neighbours.

They took Granny to what Pitouie proudly called the "undertaking chambers." The "chambers" were really part of a dairy farm made over. Granny was lain on one of the shelves where pans of white milk had once stood waiting to be skimmed.

For a shroud she wore the frilled nightgown which had lain for years in her kist, wrapped in blue paper to keep it from turning yellow. Her bristling grey hair was unnaturally meek under a fine lace mutch. On a dirty ribbon around her neck the undertaker found the small key she always wore, and gave it to Nancy. His wife half-heartedly offered to let her stay with them overnight if she was afraid to go back to the cottage alone. But Nancy was not afraid. She had been born facing the wind. So she was not afraid to go back alone. Indeed, she was anxious to get there, for she had business with the key that had hung round Granny's neck, and with the walnut box inlaid with mother-of-pearl, which stood on the red doily in the centre of the parlour.

Always she had believed that revelation and grandeur waited for her in the walnut box. Even as a child, barely able to reach it by standing on tiptoe, she felt that it held something for her. But always it was locked. And so the mystery of its contents grew, varying with the years as her needs varied. It contained a hair-ribbon grander than any ever seen before; it held a fortune (at least twenty shillings) which would buy a school-bag and a pair of skates; and finally, as she grew older, it would tell her who her father was. This last belief, once gained, never left her. The walnut box came to be a destination. As other children ran home to a fire, or to their mother's knee, she ran home to the walnut box.

The earliest thing that Nancy could recall was the feeing market on a sunny day, the heavy-faced farm-hands and farmers, the servant lasses in their Sunday-best, and the constant jerk-jerk upon her arm as her mother pulled her through the throng. There was one wonder after another all packed together in the market square—rows of stands covered with painted candy and wooden-headed dolls that clapped round brass hands when you pressed upon their breasts; a clown, with a terrifying, wide, bloody smile, shouting creakily:

"Come and see, come and see,
A horse's head where its tail should be."

A dwarf with a bucket and a monster brush scrubbing an elephant—
sight after sight, each more amazing than all that went before; but nothing
so entrancing as the tall gold-skinned gentleman, far more elegant than the
laird, even upon an Easter Sunday, who stood upon a platform, calling in
purling cadence the magic of "Jujah, the One and Only Instantaneous
Painkiller. Step up, ladies and gentlemen, only one shilling a bottle."

Between his tapered fingers, covered with rings of gold, he held
delicately a small bottle. Nancy marvelled at his hands; their blue-white
palms were many shades lighter than their brownish-yellow backs, and the
finger-nails were like none that she had ever seen, but strangely purple, as
if the blood beneath were trapped and gasping for breath. Chains of gold
crossed and recrossed his double-breasted waistcoat, and pendent from
them hung many large-pronged human teeth. His trousers were a lively
blue, traced with a fine white line, giving a jaunty note which balanced the
dignity of his black frock coat and tall silk hat, poised at a breathless angle
on his close-curled head. At intervals he would sing melodiously:

"If you've pains in the back,
        TRY JUJAH!
Or a bilious attack,
        TRY JUJAH!
If you've measles, or the dropsy,
Or the chronic pipsy-wopsy,
Try the inky pinky medicine,
        JUJAH!"

Then he would woo the yokels to step up with their aches and pains
and prove the wonder of "Jujah, the One and Only."

"One drop applied to the spot and all pain vanishes; any lady or
gentleman here with an aching tooth step this way."

The crowd began pushing a young farm-hand with a swollen face
toward the platform.

"This way, this way. Now, my pretty gentleman, where is the tooth?—
Ah, one moment, one moment, please. One drop of the marvellous painkiller
upon the spot and all pain vanishes. Watch the face, ladies and gentlemen.
See the pain disappear."

With incredible ease he whipped the tooth out and held it aloft, crying:
"Not an instant of pain—see the happy smile upon his face."

Prompted by the swarthy one's persuasive eloquence, the victim smiled sheepishly and spat a red mouthful upon the platform. He was turning away, but the honeyed voice coaxed again. Obeying it, he reluctantly handed over a shilling, took a bottle of the "One and Only" and lumbered down to his hooting companions.

"Pains in the back, arms or ribs, this way, this way, please!"

The hand gripping Nancy's slackened; she found herself alone in the crowd, and saw her yellow-haired mother mounting the platform beside the medicine-man.

Watching their meeting, an emotion blind of understanding but vivid as pain shot through her. Something was meant by that glow in the dark face that bent upon her mother's; something terrifying was meant by the glamour in her mother's face as she looked back at him. This was all that Nancy knew, but she knew it to her very core, and in her fear she screamed her mother's name.

But these two were set apart and deaf to any cry but the cry that clamoured in their blood.

What followed had faded from the child's mind. But that moment, shaken with fear and jealousy and desolation, would never fade. She came to know later that her mother had gone away with the medicine-man, but this news was only an echo of what she already knew. She had seen it with her eyes and felt it with her heart. It was a vivid spot, as if she had seen her mother consumed by fire.

The next thing that blazed a permanent mark upon her happened four years later, when she was ten. Her granny had taken her to the near-by fishing village of Rossorty for the summer holidays. At this season the fishermen had gone south, following the herring from port to port, and their wives and daughters took in summer boarders at a trifling sum if they were content to take "pot luck" and share the absent fisherman's bed with his wife or children.

For the fishing folk would make no "company" of the land folk, even if they could. They thought them an inferior people, and spoke of their coming "for our air" as if these poor things who lived inland had no air to breathe all the rest of the year. The land folk in turn despised the fishing folk for the hysteria with which they took their religion and the complacency with which they endured fleas.

To the land folk, religion was something to accept placidly, but fleas were an abomination. So they would arrive plentifully supplied with flea powder, which, however, did not seem to prevent the fleas from covering them with large itching bites, while the fishing folk never seemed to be bitten at all.

Each thought that the behaviour of the fleas proved some superiority in them. The land folk displayed their swollen bites as a proof of the delicacy of their skins, and the fishing folk bragged of their absence of bites as a proof that fleas only bit animals and human beings "with a *certain* kind of blood."

It was a gentle warfare which broke no bones. The summer visitors looked on with a kindly tolerance not unmingled with contempt when the fishermen's wives would gather with shawl-covered heads around the pump, clanging tin basins and singing:

"You must be a lover of the Lord"
       (*Bing! Bing!*),
"Or you won't go to heaven when you die."

From the noise attending these frequent meetings Nancy early got the idea that the fishermen's God was deaf, and quite a different God from the one that Pitouie, in sedate Sunday black, mumbled prayers to.

It perplexed her to know which God she should pray to on her holidays. To be safe, she prayed to both of them, but she enjoyed the noisy prayers best. It was exhilarating to bang a tin cup on a telegraph pole and roar the Lord's Prayer with all the strength of her lungs. However, she carefully made all her important requests of the Pitouie God, for, while the deaf God was more exciting to pray to, she had little faith in His ability to give the right answer. She pictured Him with a kindly, bewildered face, resembling Deaf Peter, who would listen eagerly to her question: "Have you ever seen a whale as big as the one that swallowed Jonah?" and after deep pondering, would reply gravely: "They're drowned, missy, every mother's son of them, and the boat's been sold nigh to twenty years."

Another fancy that she had was that the Pitouie God wore a tall silk hat, while the Rossorty God wore a cap with ear-flaps, which might have accounted for His not hearing so well.

She could not remember when she had been first taken to Rossorty. But she would never forget the first time she had looked on it, with eyes that saw its beauty.

On sunny days its one narrow street ran straight up the rose-coloured cliff into the sky. On dull days it had a gentler, less dramatic beauty. But never could it look like any other town.

Great rose-coloured cliffs, without a blade of green, sloped up like a reclining wall shutting off the sea, and up this rosy slope, almost to its top, marched the lime-white little cottages. The blue of the sky, the rose of the street, the white of the houses, with their yellow thatched bonnets, and, like veils upon their faces, the nets hanging to dry; nothing ever looked just like that. The seaward side was one sheer drop against which the ocean dashed and roared, eating inward in great caverns. At low tide it rolled away to show the ancient smuggling caves of the Fasseferns. But when the tide was high it sent its spray flying to the cliff-top, and the sunlight made of it a rainbow diadem to crown Rossorty.

It was on such a day that it first pierced her with its wonder. In one sharp moment she saw, and never would forget. Nothing that went before was clear, but suddenly, into the half-dark that is the narrow vision of a child, there flashed, with the clatter of hoofs, this blaze of beauty. . . .

Past her up the street rode a man, madly spurring his horse, his bare white head shining like silk, in scarlet hunting-coat and white breeches, astride an ash-white horse, and down its slender flanks the blood was trickling.

Up, up the steep street he rode, lashing the horse, and as he passed, women rushed to their doors and children scampered away.

On, on, up the rose path toward the rainbow mist.

To the top, and out of sight!

A scream went up as if from one despairing throat. And then they ran, following his path; fleet young women with children in their arms; ponderous, heavy-footed mothers of men; grey-haired grandmothers wailing toothlessly, and hobbling old men; and with them ran Nancy.

Cries and wailing everywhere: "Another Fassefern gone to his death. Suicide Fasseferns! Suicide Fasseferns! Ill luck to Rossorty and our men at sea. Woe, woe, the day!"

At the top they threw themselves upon the ground and crept forward to the cliff's sharp edge, gazing down upon the lashing coiling water. Nothing could be seen of horse or man; only the sea continuing its age-old programme, hissing up the time-worn rocks, then drawing in its breath to hiss again more wildly.

But while grey heads stared down, despairing at the sharp black teeth of the sea, Nancy looked upward, expecting to see horse and rider galloping in the blue above. For never could she quite believe that he had not ridden straight into the sky. And the beauty of this mad thing was for ever stamped upon her soul.

That night she lay in the fisherman's box-bed, spreading wide her arms and legs for the pure joy of occupying all the room possible. Soon, when Granny came to sleep on one side, and the fisherman's wife on the other, she would be folded like a portable knife, fork, and spoon, neatly flattened down to her smallest dimensions.

She thought: "When I'm rich I'll have a bed as wide as a field of barley and I'll lie in the very middle of it alone." Through the haze of drowsy contentment came the whispering of the women about the peat fire; wailing for the lost soul of the old master, fearing for themselves and the disaster it might bring to the herring nets.

Now that this had come, the herring would surely pass them by next year. Was it not three years that the herring had passed them by after the last Fassefern? The hand of God would swing the herring away. And could the hand of God be stayed while anger was in His heart?

Whispering, they told of the young Fassefern bride who was found on her wedding-morning dead in her bridal robes, lying upon the altar of the chapel, lilies heaped about her, and candles burning at her head and feet. And of the youth, naked in the rose stone fountain, dead in the moonlight.

For long they fretted with prophecies and lamentations, huddled over the peat fire. As her eyes were closing, Nancy heard them say her name, and then her mother's name. Listening, she sensed that in some way they thought her linked with this mad race that threw life away in a flash of beauty. And as they talked, always they came back to her and wondered, and Nancy wondered at their wondering, and ached to grasp the vague thing and know what it meant.

Through the years that followed it came to her in half-told tales and pregnant pauses. Piecing the tattered ends together, she learned the story. At sixteen her mother had gone to Castle Fassefern as second upstairs maid. From somewhere Nancy gleaned a vision of her, girlish and dainty in a grey alpaca gown, with white frilled apron and cap. And then came a picture of her, the frills all suddenly bedraggled and dim, pitiful, as she once had seen a white Minorca hen, pitiful, after a fight.

Soon Nancy came to see that the gossips of Rossorty and Pitouie were venomous toward her mother, not because she "had given birth unblessed," but because she would never tell them whether the father was Willie Weams, the groom, or Ramsey Gordon, the young lord of Fassefern. Some said it was the groom, pointing out that he had left the castle and had gone outside the parish the very week that Bella Pringle came home. Others declared it must be young Ramsey of Fassefern himself, for did he not go suddenly to Europe? And, though his father said that the lad was outgrowing his strength and he was sending him to Switzerland for fear of his lungs, one excuse was as good as another, and it was not likely he would be telling the real reason.

They were prepared to believe either story, but Bella Pringle would not tell. So they, who would have liked to take sides with her and bewail the injustice of the gentry against a humble servant lass if it was the young master, or insist that he make an honest woman of her if it was the groom, were left with their good intentions on their hands, and no use to put them to. They vented their annoyance by saying that she had doubtless been free with both of them and didn't know herself which was the father to the bairn.

Their tongues never troubled Bella Pringle. For there was no lack of lads to take her to a dance, bairn or no bairn. And no lass in the parish made a bonnier show than she, in her spotted muslin gown. Burnside's son himself was not above leading the lancers with her. And even the banker, pompous and round as a Toby-jug, would meet her secretly at the turnpike bend after dark. No lack of kisses, and maybe more than that. No lack of pretty boxes with shell-encrusted lids, or ribbons for her neck. But no man came up to the door and knocked in broad daylight. And none asked that she would wed with him.

Other lasses with just as lively evidence of their sins were wed, and soon forgot that "little Jimmy" or "Mary Ann" had been a misbegotten bairn, and the neighbours gladly forgot it with them. But a mystery will not be easily set aside, and so the sin of Bella Pringle would not be laid away.

Nancy was nearly twelve when she heard word of the groom that sent her all the way to Callochie in her bare feet to get a look at him. It was in the late afternoon. A neighbour chanced to remark that the groom was "walking a stallion" on his way to Callochie Fair, and wondered if he had forgotten Bella Pringle, or if he had a reason too good to remember her, adding that it was safe enough for him to come back, either way, since the woman had shown that she was no better than a harlot, and nobody would be expecting him to make an honest woman out of her. Though, if the minister got wind of his coming, he might ask him to provide for the bairn.

On hearing this, Nancy ran out on the turnpike leading to Callochie, her shoes dangling about her neck, where she had hung them while wading in Menzies' burn after school. She was confident that one look would tell her if he was her father.

She made the ten miles in a series of runs, pausing to ask occasional farm-hands if they had seen a big man walking a stallion, always to get the same answer: "No, lassie, but I saw a wee mannie walking a stallion."

If it was a "wee mannie," it would not be her father, that she knew well, and she ran on with a lighter heart after each answer. For there was a fever in her crying that she was no child of a groom, and urging her to look upon his face and know this for the truth.

The long dusk had thickened into black when she reached Callochie, and, by the instinct of those born in little towns, found the market square. Already it was criss-crossed here and there with skeletons that to-morrow would blossom into balloon stands and sweetie vendors' tables.

She wandered among the ghosts, looking for some one to question, but all Callochie was in bed, squeezing its eyes tight in an attempt to be asleep two hours before its accustomed time. For not a man or bairn but would be up at the first cockcrow, and not a mother but would be up long before that.

It was here that he would come in the morning, so it was here that she must stay. She found a load of hay laid down near the ring for the circus tent, and pushed her way into it, wondering if rats would be in it already, or if they would find it in the night and come jumping in on her.

She remembered terrible tales of travelling tinkers who had their toes chewed off by rats while stealing a night's sleep in the hay. And, as a caution against this, she removed the shoes from her neck and put them on. She lay down with her hands pressed against her stomach, where it kept thinking of "tatties and herring," and other sweet-tasting foods. But the remembrance of earwigs made her start up again; for well she knew that if an earwig got into your ear, it burrowed and burrowed until it came out at the other side. And that was not the worst of it. Often it laid a trail of eggs from one ear to the other, so that for ever after little earwigs, bleached white in the dark, kept hatching out and wandering about in the unfortunate body's head, till at long length the poor creature went mad with the way they itched and no means of getting in to scratch them.

So she sat up in the little hole she had made, and looked straight out at the brooding square. The thought of food overcame her at last. She stopped wrestling with it and sat repeating toothsome dishes one after the other. Many of them she had never tasted, but she could be as extravagant as she liked with no one to hear her: "Bannocks with treacle, tatties and herring, cabbage brose, kale brose, pease brose with cream, chappit tatties with sise, stovers, hare soup, a boiled egg—two of them (though she knew that was out of all reason), bloody pudding, skirley, suet pudding, dumplings and broth, meal and ale, tripe, potted head, skate, fried roe, finnan haddie, *kippers.*"

That last was too much. She could not swallow fast enough. She would have to stop or her tongue would be washed away.

She woke so cold that her heart was almost shaking loose from its moorings, and her legs were two lead things with wooden feet at the far end of them. Wheels were rumbling toward her. It was beginning to be faintly light. She looked out from her hole, surveying the square. Shapes and sounds were moving into it from everywhere, dusky elephants and swaying camels, a cluster of white ponies moving like four-footed ghosts, caravans rumbling perilously, carts clattering, and strident voices issuing orders.

Someone was building a fire. Nancy pulled herself out of her chill nest, twisting her tortured feet to hasten life into them, and limped toward the blaze.

A woman was bending above it, arranging a kettle upon three stakes. Her curly black hair hung about her face. A small shawl, crossed upon her breast, was fastened by a large brooch of dazzling diamonds as big as robins' eggs. Nancy at once decided that she had stolen it, for a brooch like that must belong to a queen. Her skirt, dragging in the dirt, was torn, and on her feet were rubber boots big enough for a man. She looked up and saw Nancy standing in the outer circle of light, and cried:

"What do you want, bairn?"

It shocked Nancy to hear her speak a tongue that she could understand. She had expected her to say: "Fee fi fo fum," or other witches' talk; although it was true that she didn't look like a witch, but was young, and had a warm brown smiling face, such as witches never have.

"Have you lost your tongue?" she taunted good-naturedly.

Nancy drew a little nearer and smiled timidly.

"Ho, left your mouth open at night and the mice ate it, I suppose."

Nancy smiled.

"Are you cold?"

Nancy nodded.

"Like some tea?"

Nancy came forward eagerly.

"I'm cold, I'm awful cold, and hungry," she chattered, holding her hands toward the leaping flames.

"Just got up, or never been to bed?"

"I slept in the hay."

"Why? The camels might have bitten you."

She drew the child's attention to the camels, tearing hungrily at the hay.

"Snap, there, took a bite out of the chief clown last week—not that I would have shed a tear if he'd taken the head off him."

Nancy wondered at that, but said nothing.

"Don't stand there staring like an owlet. Tell me what you were doing in the hay, and why you couldn't be sleeping in your bed—you're not in the profession."

A look at Nancy's well-mended apron and neat wincey dress proved to her that her assertion was true. People "in the profession" did not mend their clothes, though it was a point of honour with them to wash them occasionally.

"I came to look for my father," the child volunteered. The woman set the kettle down hurriedly in the middle of filling the teapot.

"Is he with the circus?" she asked sharply.

"No, he's walking a stallion. I mean—you see, he's not my father, but I came to make *sure* that he isn't. His name is William Weams."

"So your name is Weams."

"No, it isn't, because he's not my father."

"Then why are you looking for him?"

"Because I want to be *sure* that he isn't," Nancy repeated.

"And how will you know? By asking?"

"No, by looking."

The woman gave a short dry laugh.

"Well, you're a queer bairn. Where's your mother?"

"She's away with a medicine-man that does the fairs."

"So you *are* in the profession. You might have said that first as last—well, take that mug and drink some tea. It'll warm you up."

It *did* warm her up. It was like a spot of fire in the middle of her, that began to spread and spread, until the shaking about her heart and the chattering of her teeth were lulled in a sweet glow.

"Would you like to join the circus? We need a tight-rope walker and a girl to play beauty and the beast with King Leonard, 'the biggest and most savage lion in captivity; the very king of jungle beasts, more savage than the tiger, more deadly than the snake.' It's a good trick; the girl puts her head in his mouth. But she has to be young and pretty. When Mattie died, old Julie did it, but the audience cried: 'Bite her head off.' You've got to be young and pretty for *everything* except telling fortunes, and for *that* the older the better."

"But doesn't the lion bite?"

"Bite!—Can't chew his food. We have to feed him with a milk-bottle. His teeth are false—put in for the performance. We got him from a zoo for a song because his jaw-bones were festered. I'd advise you to apply for the tight-rope, there's no future in the animal acts."

Nancy was sipping her tea gratefully, paying much more attention to the woman's actions than to her words. From a push-cart near she had taken a frying-pan and a box of kippers. Pulling some of the fire forward, she set the pan upon it. Soon the sweet odour of frying kippers was in the air. Nancy felt weak with its deliciousness. The woman tore off a hunk of bread, tossed a sizzling kipper upon it, and handed it to her. It was heavenly fare! She ate it all, and sucked the fins and tail in silent ecstasy.

A man approached them, hungry for his breakfast.

"Who's the kid?"

"She wants to train for the rope."

"Had any experience?" the man asked through a full mouth.

"Her mother's in the profession."

Nancy wanted to tell the truth. But how could she contradict the woman after having eaten her kipper? And now maybe she would be obliged to go with the circus out of gratitude. It was well the woman had said the tight-rope. She would not like to put her head into the mouth of a lion with festered jaws.

While the woman was busy handing kippers here and there among the troupe that came up to the fire, Nancy stole away, for she *had* to see Willie Weams, circus or no circus.

The market square was now a bustle of people and carts, elephants and camels, hurdy-gurdies and shooting galleries, everything that could be named, but no stallion. At last she stopped a farmer with a laughing face and twisted staff, and asked where a stallion would be kept at night, and if it would be likely to come to the fair-ground.

"A stallion?" he roared, laughing lustily, "not with all the circus mares there are about, I'm hoping. What were you wanting with a stallion, bairn?"

"I'm wanting to see the man who walks it," Nancy explained. "I'm wanting to see Willie Weams."

"Well, well, tastes do differ, I must say," he marvelled drolly, surveying her. "But if you're bound to see him, though I'd sooner see a twice skinned ape myself, I'd look in Bizzet's barn."

As she went he called after her some quip which bent him double with mirth, but it had no meaning for Nancy.

At the barn she met several men with thick short necks and red faces. She thought they must be brothers. She asked the man with the whitest face if he was the man who walked the stallion.

"No, he's in the yard behind the barn."

"He's not receiving ladies—only the four-footed kind," another announced, and at that they all laughed as if some great joke had been made. Something in their laughter made Nancy conscious of her bare knees.

"I'm only wanting to look at him. I'm not wanting to speak to him."

"She's wanting to *look*," the reddest one cried, and they all howled again.

"All right, I'll lift you up and let you look."

"Leave the lass be," ordered the one to whom Nancy had spoken first.

"Away you go, bairn; this is no place for a lassie," he advised.

"But I *have* to see him," Nancy said firmly.

"Let her see," said the reddest one. "I'll lift you. He's the short one."

He lifted her up as he spoke. The others crowded with them up to the wall. As Nancy looked over, they broke out in leering cries and laughter. She had a confused flash of some strange struggle between the stallion and a smaller horse. A stout squat man was near the wall. He turned his face upward as Nancy looked down. She saw it full and freely.

"That's him," they told her.

"Let me down," she screamed, kicking the one who held her.

Their bawdy laughter followed her as she ran.

She ran, and ran, crying at something, she knew not what, sick at some odious thought which would not form itself clearly.

"He isn't my father, he isn't my father!" cried every beat of her heart. On and on flew her feet.

"He isn't my father, he isn't my father!"

Faster and faster she ran. On and on flew her feet, trying to leave that face behind. But it swam before her, red and pock-marked, as she had seen it when she looked down from the wall.

"*You are not my father!*" she stopped and screamed, as if to pin the face upon the road with that sharp cry.

"You're not! *You're not!*"

She stamped the loathsome face into the road with angry passionate feet. Then she ran on, often looking back fearfully to see if it would rise, battered and purple, to follow her.

But it lay there.

Out of breath at last, she sat down by the roadside. Already she was almost half-way back to Pitouie. The woman at the circus would be expecting her. It was almost like stealing to have taken her food unless she went back, but nothing could make her pass the place where the face of Willie Weams lay stamped into the road.

When she got home, she found Granny in the midst of her first heart attack. Whether she was missed, or what punishment might have been in store for her, she never knew. From that day all things were changed. Her school-books hung in their canvas bag behind the door and were never opened again. Baking and washing and sweeping filled her days, and querulous scolding from the bed dinned in her ears. At first she tried to be everywhere at once, stirring porridge on the fire, shutting the door and rubbing the old woman's knees all in one breath. But soon she gave this up. No amount of effort could please Granny. Complaining was the only thing left that she could do, and she did it with all the strength at her disposal.

Nancy accepted the wailing and upbraiding as a sign that all was going well, and kept about her work, doing each thing in turn as she came to it, despite the demand for *this* now, and *that* then, which came like a dirge from the depth of the curtained box-bed.

There was nothing in the walnut box, nothing that she had hoped to find there. Its pitiful contents lay at last in her lap. She turned them over, unbelieving: her grandmother's marriage certificate, her grandfather's obituary notice, her mother's birth certificate, an envelope with some pressed seaweed, a pink shell with forget-me-nots painted upon it, a piece of very flaxen hair, and a gold brooch with the pin broken.

Nothing to tell her anything. There was nothing written upon them anywhere. Nothing!

It was not until she was sure of this that she felt completely adrift, completely alone. In all the world there was nobody who belonged to her, in all the world nobody to whom she belonged. Her long-nourished hope about the walnut box stiffened in her throat, making a lump which no amount of swallowing would drive away.

She had dreamed of this moment a hundred times, dreamed of finding a cue, some frail wisp of evidence too delicate for Granny's understanding: a few words arranging a tryst, words written with sweeping arrogance bespeaking the master beneath the lover; a small lace fan, a useless gift for her mother, to be sure, but one that told the giver's rank; a handkerchief with finely embroidered initials; a withered rose (no groom would send a rose). No matter what it was, it proved for ever, beyond all reach of further doubting, that she was not the daughter of a squat-bodied, pock-marked groom; and it told full and freely that she was indeed a child of the Fasseferns, and well might she walk high-headed, knowing the grandeur and the pride of that wild blood.

And now the contents of the walnut box lay before her and said not a word of groom or lord. Granny lay dead and strangely clean upon the stone shelves of the dairy farm, the box-bed opened deep and black, giving forth no wailing cry from the toothless gums. Nothing to right or left beckoned her to do this or that. She need not rise from her chair to make the tea for hours. She need not even make it at all. No one would reproach or comment. No one would even care. Suddenly her freedom became only loneliness. She looked about for something to cling to. With all her heart she longed for a cat. But Granny would never have one for fear it would get on the bed and "steal her breath" in the night. And now Granny's breath was gone anyway, though there had been no cat to steal it, and she was alone, all alone. It was getting dark, and Granny's bed was gaping in the corner. Tears came up in great gusting sobs. She cried, not knowing if her tears were for the cat she had never owned, or for Granny who was gone, or for herself left so alone.

But next morning she set buoyantly about rearranging the furniture in the little house. The sun shining in at the squat window cast upon the floor the shadows of "weary willies" and geraniums growing in little red pots on the window-sill. She paused to water them, and the thought came over her that now she was watering them for herself, not for Granny, now they were her own.

"I'll be a widow-woman with flower-pots in my window," she thought to herself.

Already she could see herself grown into a portly placid woman with a shiny black satin apron for afternoons. It was a comforting picture, and gave her a sense of being some definite person instead of just Granny's grandchild. She took on a new mannerism, walking about the house saying, "Tut, tut," and "My certies," with the right degree of indignation at each fresh speck of dust.

She was elated at being "mistress of the house." Any rap that came at the door now would be for her. She almost wished that one would come so that she could demonstrate this authority by answering whatever was asked without relaying it to the box-bed.

She remembered how when she was little she had read that "The Holy Ghost visited the Virgin Mary, and she had a son." This formed a picture in her mind of the Holy Ghost looking very much like Tinker Tom, with a hamper covered with oilcloth in which he kept his wares. While Tinker Tom cadged china cows with blue-coated cowherds leaning against them, and Toby-jugs with pewter lids, the Holy Ghost peddled little boys. She could see him leaning his heavy hamper against the door-post, smiling the coaxing smile of a tinker who has wares to dispose of, as he beguiled Mary saying:

"Good day, ma'am, would you be wanting any boys this morning?"

And Mary, looking very tidy and capable in a wincey dress and striped shirting apron, for it was morning yet and all the housework to do, so a shirting apron made from the back of her man's old shirt was surely good enough, would "hem" non-committally. For, in the first place, if the cadger was disposed to make her a present it would be ill-advised to discourage him by saying "no" right away. And if the boys were for sale she could always refuse on the score that her man was set against boys.

Tinker Tom, sorting the boys over appraisingly that she might see, he chose the best for her, said:

"I've a nice little boy here called Jesus——"

And Mary, sensing that a price was to be asked, interposed:

"But, my man——"

The peddler smiled, raising his hand to stop her words. Supporting the hamper between his knee and the door-post, he carefully lifted the little boy out and deposited him in Mary's still hesitating arms, with the words:

"You'll never miss his food, ma'am—and only two shillings—and forby that, no need to pay me this time—spring is soon enough."

So just as simply as that, "The Virgin Mary had a son." Nancy, yearning for something to play with, had wished that the Holy Ghost would "visit" her also. But that was out of the question, she knew. For you cannot "visit" anyone unless they have a door of their own to rap on. And Granny would claim any baby that was brought to their door. She was so sure that this was all that held him back that for a time she prayed:

"And, O God, give me a door of my own—so that I can have a son."

She had long since outlived that childish notion but she had never outlived the desire to have a door of her own. And now at last she had one. If somebody would only rap on it!

To her delight, a brisk rap sounded on the door. Arranging her face into the look that Mistress MacIntosh usually wore when gentry came into her shop to buy candy, she minced to the door, holding back imaginary long skirts as she walked.

The Reverend William Anderson stood on the doorstep, his green-black umbrella with the yellow worn handle clasped against his bosom.

"My poor child."

Nancy's heart sank as she stepped aside to let him come in. So she was still only "my poor child" despite the proud possession of a personal door.

She sat primly opposite him, her heels held in the rung of the chair, her hands folded in her lap. But she was not listening. This was her church manner. She fixed her eyes steadily upon his face and thought of something else. Stray bits of what he was saying came to her as she watched him fiddle with the umbrella. First he pressed the cold ivory end of the handle against his chin, then pressed it into either cheek, where it left a white ring in the gaunt yellow surface of his thin face. For the Reverend William had a weak digestion, and it was necessary to weigh his food out to him in meagre ounces; in consequence, he had a pinched cold look, and his clothes hung upon him listlessly. From where Nancy sat she could see his Adam's apple bobbing about in his wide collar. All her life afterward the sight of a man with a thin neck depressed her.

"Of course the parish allowance will stop now that your poor dear grandmother is beyond the need of earthly kindness." He chewed his words leisurely, seeming to find a tired pleasure in their sound.

So there had been a "parish allowance"! That explained why the Reverend Anderson had called upon her grandmother every week. Nancy had always thought it was because he liked her better than the rest of his flock.

"So Mrs. Anderson and I have decided that for the present we will take you to the parsonage."

He was pressing the umbrella against the tip of his nose now.

"Our dear mother is not so well as we would wish her to be. We feel sure that you will do your best to be of great comfort and assistance."

"I'll not look after another old woman," Nancy rebelled inwardly. "I'll lead an immoral life first."

It was well that she did not say this aloud. The Reverend William Anderson might not have understood that in Nancy's conception of it, gathered from illustrated papers, an immoral life consisted of sitting in a restaurant, eating olives, with your elbows on the table and your legs crossed to show too much of your stockings, which must be silk. And she was quite prepared to dash into this form of depravity rather than humour another old woman. But, as she reflected soberly, she *had* no silk stockings, and she did not know if she would like olives because she had never tasted them.

"So to-morrow we will send for your things, and the next day we'll sell all this."

She was not going to be allowed to keep her personal door! He was sweeping her life away as if she were nothing more than a maggot on cheese. But she would not submit. She pulled her heels out from behind the rung and stood up, saying:

"Thank you kindly, but I'm going to stay here. This is my home."

There was a strengthening sound to the last sentence, "This is my home." She almost added, "And that is my personal door," just to vanquish him completely.

"But, my poor child, what will you do for a living?"

"I'll—I'll take in lodgers."

With a meagre smile the Reverend William dismissed this announcement:

"Due to the unfortunate circumstances of your birth, I am your guardian, until you attain your eighteenth birthday."

There was no hope, Nancy could see that. Her life was to be taken out of her hands again. Once more would begin the dreary business of carrying tea to an old woman. Once more the wrangle about fresh air and soap and water.

She determined to leave in the night. She would get away before they came for her in the morning.

But when this first wave of rebellion had passed, she remembered one alluring thing about the parsonage.

It had a bathroom!

Not just a place below the stairs where you washed in a tin tub. But a room made especially to take a bath in, and hot water, and cold water, running into a bath that was as white as a china plate, and big enough to drown in if you took the fancy.

So Nancy moved to the parsonage. Her bedroom was the tower-room of one of the many turreted gables into which the fretful grey house was divided. Narrow oblong windows encircled the room, too high for her to see through, unless she stood upon the bed. Often she would do this, feeling that she was a princess imprisoned in a tower. Or, in a more triumphal mood, she would be a monarch in her lookout tower, viewing her domain. Once she thought, as she looked at the other gables rising close to hers: "In my Father's house are many mansions," and it gave her a comfortable conviction that Heaven was a cosy place where each had his own spired gable.

She came to love this room, although almost everything in it was there because it was rejected by everybody else: a large wooden bed that took up too much of the space, a broken spinet like a jolly old lady with missing teeth, a hand-woven rag rug with a gay tiger prancing knee deep in yellow daisies, a horsehair settee, a small table with a marble top, and on it a rose-coloured glass oil lamp with a fluted chimney and white frosted globe. She trimmed the wick and filled the lamp herself, so that it never smoked as the other lamps in the house did. On the sill of each high window she set a pot of blooming red geraniums, and upon the marble mantelpiece which overhung the tiny grate she put her red and white china cow attended by a cowherd in bright blue coat and yellow trousers. This was all she had saved from the sale of Granny's things except the walnut box, which she kept because it had a key.

No old woman could have been less like Granny than old Mrs. Anderson. A black-eyed old lady with a thirst for clandestine pleasures, she lived in a kind of furtive gaiety. Her room was honeycombed with pigeonholes, band-boxes and other hidy-corners in which she kept forbidden things: bits of cheese, sealing wax, odds and ends of string and paper, half-burned candles, broken china, nut candy, brandy snaps (which she bought because the name sounded devilish), pictures of actors, and divorce scandals clipped surreptitiously from the newspapers.

Every now and then the mice, attracted by the edibles, became so bad that the minister's wife would invade the lair and clear out the accumulation, leaving the room bristling with mouse-traps upon her departure.

These invasions would infuriate the old woman, who would sit silent while they were going on, but when her pallid daughter-in-law withdrew she would say distinctly and with relish: "Face like a boiled suet pudding." This never failed to restore her temper. The raids had no permanent effect upon her. As soon as the mice were subdued she would begin collecting again. To prevent her doing this was one of Nancy's duties. But the old lady had a persuasive way of holding on to things. No matter what it was, she would be "sure to find a use for it later." Her greatest joy was to sit blandly upon a book, a pair of scissors, a piece of sewing, or anything at all, while her daughter-in-law hunted for it from ceiling to cellar.

She held herself quite aloof from the floor below, having her meals sent up on a tray. Nor would she descend for morning and evening prayers, maintaining that her knee was too stiff for this effort, although her agility was astonishing on less religious occasions. She could not forgive her son for being a minister instead of a soldier. And, above all, she could not forgive him for being such a *spiritless* minister. If his had been a God of lightnings and thunderbolts, she could have borne with it, but William Anderson's God was flaccid, and a little bilious; His character was determined by William's hepatic torpor.

William was the second disappointment that religion had brought her. She had married a lusty young Captain in the Argyll and Sutherland Highlanders, her warm blood stirred by the swing of his kilts, and the forceful passion of his courting.

A perverse fate took them to a small herring village in the north to spend their honeymoon. It had been a bad year for the herring, and the fisher-folk were swept with a passion of repentance. Figures prostrate in prayer lined the beaches from sunrise to sundown. Wild-eyed fishermen with bristling salt-bleached beards walked the streets in the night singing psalms. Young women smote their breasts and cried their sins to Heaven in shrill hysterical voices.

In the midst of this the lovers loved madly, climbing to heights of frenzy, unbridled and ever rising. The passion of repentance about them blended with the passion of love, spurred it on, until on a high note of delirium it snapped, and the young bride found herself facing a groom gone suddenly mad with the need of prayer and repentance.

That was the end of fleshly love between them. In a way they became enemies, he regarding his passion for her as a weakness to be overcome, and she resenting and never understanding the sacrificial fervour that made him put their love aside. She was always faithful to him, and for this also she could not forgive him. Soon she began to do little things in a clandestine way just for the pleasure of cheating him, and the habit grew. Now that he was dead she did the same thing with her son. But William, wrapped in the blinding dogma of his faith, never suspected his mother's antagonism nor sensed the irritation she felt about his God. He attributed to her a deeply religious, silent nature, and so kept for himself the image of the mother he wished to have.

His wife was a weary blonde, curved inward like a sickle from the waist up. She was short-sighted, and was for ever struggling with her glasses, never seeming to find the place upon her nose where they would give satisfaction. Her voice was neither high nor low, and left no memory of its sound when she had finished speaking. It had the quality of opaque glass or mist. She would end each remark with a deep sigh, which she followed at once with a brave Christian smile. It was as if she were saying: "My life is very, very hard" (sigh), "but I always bear it bravely" (smile).

Nancy learned to imitate this sigh-smile mannerism, to the great joy of old Mrs. Anderson. At other times she would array herself in a floppy top coat and give an impersonation of the Reverend William reading prayers. But this was only indulged in when the family was safely out of earshot. For on one occasion Mrs. Anderson's loud cackles of mirth at this performance had brought the Reverend William himself on the scene at a too revealing moment. For weeks afterward Nancy ceased to be "my poor dear child" to him, and became something that had neither name nor substance.

The other member of the household was Mary, who had a harelip. She would explain this by saying that her mother had been kicked on the belly while carrying her. She had a passionate longing to be able to do drawn-work. Nancy tried to aid her in this. But Mary's hands were designed for doing things on a larger scale—great, puffy, red hands, each finger jutting out like an infuriated sausage. The more Mary tried to make them hold the needle, the more they would sweat and fumble. She never managed to make anything. But she always kept by her a soiled and rumpled square of linen with a rusty needle stuck in it, which she referred to affectionately as "my fancy work."

The minister's wife and Mary between them created a mourning dress for Nancy out of Granny's black alpaca skirt. It smelled strongly of peat smoke, and in the sun it had a greenish cast. The seams rasped her armpits viciously. She was miserable in it until, to ease the pain of wearing it, she conceived herself to be in mourning for her sweetheart who had died in her arms.

He had died in her arms at sunset, upon a mountain-top. The cause of his death kept changing from time to time, but the mountain-top always remained. At first he had been drowned while swimming to keep their tryst. But that had to be set aside because the nearest water was the North Sea, and it was hardly likely that he would be swimming the North Sea to keep a tryst on a mountain. So he had died of heart failure as the sun went down. But that did not quite satisfy her. She kept trying various deaths for him, but most of them demanded a bed, and nothing would make her abandon the mountain. At last, after she had been mourning him several weeks, her search came to an end when she heard the words "galloping consumption." So it was finally from this ill-omened, hopeless disease that he had died, saying with his last breath: "I love you." She took to going every day to the kirkyard to visit his grave.

"His grave" was any grave at first. But, as the legend grew and deepened, she found herself searching for him everywhere, turning away always from "Beloved Husband" and "Beloved Son," for her love must belong only to her. Searching, searching, tears filled her eyes as she murmured in the words of Mary Magdalene:

"They have taken away my Lord, and I know not where they have lain him."

One day, in a far corner of the churchyard where the sexton's scythe never came, she found at last her lord, her love. High-grown grass and a low-hung weeping willow kept him safe and secret. When she had torn away the grass from the flat slab sunken deep in the earth, she found the words embroidered in green moss: "Hector Campbell, who died Nov. 6th, 1774, Aged 19." Aged nineteen! So young, so handsome, her Hector who had died in her arms!

After that she went daily to see him, carrying a white rose. No one interfered with her visits. They believed it was devotion to the memory of her grandmother which took her up the steep road between the overhanging beech trees to the little graveyard behind the kirk.

It was when she was returning from one of these visits that she first met the Whistling Boy. She had seen him of course in the druggist's shop many times when she went to get "Elman's Embrocation" for Mrs. Anderson's knee or peppermint for her stomach, but she had never really spoken to him until this day.

He came toward her, his hands deep in his pockets, his head lifted in fine ecstasy as he whistled a cataract of sweet sounds. Other boys could whistle a tune, making lamely one note after another, but the Whistling Boy could shower the air with a cascade of harmony.

He was from Edinburgh, and would be going back there again to college after a year's apprenticeship at the druggist shop. She knew this and more from talk she had heard. It was said that he could whistle ten operas from start to finish; that his underwear had his full name embroidered in fine thread upon it, and that he had brought fourteen pairs of socks with him, not a pair of which had even so much as been worn once.

He came to a stop in front of her, timing the last note to finish as he did so.

"Do you like whistling?" He looked at her laughingly as he spoke.

She felt suddenly clumsy. His hands, now that he had pulled them from his pockets, were very white. She saw for the first time that hands might be something more than just useful, and she tried to shrink her own red hands out of sight up her too narrow, too short sleeves.

She nodded in reply to his question, her eyes making little flying looks at him, but not settling on him for long at a time.

"Do you like Chopin?" He pronounced it "Shopping."

"I don't know—you mean buying things?"

"My God, no." A gleam came in his eye. Here was ignorance, unbelievable, profound. A white page for him to write upon.

"Did you ever hear of George Sand?"

"No, what did he do?"

"*She*, not *he*! She led a wanton life with Chopin and wore trousers. But after he got away from her he wrote a lot of music."

She sensed a slur upon her sex and bridled.

"I suppose he could have got away before if he had wanted to."

He waved away her irritation. The passion to inform was upon him.

"Would you like to hear the Grand Waltz in E Flat Major? It's best on the mouth organ, but I can whistle it as well."

But before she could reply, he asked eagerly:

"Do you know any music at all?"

"Only hymns, and I can sing a song. At least, I can sing the chorus."

"What song? Can you sing the 'Barcarolle'?"

She shook her head. The song she knew was one that Mary sang as she laboured about the kitchen, puffing and sweating. The words of the chorus were:

"I wish, I wish, but I wish in vain:
I wish I were a maid again.
But a maid again I never will be
Till an apple grows on an orange tree."

101

The tune was very mournful, and there were nineteen verses all about "my fair, false love who deceived me." But she had no time to tell him this because indeed he did not want to know what she knew. He only wanted to be assured of her ignorance so that he could have all the more joy in enlightening her.

"I'll whistle the 'Barcarolle.'"

He looked about for a good setting. "Come on." Taking her by the hand, he pulled her briskly toward the grey stone, moss-grown dyke which separated the wood from the highroad.

"There's a place with rocks. It's like Italy. I'll go first, or do you need a leg up?"

But he did not wait to see if she needed help. Setting his toe in a crevice between the stones, he leaped over, arriving on the other side with a great crunching of dried beech-leaves.

"Come on," he cried, and she heard his feet crunching away from her with invitational eagerness as he sought the place, the right place to whistle the "Barcarolle." She climbed over and followed him.

Spring was upon the beech wood. Through the bronze crackling carpet of dried leaves white anemones looked up like wakeful stars, and overhead the trees put out sticky fingers to see if the world was warm enough. An amber torrent of melted snow fell clamorously down to a frothing pool below, then sped away, whispering between the tall beech-trees. Slender pale rods of bride's breath scented the air, and pungent bracken broke beneath her feet.

She found him where the water clamoured loudest, whistling a thread of melody that lay against the sound of falling water as pearls lie bright against black velvet.

She sat upon a boulder, looking at him as he leaned against a tree, his bare brown head held high, his mouth red as a rowan-berry. There was that about the corners of his mouth which assailed her with a blind sweet anguish. She folded her arms and pressed them against her middle where it seemed to be melting away. There was a glamour upon his face, a madness of joy upon his pulsing throat. It seemed to her that he was fringed with light which lost her in its outer shadow. She tried to rise and go to him, to say some simple thing like:

"Is it true that you have fourteen pairs of socks?" That would make him see her, would widen the light to include her. But she did not dare to interrupt because she knew that she was here only to listen. That was her only use. When he had finished she would be important for a moment if she praised. But now, while he was whistling, she did not exist. At this moment the waters tumbled for him in wild applause, for him the high

102

trees waved bare arms in rapture, and he was one with the glory of the spring.

All her blood ran toward him. "Like treacle on hot bread," she thought. She spread her hands wider on the front of herself, and held on, trying to keep back the main portion of herself.

He came to the end of the "Barcarolle" and went right into another tune. He did not even need her to praise him. It was easy to see that he had forgotten her altogether. She thought of getting up and leaving; picturing his dismay when he looked down and saw the empty boulder. But she knew that she could never move away from him so long as he was indifferent to her. If he were to turn and reach for her with a look that valued her, she could gather her precious person into a stiff haughty ramrod and move off disdainfully. But not now, while he did not even know that she was there.

He reached the end with a flourish and smiled widely down at her.

This was the time for her to leave. But she sat mesmerised, saying nothing to his waiting face, but only looking up at it, gleaming as it was. He took her silence for tribute, and came to her, seating himself on a boulder at her side.

"If I only had something to play on," he cried, pressing his clasped hands between his knees as if to control the desire in them.

"I'm going to write music like Chopin, and Liszt, and—and those fellows."

"I thought you were going to be a druggist," she ventured.

"Only till I get my money. . . . You see, I'm a ward in Chancery."

She did not see, but she hoped he would go on and explain.

"I'm an orphan. When I'm twenty I'll be rich. But just now I have ten old buzzards who decide what I have to do. I have to 'study some useful trade or profession' until I'm twenty. They don't think music is a 'useful trade or profession.' But when I'm twenty . . ."

"Is it true that you have fourteen pairs of socks?"

Immediately she wished that she had not said this, but it just popped out of her mouth. If she could, she would have reached after it and popped it back in again.

But already he was answering her.

"No. I've fourteen shirts, and twelve pairs of socks."

She was glad now that she had asked. This was a real, a tangible thing to know about him. If in the wakeful night she was wondering and beglamoured by the mystery of him, she could say firmly: "He has fourteen shirts and twelve pairs of socks," and so get back to solid ground again.

"I'll buy a pipe organ when I get my money. But I'll have a piano for composing on."

He was not so much telling her this, as he was telling it to himself. But it was too vague and distant a piece of information to warm Nancy, who needed to know closer things.

"Why have you so many shirts?"

"That's only a reasonable number," this shortly. Then back to his dreams again.

"I'll have more than one piano."

She could not stand him soaring out of her reach like this, borne aloft on many pianos, so she reached after him again with:

"Is the druggist's wife your aunt?"

To have to acknowledge the druggist's wife as an aunt would be something of a downcome, would in a way put a blemish upon him, and so bring him nearer to herself. Not that the druggist's wife could be looked down upon. Far from that; but she could be laughed at. Indeed, she was laughed at for her mincing speech and such pretentious havers.

She was a large woman with a "fainty" voice, and an air that butter would not melt upon her tongue. But it was well known that she flew into such rages and screamed so loudly that the druggist always kept a tin basin in the back shop so he could rattle it to keep her noise from reaching the customers.

Once she had been so angry with the servant lassie for serving the porridge without salt that she repaid her neglect by clapping the hot porridge upon her head. The poor lass ran screaming into the street with porridge streaming down her face. And it was the best part of a month before she could so much as put a comb upon her scalp. But the lassie paid her back by telling far and wide that the druggist's wife grew a beard, and that she would remove it now and then with some paste that smelt strong of rotten eggs. So at last Pitouie knew the real explanation of the red marks that would come from time to time upon her chin and lip.

The lassie further told that some nights the druggist would be driven out of his bed, and would have to finish the night lying on a bag of sugar in the back shop. But this was hardly likely, for the druggist did not sell sugar; and anyway a bag of sugar was an unlikely bed even for a little man such as the druggist; although that might well account for the chilblains that he was plagued with both on his hands and his feet. He had a way of scratching the ones on his hands against the sharp edge of the counter, holding his head well up and talking in lofty accents while he did so. As if by doing this he could hold the customer's head up also, and so prevent him from seeing the chilblain-scratching.

So, if the druggist's wife should be his aunt. . . . But no, he was already telling her that the druggist's wife was *not* his aunt. Neither was the druggist any relation to him. He came here because one of the "buzzards" knew the druggist and thought this was the best place for him. He would not mind it if he had a piano and could go on with his lessons.

"I had a piano in Edinburgh. . . . It wasn't really mine, but I could play on it whenever I liked. It belonged to a girl I went to school with."

A queer resentment took her against this Edinburgh girl who could give him a piano to play on.

"There's a pipe organ in the kirk." She wondered at the desperate plan that rose in her mind right on the heels of her words.

"I wish I could get a crack at it," he cried fervently. "I've played an organ. . . . I could play all this, if I had an organ . . . this water." He finished up at a loss for words, and sat gloomily haunched.

Committing herself past all reason, she said:

"The key of the kirk hangs on the hat rack just beneath the minister's hat. Some night I could give it to you."

"It wouldn't be any use to me. I have to have somebody to blow the organ."

He pulled a hoarhound drop from his pocket and chewed it desolately.

Gasping a little as if she had taken a leap into cold water, she said:

"I'll blow the organ for you."

He regarded her. His blue eyes suffused with hope. She marvelled at the neat whiteness of his nose as it merged into his fluted upper lip, at the fine down like golden feathers that grew faintly on his cheeks, and, marvelling, forgot the wildness of her promise.

"But somebody might hear the playing," he said in a tone that begged her to contradict him.

"Oh, no," she plunged, lost to all caution. "There's nobody to hear at night. We can keep the windows and the door shut. But nobody passes at night but the farm servants going back to Menzies' Farm, and they go by in a bunch, whistling and singing for fear of ghosts."

So her promise was given past recalling.

A mist was rolling down from the hills, carrying the dusk in its cold grey arms, as Nancy hurried up the steep brae to the parsonage.

It must be nearly six; after six perhaps. Time had gone by in a warm flash that wiped out thought. She should have been home two hours ago. What explanation could she give?

She hurried in through the iron gates already greyed over with the sweat of night. The glow of the afternoon was leaving her. A chill fell upon her heart, and she thought desolately: "I am always going home to a cold fireside."

They were already seated at the table when she entered the dining-room. Miss Clark had come to supper. She was a genteel spinster who kept a boarding-house for "selected gentlemen." She suffered from asthma, and always wore a respirator covered with black velvet over her mouth.

From the pause that marked her entrance Nancy knew that they had been discussing her, and she hesitated whether to go forward to the table or go to the kitchen and ask Mary for supper.

Her position in the household had never been clearly defined. It seemed to be for ever suspended in air awaiting a solution. Each day Mrs. Anderson would say: "You might as well eat with us," but always as if this decision was made for that day only. Old Mrs. Anderson had her meals in her rooms, and Nancy would gladly have carried another tray upstairs for the pleasure of eating with the gay old lady. But it seemed that the minister's wife could not forgo the joy of showing daily that hers was a true Christian heart which could treat this despised orphan as a member of the family.

So Nancy waited irresolute, everything inside her crinkling with hateful anticipation. Miss Clark, perking her head like a frowsy bird, looked brightly at Mrs. Anderson with a look that said: "I *know* that you are going to be as kind as kind can be to the poor thing."

And Mrs. Anderson, giving back a sad sweet smile, said to Nancy:

"My *dear*, I wish you would endeavour to be here at six o'clock" (sigh). "However" (smiling bright forgiveness), "better late than never, so we'll say no more about it."

The table overflowed with Christian charity as Nancy slipped into her place. All was forgiven: the sad fact of her existence, the crime of her late arrival, even the ingratitude which they knew was lurking in her breast; all, all was forgiven. The weight of their goodness to her sat upon her head like the stone placed on cheese to squeeze the milk out of it. She sat as far down in the chair as she could to escape it, and soon they forgot her.

Miss Clark's respirator hung round her neck from a black ribbon as she ate. It was strange to see her without it. To Nancy the oblong black velvet mouth protector had become one of the features of the spinster's face. There had been a time when she believed that Miss Clark wore it for quite another reason than asthma.

From some vague source she had got the idea that there was a germ in the breath of men who had moustaches, and that if by chance a grown woman breathed this, she willy nilly got a baby. Miss Clark had so many men boarders with moustaches that it was easy to see why she took this precaution. But since the card in her window read "Lodgings for selected gentlemen," Nancy had often wondered why she did not select them without moustaches, and so do away with the need for a respirator.

But looking at her now, so brittle and thin, with the black respirator pendulous upon her sunken breast, Nancy reflected: "Even if it were true, there is no danger. She hasn't got juice enough." For a mad minute she wondered what would happen if she sang out: "She hasn't got enough juice." But this peril passed when Mary, like a genial gargoyle, came in, bearing a fragrant dish before her.

There were fresh herrings and hot scones for supper. It was always "supper" except when the Bishop or some visiting minister came to stay, and then in the twinkling of an eye it became "dinner," and had soup at the beginning of it. It was still only "supper" to-night. A mere Miss Clark could not change its name. But the herrings were crisp and brown, and the scones delicious.

Nancy often watched Mary make the scones. From the way her fat red fingers bungled back and forth in the dough you felt sure that no good could ever come of it. But always they were lighter than any scones you ever tasted.

Mr. Anderson could not eat the scones, of course, nor the fried herrings. Nancy felt sorry for his cold bluish face as it contemplated the dried brown bread and hot milk which was its share of the feast. But it was probably the coldness of the room that made his face look bluish. The only warm place in the parsonage was the kitchen, and he, poor thing, could not go there to get warm on the pretext of watching Mary baking scones. The grate in the dining-room was an economic little cage barely able to hold three lumps of coal. One spot of red was all the fire there was under the great overhanging marble mantelpiece. It gave the effect of a small malevolent eye beneath a monster eyebrow.

Miss Clark separated the bones from her herring with a self-conscious daintiness which said: "It is easy to see that I'm a lady-born," and offered little bits of information about her lodgers between wheezes. This was how she paid for the invitation to supper, and was the real reason why she was asked. For Mrs. Anderson had that quivering curiosity about the private lives of others which drab women have. She called it "taking a kindly interest in the young people of the village."

"And how is the new watchmaker turning out?" She prompted.

"Oh, he writes to Callochie twice a week, to a Miss Shields. I've seen the name on the envelope a couple of times, by chance. And there was 'my own girl' as plain as could be on the blotting paper. So that would mean marriage, I'd say."

"It should," sniffed Mrs. Anderson, as who should say, "my own girl," indeed! A fine hussy she must be.

"Of course, you never can tell," agreed Miss Clark. "Girls are not what they were in *my* young days."

"That will be a fine flea in the ear of Bella Fraser, when she hears *that*." There was almost a throb of exaltation in Mrs. Anderson's pallid voice. "Somebody should tell her to prevent her making more of a fool of herself than she's done already."

And you could hear the conviction growing in her, that *she* was the one to take Bella Fraser aside and say sweetly, oh, very sweetly:

"You've met Miss Shields, I'm sure, the watchmaker's—well, I suppose one should call her his fiancée."

"Well," admitted Miss Clark, "I did think of mentioning it. In a way I suppose it's my Christian duty."

But Mrs. Anderson would have none of this. Who was Miss Clark to think she had a "Christian duty"? Such presumption!

"I *think* I had better do it myself"—smiling with icy sweetness. "It will come better from *me*. The young people know I have their interests at heart. Don't you think so, William?"

William did not interrupt his fifty-six chews, but simply nodded. Meal-time for William could never be conversational. Each mouthful had to be guarded lest it slip down without proper mastication. "Forty-nine, fifty, fifty-one, fifty-two, fifty-three, fifty-four, fifty-five, fifty-six, swallow! Bite, one, two, three——" Unless you caught him at "swallow" it was useless.

"I'll mention it to-night after choir practice. No use letting it go to greater lengths."

There was something in the way she said "greater lengths," that made you see the need of having Bella Fraser told at once. If, indeed, it was not *already* too late.

The arrival of the new watchmaker had caused a great flutter by reason of the fact that he was single and had a business of his own. He was a little man, with a bantam-like briskness, but when he sang "Oh, let me like a soldier fall," you could well believe that he was over six feet.

What a traffic there had been the first few weeks, with watches to be cleaned, and brooches to be mended. Gewgaws that had never seen the light of day in twenty years were dragged from shell-encrusted boxes and taken to the watchmaker's to be cleaned. And each one wore her Sunday hat, thinking to put the others in the shade.

A whirlwind of parties took the town. At every one the new watchmaker begged melodiously that they let him "like a soldier fall upon some open plain." At first it seemed that the oldest Webster girl would get him. She was pretty, or would have been if she had not sucked her thumb in her cradle, and she could accompany him on the harmonium. But the Robbie girls outshone her with a piano that was always in tune, due to the fact that their brother was a piano-tuner. This gave them an artistic tang which seemed to please the new watchmaker. But finally it was red-cheeked Bella Fraser with whom he walked out on Sunday afternoon, and took to choir practice at night. Not that Bella could sing a note. It was well-known that she could not hold a tune, and only sat with the choir to give the seats a filled-up appearance. So it was not music that had brought them together. And now, in the face of all the Sunday dinners he had eaten at the Frasers' house, he was corresponding with a "Miss Shields at Callochie"!

In her gratitude at this piece of information Mrs. Anderson pressed Miss Clark to take another herring. A gratified smile tried to express itself upon her unaccustomed face, and the sharp needles of her eyes behind her thick glasses pricked here and there in excitement. She was going step by step through the scene as it would occur after choir practice. "*That* will drive some of the red out of her cheeks," she thought triumphantly.

In this lay the secret of her hatred for Bella Fraser, the warm gay red in her youthful cheeks. This hatred had been born suddenly full grown one Sunday morning. It was just after service, and they were walking back from the kirk over the powdery snow that squeaked frostily under their feet, when they met Bella Fraser. She wore a white tam-o'-shanter of furry wool upon her dark curly hair. A coat of the same white wool was belted about her slim waist, and a scarlet woollen skirt completed the gay picture. Her bright cheeks glowed with the bold beauty of health, and her teeth glistened between the silky red of her lips.

Every instinct in the pastor's wife told her that this was a wicked sight. She stiffened righteously and turned to William to hear the disapproving words this flaunting dress would surely bring.

But there was a light in William's eyes that she had never seen there before. He was strutting like a cockerel in a crowded barnyard, his shoulders held four inches higher than normal, a silly smile upon his face that gave him the look of a sick duck. From very shame for him she looked away, not wishing him to know that she had seen. She felt him watching Bella as far as he could see. For a moment she thought that he would even turn and look after her, but he won the struggle with himself, and they plodded forward side by side in silence. Presently a long sigh escaped him, and his shoulders drooped down to their accustomed place. He turned and looked at her, his wife, his spouse, with leaden eyes; and then her hatred for Bella Fraser was born.

Often she had dreamed of her revenge, when Bella would marry, and one child after another would make of her a gaunt pale drab. Or, better still, no man would want her for a wife, until at last, as one man after another passed her by, she would sicken with a lung disease and waste like a ghost. Then when at long length she lay in her coffin there would be nothing left to remember her beauty by.

But now she wondered if William had heard what they were saying, and realised that Bella Fraser had been making herself cheap like the hussy that she was. You could not tell if William listened or not. Often she suspected that he lived in a part of himself which he never let her see; held conversations, and met people she had never known, was untrue to her even, right under her nose while she was speaking to him.

It was as if his face were a screen with "interested listener" printed on it, which he held up as a blind, while he went on doing, heaven knows what, behind it. He had that look now, and it drove her to say tartly:

"William, did you hear what Miss Clark was saying about Bella Fraser?"

"I heard what you were saying about her, my dear."

Now what did he mean by that? Was there an emphasis on "you," or did she just imagine it? Now he was talking to Miss Clark in order to change the subject.

"I never see your youngest lodger at the kirk, Miss Clark," he was saying. "I had hoped that your good influence . . ."

"I have spoken to him again and again," Miss Clark assured him. "I asked him if he didn't feel the need of meeting God once a week. And what do you think he said?"

Nancy was aquiver to hear what the Whistling Boy had said. But Miss Clark was in no hurry to rush to her climax. She looked from one to another in a sort of scandalised delight, and her voice quavered with the attempt to make it sound shocked instead of pleased:

"He said, 'I don't believe God goes to your kirk, and the music is so bad that I don't blame Him!"

In the indignant pause that followed the minister held Miss Clark's eyes with a chill reproving look, which told that he was not deceived by her attempt to sound shocked. He knew that she was thrilled by the daring of the blasphemy, and liked to repeat it to show the mettle of which her lodgers were made.

It was a pitiful weakness in Miss Clark that she could never bring herself to condemn any member of the male sex, no matter what his guilt. The bare fact that he was a man put a glamour upon him and called forth her admiration. She admired men extravagantly, perhaps because no one of them had ever admired her. Never had she been able to acquire that easy contempt toward a man which women have toward men who love them too much. For her they had remained bewildering, arrogant gods.

It was fifteen years since her father died. Fifteen years since she had decided on the bold scheme of turning the house where they had lived all their lives into a home for "selected gentlemen."

Her father had been the veterinary surgeon for Pitouie. Also he pulled teeth for anyone who wanted him. Indeed, after the village had presented him with a full set of dentist's forceps, there had been no holding him. Often just for the joy of using one of the shining instruments he would coax a loafer in off the street to have his tooth pulled with the assurance: "All teeth get painful sooner or later. If it doesn't hurt now, it will some time." So that if death had not taken him, there would not have been a tooth left in the village.

While he lived, there had been men knocking on the door, asking for him every hour, so that Miss Clark had lived in a quiver of excitement from one day's end to the other. But when he died and was finally laid away, and she had made the last excusable visit to the banker to ask for advice, and the doctor had called for the last time to soothe her nerves, she found herself facing a life gone suddenly arid.

Across the street, where the new veterinary made his home, she could see her father's sign repainted with the new name, and at the door the stalwart male backs as they waited for admission. But never more would she go palpitating along the passage to answer the summons.

She sat at the window day after day, watching the activity in the house across the street, till it seemed to her that in taking the sign they had taken also the very breath out of her life, and left her the corpse to hold upon her knee.

After a month of this, she could bear it no more, so, despite the fact that she was a lady-born and had an annuity that would keep her to the end of her days, she gave up watching the house across the way, and put the printed card in the parlour window.

Her very first lodger was Mr. Robertson, the schoolmaster, as fine a figure of a middle-aged man as Pitouie had ever seen, and single in the bargain.

Never would she forget the panic-stricken moment when she saw him coming up the sanded path between the daisy borders straight to her front door. She had been sewing some white ruffled edging into the sleeves and neck of her best black cashmere frock, and had just finished the last stitch as he turned in at the gate. What was she to do? Here she was in her oldest wincey, for it was the morning that she turned out the parlour, and there was *he*, knocking at the door and nobody to answer him. Little Jessie, who came in daily to take out the ashes and do such unladylike work, had that minute gone out to the butcher's to buy three-pennyworth of liver for the noonday meal. It was not likely that he would stand knocking till she came back.

Before she knew it she was tearing open the buttons of her bodice with hands that fairly shook with panic. In the wink of an eye she was pulling her best afternoon frock over her head. She heard him turn to leave, and ran pulling the frock into place as she went. The hook of her placket caught in her hair-net. She gave it a flustered jerk and off fell the three braids of her dead mother's hair which made such a luxuriant knot at the back of her head, leaving nothing but her own little wisp, looking like a dormouse-nest tied up with string. There she stood with half her head in her hand as you might say, while his feet went crunching away from her, maybe never to come back!

Such a thing must not be! She opened the door and called. Not a moment too soon! Already he was almost out of earshot, but he heard, and turned back. Heaven help us! He would be on the doorstep, and she with three buttons to fasten yet and the lump of hair in her hand. No use to try to fasten it on now.

Her eyes darted here and yonder looking for a place to put it. Then, like an answer from Heaven just in time, she saw the ornamental flower-pot that stood on the end of the banister. Plop! It was safely inside, just as he was raising his hat and saying:

"Good morning, Miss Clark."

Oh, the time she had had to keep him from seeing the back of her head! Especially when it came time to go upstairs and show him the bedroom. His politeness would not let him go ahead of a lady, and she could not possibly let him come behind her. They stood at the foot of the stairs arguing about it till, of a sudden, she realised that any minute he might glance into the flower-pot and see the hair lying there. This put her in such a flurry that she clapped her hankie to her mouth and told him between gasps that she could not bear to have anyone walk behind her ever since her father died. He was so sympathetic about this haver that she could barely keep from telling him the whole truth. So, true gentleman that he was, he held out his arm, saying to her:

"Then, dear lady, we'll climb the stairs together."

And up they went, arm in arm, for all the world like a bride and groom coming from the altar, though, of course, they would have to be going in the other direction for that. But nevertheless there was something so intimate about it that she felt she had overcharged him for the room. While her hand lay on his arm he looked down and saw the clean white frilling about her sleeve, and said appreciatively that it made "a lovely setting for a woman's hand." That was how it came about that for the last fifteen years she had worn frilling on all her frocks at every hour of the day, instead of just on her best frock. It was a great expense. A yard of frilling cost one-and-sixpence, and it took a yard and a half to go round the neck and sleeves. With the dusting she had to do it would never last clean above two days. And it was harder and harder to get. They would tell her it was out of fashion and not being made any more, but she always managed finally to get some. Often she had been tempted for economy's sake to go back to her old plan of just having the frilling on the neck, and not on the sleeves except for rare occasions. But she would think of his words, and that moment when they had walked side by side up the stairs, and she could never bring herself to do it, no matter what the expense.

He had never said another word about it, though every morning since then she had poured his breakfast tea with spotless frilling on her sleeves. But at any rate he had stayed with her, and had not gone off to get married as the others were always doing. And who could say that it was not the white frilling that had held him?

When Nancy told old Mrs. Anderson what the Whistling Boy had said about the music, and gave an imitation of the scene at the supper-table, the old lady laughed so hard that she brought on one of her hiccoughing spells—the worst she had ever had.

She tried holding her breath while Nancy counted to a hundred, and other remedies that rarely failed, but nothing would stop it. She rolled in her chair in painful mirth, the tears dropping down her face as the hiccoughs almost strangled her; Nancy at one moment wildly laughing with her, and at the next wringing her hands in dismay.

Beside herself at last with anxiety, Nancy ignored the old lady's gesture of refusal and ran to the door, calling over the banister for the others to "come quick."

William came first, pallid and startled, and behind him his wife, with that air of triumphant malevolence which she always felt on being summoned to her mother-in-law's room. Her whole air seemed to say:

"*There* you see, William! *I* never have these attacks! Why should *she* have them?"

"How did it happen?" William inquired.

Stammering, Nancy tried to find some plausible thing to say. But before she could speak the old lady cast a look at her lugubrious son in his loose-hanging clothes; this sent her into such a spasm of laughter that she grew purple in the face and her clenched fists beat wildly on the arms of her chair.

Her daughter-in-law swiftly crossed the room, picked up the ewer of cold water that stood on the marble-topped washstand, and flung the water in the old woman's face. There was such venomous hatred in her eyes as she did this that Nancy caught her breath, expecting her to scream terrible curses at the gasping old lady. But instead she stepped back and said smilingly as the hiccoughs ceased:

"That's better now; 'desperate diseases require desperate remedies,' you know."

Her mother-in-law made no reply. She knew exactly with what emotion her daughter-in-law had flung the water in her face. But she gave no sign. She looked at the peering, short-sighted wife of her son, and wondered why she could never see her without thinking of a pale green caterpillar reared upon its tail, blindly feeling for the next leaf.

"Mother will want to change her wet things. We'd better be going, William." She hooked him possessively by the arm.

"Can I do anything, mother?" William's tone was baffled. He knew that some emotional encounter had taken place, but he was too confused to understand it. He felt sorry for his mother, sitting silently with her hair clinging wetly to her head and her hands picking about aimlessly in her lap. She had a meek look as if brute force had been used to subdue her. But that was nonsense. It had been necessary to throw the water on her. His wife had done right, had done it out of kindness. Hadn't it cured the hiccoughs?

"No, there's nothing you can do." She closed her eyes and leaned back in her chair. She did not want to look at them any longer. When the door had closed after them she opened her eyes and said so loudly that they must have heard:

"Suet-face!"

But her face quavered and broke up as if she wished to cry.

She was very quiet while Nancy brought her dry things and rubbed her damp hair with a towel, almost childlike, and Nancy felt greatly drawn to her. She longed to speak to her about the Whistling Boy. She needed to say things about him aloud to ease the things that swelled her breast.

"Did you ever study music, Mrs. Anderson?"

With characteristic quickness the old woman pulled her head out of the towel, the better to see Nancy's face, and asked:

"What makes you suddenly interested in music?"

Nancy reddened. No, she could not speak of him yet. Besides, what could she say about him? Nothing! Nothing! But the old lady's bright eyes were demanding an answer.

"Have you met this Whistling Boy? . . . But I see you have, so don't tell me any stories."

"I don't tell stories." Nancy seized on this to escape, but she did not deceive old Mrs. Anderson.

"Where did you meet him?" she demanded, her eyes sharpening suspiciously.

At bay Nancy replied:

"On the way back from the kirkyard."

"How long has this been going on?"

"What?"

"How long have you been meeting him?"

"To-day's the first day I've spoken to him. . . . He whistled tunes to me."

The old lady relaxed, the sharpness left her eyes and she smiled.

"Never mind me, I'm a stupid old woman. . . . I forget you're nothing but a bairn. . . . So he whistled tunes to you?"

"Yes. He's going to be a great composer when he grows up. As great as Chopin and—and other names that I can't remember."

"So he was telling you that?"

"Yes, and when he's twenty-one he'll be rich, and then he's going to buy organs and pianos galore and play on all of them."

"My certies!"

"And he'll play things like water, and the sky, and everything."

"I'll warrant he never had time to ask what *you* were going to be!" laughed the old woman.

Some bitter amusement in her voice pierced Nancy. Suddenly she wanted to cry. It was spoiled, spoiled. Oh, why had she spoken about him?

"Don't look so tragic, bairn. . . . I must get you a new dress; you look like a tragedy queen in that black thing. . . . We'll take a jaunt out to-morrow and see Betty Murry. . . . What colour would you be wanting?"

Perhaps if she had a new dress the Whistling Boy would be interested, would ask her what she was going to do when she grew up. But what *was* she going to do? What could she tell him if he asked? She had nothing, no education. . . .

"Don't stand staring like a warlock. Answer me!" demanded the old woman.

"I was wishing I had more education. I don't know anything about music . . . or anything. I'll be nothing—nothing at all when I grow up."

Old Mrs. Anderson regarded her thoughtfully, even sorrowfully, as if she were seeing the doubtful road her feet must travel, before she said with a sigh:

"If you think education will help you, bairn, I'll speak to Mr. Robertson. He can give you home lessons to do."

Nancy smiled her thanks then: "Why were you sighing about me?" she asked timidly.

"Nothing, nothing, bairn. I'm a fanciful old woman . . . always seeing warlocks and the like. Never mind me. We'll get you a new frock, and an education, since you're so set on it. . . . Now, fix up my bed; it's been a hard day."

She walked close to the banister, to avoid the creaking middle portion of the steps. Her shoes, tied together by their laces, hung around her neck.

She reached the lower hall and stood listening. Her heart boomed like the distant pounding of the sea. She could hear no other sound.

From where she stood she could see the gleam of the brass knob on the door of the bedroom where the minister and his wife slept. It was the one bright thing in the crouching dusk. It winked at her evilly. She stared it in the face to show that she was not afraid. Subdued at last, it gave up and became a quiet brass knob again.

The hall was covered with linoleum patterned to look like inlaid wood. Under it there was a loose board. To step on it meant discovery. Earlier in the evening she had counted the squares on the linoleum, noting under which square the loose board was. But now she could not remember. Was it seven and eight that she must step on? Or was it seven and eight that she must *not* step on? Even if she remembered could she be sure of the squares in this dim light? They blurred and ran into one another. Better not try.

On tiptoe she skirted the middle floor, keeping near to the wall. This took her close to the bedroom door, but better that than risk the loose board.

The minister's black hat, like a mournful mushroom, occupied the centre of the hat-rack. Under it she found the key.

A breathless moment and she was outside.

The swarthy night crept sniffing to her feet, a cowardly dog, ready to bite her if she showed fear.

The chill damp gravel struck through her stocking soles and sent a shiver up her thighs.

She dare not put her shoes on yet, gravel had such a way of crying out under the press of shoes.

There were two ways that she could go, down the long path that led to the garden's end, or out by the creaking iron gates.

But she must not risk the gates.

She went forward along the gravel path, treading as soft as a cat in her stocking feet.

Her eyes strained wide open as she passed the rhododendron bushes, fearsome tents of darkness, out of which could come a long clawing hand to seize her.

The dark red rose-bushes, so friendly by day, now swung black clenched fists and whispered together.

The daisy border that winked so cheerily in the sunlight now wound like an endless snake on either side.

At every step she faced a new terror, staring it down, only to have it glide behind her, to join the throng of creeping fears that whimpered at her heels.

Reaching the garden's end, she squeezed through a hole in the hedge and won out to the road.

She could put her shoes on now, but for that she must stop, and all the creeping things behind would nuzzle up to her elbow. Oh, to have some friendly wall to put her back against, to get them all in front of her and hold them with her eyes while she tied her shoes. Should she swing round and drive them off? No, they would know she was afraid. Better to stop quiet-like, humming a little tune to drown the nuzzling.

It was done!

She started on again, dismayed at first by the sound of her own feet, yet strengthened by it. At least she could make more noise than the things that followed, followed. . . .

Heartened by that thought, she set her feet down more and more loudly, challengingly, threateningly. The terrors fell away discouraged. The darkness drew in its evil breath. A clear space came about her. She walked on swinging her arms now.

He was waiting at the bridge as they had planned. His shadow came out of the bridge-side and spoke as she drew near.

"I thought you would be scared to come."

"I wasn't scared a bit."

"Have you got the key?"

The key? Yes, of course she had the key. This was it, burned into her hand with gripping it. She gave it to him.

He started on ahead of her without a word. She felt dismissed, forgotten. Maybe she should go back.

By the way he bore his head she could see that all his thoughts were already up the brae and sitting at the organ. The organ! He could not play it without her. He needed her to blow. So there was a reason for her to follow. Just then he looked back over his shoulder and cried roughly:

"Come on."

She bounded toward him, a joyous little dog, and trotted gladly at his side, glancing up for ever at his forward-looking face, which swung misty and remote above her.

It was nothing to walk between the graves with him striding just a step

117

in front of her. She panted a little, but not from fear.

"You're out of breath." As he spoke he turned and peered down at her. There was accusation in his tone, not sympathy. She resented what he meant by it, and cried:

"It's only because your legs are twice as long as mine."

He must have liked that, because he grinned and walked more slowly.

She was quiet in her breast when he opened the kirk door and nothing but black holiness stood before them. She would never have dared to walk into it alone, and never, never have dared to speak in it, but with him she could do anything.

He pulled her in and closed the heavy door.

They groped their way, hand in hand, through the sacerdotal gloom toward the organ.

He left her and went clacking with impious heels across the tiles of the altar floor.

In the ghostly box behind the organ they found a small oil lamp. There was nothing else in this small space. Nothing but the great bellows, its handle grown slippery with the sweaty hands that had pushed it up and down.

Pendent from a string there hung a small lead weight. She must keep her eyes on this ever watchfully. When she had pumped with all her might, up and down, up and down, the weight rose up and stood at "full."

But one blast upon the organ would send it skipping down perilously, oh perilously, near to "empty."

Up and down, up and down, up and down . . .

She wished that she could hear the tune that he was playing and see his face.

But, up and down, up and down, up and down . . .

Was he pleased with the way that she was blowing? My, that must be a loud tune, it used a lot of air.

Wildly, up and down, up and down, up and down . . .

A quieter one now.

So patiently, up and down, up and down, up and down . . .

Up and down, hour after hour. He must have played all the tunes in the world by now . . . That smarting on her palms was because the skin was off and the sweat was salty . . . They put salt on a sailor's back after the cat-o'-nine-tails. Was that to heal the cuts or to make them hurt more? . . .

Oh, the weight!

Madly, up and down, up and down, up and down . . .

The lamp was almost out. She would not be able to see the weight. If she could only straighten up for a minute . . . There was a carving-knife between her shoulder-blades. A rusty carving-knife. "She died of a rusty carving-knife between her shoulder-blades, regretted by all."

Up and down, up and down, up and down . . .

She would not mind so much if he would leave the air in the bellows for a minute. But no, the more air she pumped in, the more notes he played, and sucked it out . . . He was a vampire that sucked air.

No, it was blood they sucked . . .

The lamp was beginning to smell. The smoke from it was getting in her eyes. They smarted. She could close them and pump . . .

Up and down, up and down, up and down, endlessly up and down . . .

It was her breast he was drawing the air out of. She was pumping to keep him from stealing all her breath. It was a fight between them.

A queer hatred for him began to grow on the same stem alongside her love.

Up and down, up and down, up and down, he must not win. She must keep the breath in her body as long as she could.

Up and down . . . But she could not, could not do it any more . . . Up . . . and . . . down . . .

"Hey, you'll have to pump steadier than that."

He was clambering his way through the dark vestry toward her dim-lit cell as he called. His voice was laden with reproach and irritation.

She did not care. The floor on which she lay was soft as down, and she was melting into it.

"Why, what's the matter?"

He pulled her up to a sitting posture, bewildered concern on his face.

She opened her eyes. Beyond his head she caught the faint first rays of dawn in the high little window of the cell.

It was day.

She had been pumping all night long. A wave of pity for her poor throbbing hands rose up in her throat, and great unrestrained tears rolled down her face.

"The matter is that I'm tired . . . and my hands . . ." She lifted them pitifully for him to see. Letting them fall again in her lap, she gave herself up to a quiet spent weeping, while he sat by, penitent, trying to find words to explain his forgetfulness.

He left her at the garden's end as the slow-coming day began to lift the black night-clothes from the rose-bushes.

She won silently into the house and hung the key under the minister's black hat. In a minute more she would have gained the turret room

119

and safety.

But crack! The loose board shouted beneath her feet. Shouted with venomous glee as if it had been waiting all night to betray her.

There was a fumbling sound from the bedroom behind her. She scurried up the stairs, winning the first landing as the door below opened. Even now she might evade discovery.

But no, looming in her path, looking larger than human in the morning half-light, stood the night-gowned figure of old Mrs. Anderson.

"What's that? What's that?" came querulously from below.

Nancy shivered between two enemies and stood still.

"Nothing, William . . . I went down to get a drink."

As she spoke the old lady was pushing Nancy toward the turret staircase, pushing her out of sight.

The noise below subsided into a negative mumbling, and the bedroom door closed again.

"Come in here, *miss*."

Nancy was too tired to wonder at the hard ferocity in the old woman's whispered words, or to resent the passionate grip upon her arm as the old lady steered her into the room and shut the door behind them.

"Well?"

The old woman was glaring a question at her, but even this did not greatly disturb Nancy. To be out at night would bring her a scolding, she knew, but it would soon be over with. That she had taken the key of the kirk was more serious. But how could the old woman know that she had taken it? Maybe she had been thirsty in the night and was angry to find her gone. That might account for her fury. But it was too much trouble to reason it out now. Her back ached and her blistered hands stung angrily. It was senseless of the old woman to stand glaring at her like that in the chill morning. She felt behind her for a seat and sank into it, saying:

"I'm tired."

But this, instead of stopping the glare in the old woman's eyes, only added new ferocity to it.

"Tired! I don't doubt you're tired . . . you slut! You dirty little trollope . . . you . . . fauch! You brazen hussy!"

Nancy was perplexed now by the violence of her anger, but not at all by her words. Granny had always called her a "slut" and a "trollope" every time her tea was not as hot as she liked it. The torrent of abuse meant only that Mrs. Anderson was angry. So she sat still getting what comfort and rest she could out of the back of the chair while the old woman's rage hissed about her drooping head. She had found it best to sit so when Granny scolded. In time the old lady would stop for want of breath, and then she could go to bed.

But in Nancy's stillness Mrs. Anderson read only a deeper guilt, and her fury passed sane bounds. The love she had for Nancy and the pride she had in her made her anger against her a blind hot madness. She could have torn the girl limb from limb. No words were too cruel for her tongue to utter:

"What's bred in the bone comes out in the flesh. . . . Easy to see the trull of a mother that bore you . . . First a stallion cadger, then a nigger medicine-man. . . . By now, doubtless, you've half a dozen nigger sisters . . . and *you*, I suppose we'll have to get the midwife for you before the snow flies. . . . Say something! Where have you been? . . . Tell me *that*! . . . And none of your lies. . . . How long have you been doing this?"

Nancy was prodded out of her tired stupor by the knife-edged voice.

"I never took the key before."

"The key?"

"Of the kirk."

"The kirk? So *that's* where you go for your dirty traffic?"

"That's where the organ is."

"The organ?"

"Yes."

Brought close to tears by this buffeting which she could not understand, Nancy lifted up her swollen hands in mute explanation. Again she was overcome by their pitifulness, and her voice quavered as she cried:

"I've been blowing for him all night."

The old woman seized her hands and peered at them in the grey light. On their blistered palms was written clearly the simple story of the night's "traffic."

"The skin's all off them," sobbed Nancy, as she felt the hostility toward her die out.

The old woman made a queer sound in her throat, and stood trembling and uncertain. It was as if she had rigged her sails for a stormy sea and suddenly found herself upon a placid lake. She wanted to take the child in her arms and weep over her, but caresses did not come easy to her hand. She reached out to touch Nancy's head, but drew back. She said in a flat voice to disguise her tenderness:

"You better away to your bed, then. . . . No, better creep in here with me. It will be warmer."

She pulled Nancy's clothes off with hands that trembled to convey their remorse, and finally, using the cold as an excuse, she held the child against her breast in the large feather-bed.

"Was the man my mother went away with a nigger?"

This came in a voice husky with sleep from the region where Mrs. Anderson's flannelette night-gown was fastened with three large pearl-buttons.

"Well, he wasn't a full-blooded nigger, but he was part nigger they say."

After a long pause, as if the thing had been turned over well in her mind:

"Maybe she wanted to do things for him to make him happy."

"I suppose she did." This came very dryly from Mrs. Anderson.

"I think she was right to go, then."

"Well, she had *you* to do for. It would have become her better to stay and tend the bairn she'd brought into the world already than to go gallivanting——"

Mrs. Anderson put a check upon her tongue.

Silence from the region of the pearl buttons. Then clearly, as if the thing that troubled her had been understood at last:

"And *I* should have stayed and tended to you instead of going out to blow the organ for him!"

Tears came to Mrs. Anderson's dusty old eyes, tears of thankfulness that Nancy had found such a simple explanation for her anger, and tears of grief that age is given so little understanding of youth, that age must always look at youth through the muddy eyes of experience. It was a mercy of God that the child was too innocent to know what she had been thinking. But why had she thought ill of Nancy? It was not like her to suspect evil. With the mother Nancy had, evil would be expected of her. But it was something more than that. There was in Nancy herself something keyed too high. A look about her, an overthrowing look, an air that she was neither to hold nor to bind. She must talk to her about it, warn her.

She searched about in her breast for some wise way to say the thing that she must say, tightening her arms about the child in a convulsive wish to guard her from life.

But Nancy took the tightening of her arms for forgiveness, and was comforted. It was nothing that Mrs. Anderson had called her mother a "trollope" and a "slut." She had heard the words too often for them to have any harsh meaning. When people are angry they call you "trollope" and "slut." They call your mother that also, and if you have a father and a sister, they come into the scolding as well. When their anger is over they say something nice or put their arms about you, and it is forgotten. That is the way of life. Nancy was willing to forget.

But Mrs. Anderson had a burden upon her heart that would not be laid away. She sighed deeply. Misunderstanding the sigh, Nancy said:

"I won't go out at night and leave you any more."

"That's not the worst of it," said the old woman, feeling her way cautiously to what she wanted to say.

"Taking the key, you mean?"

"That, but more besides. There's the 'appearance of evil' to be considered among other things." She stopped, afraid to go on. How was it possible to speak of danger without naming the thing itself? She waited a while, and then took up the burden again, haltingly:

"My son's wife would never understand your reason for taking the key, or for going out. . . . She wouldn't believe your explanation." . . . Feeling herself on delicate ground, Mrs. Anderson hurried along to a new reason. "Besides, she wouldn't approve of the Whistling Boy playing the kirk organ, especially in the dead of night. And she would think it a reflection upon herself to have you trapesing hither and yon. . . ."

Again she paused. This was leading her away from what she wanted to say. She would have to be more direct.

"It would be ill advised for you to meet the Whistling Boy again."

Nancy stirred as if out of a half-sleep.

"Why? I won't go out at nights any more. But in the days when you aren't needing me."

"It isn't so much my needing you. It's the 'appearance of evil' that I'm considering. Not that there's an evil thought in your head, but you're one that will have to walk a chalk-line all your days."

She gave it up once more, and lay brooding helplessly. Nancy, lying against her breast, reflected that the poor old woman was getting like Granny in some ways. It was age likely that made them talk so aimlessly. She felt sorry for the old woman. She reached up a timid hand and bashfully caressed her withered cheek.

The old woman sighed deeply and said:

"I sorely misdoubt, bairn, if you were born but under a dark star."

Humouring her, Nancy asked sleepily:

"What's a dark star? I've never seen one."

Heavy with prophecy and foreboding, the old woman answered:

"No, nor ever has any man. But there're dark stars, and there're light stars in the sky. . . . There're some that are born under light stars, and for them the road is fair and lightsome. . . . Their very sins turn into glories upon their heads. . . .

"But woe betide the bairn that's born under a dark star, for she is for ever taking the wrong turn in the road. Her simplest move takes on an evil look and is held against her for a sin . . . and love never shows its face but it comes sharp-thorned with grief. . . ."

The old lady broke off and lay still. Her eyes, grown old and bewildered with wisdom, watched the young day come in at the window. The head upon her arm was heavy and limp. Nancy was asleep.

The next day there was no time to return to the subject even if she had not already lost her courage for it, for the minister's wife got up in a bad temper. This meant that Nancy must dance at her heels every minute of the day. The minister's wife felt herself put in the wrong in William's eyes. This could not be borne.

Miss Shields of Callochie had turned out, after all, to be only the watchmaker's aunt. And, more than that, she fully believed that William had known it all the time and had never said a word to warn her.

Just after choir practice, while they were standing near the lectern, she had seen her chance to prevent Bella Fraser from making herself "cheaper than ever" by letting the watchmaker see her home. Turning to the two of them as they were leaving together, she said playfully to the watchmaker:

"I'm going to take Bella away from you. I want her to walk home with me."

The lovers had looked one at the other with the clear admission that they didn't favour the proposal. So to let the watchmaker see what she meant, she said with a smile: "I suppose you will be running away to Callochie anyway now."

"I will that," he admitted. But he did not give ground or seem back-set. So she turned to Bella and said lightly (the way such things must be said):

"And how will that suit *you*, Bella?"

Bella laughed a little simperingly:

"Oh, fine. I'll be going too. I've never met his aunt." And as she spoke she raised her left hand to push back a curl which did not need to be pushed back. It was then that Mrs. Anderson noticed the engagement ring on her finger, and looked up in time to catch the very edge of a smile on William's face; or was it only the shadow of the lectern that gave his face that look?

It had been gall upon her tongue to wish Bella Fraser joy, not knowing all the time what William was thinking behind his face.

So next day she got up with the need to prove herself a Christian martyr before evening. This meant that from early morning till supper-time she would "visit and cheer the sick of the congregation", carrying jars of jelly and cheerfully worded tracts to the righteous ones, and to the sinners those passages from the Bible that best accorded with their sins. At evening she would return, pallid and limp, to creep supperless to bed, and no amount of coaxing would make her eat a bite of food. Quite wordlessly she could convey to William that it was some lack in him that kept her slaving all day. With a troubled sense of guilt he would carry tasty bits of this and that to the darkened bedroom, only to be sent away with the pensive sigh:

"I can't, William, after a day like *that*."

And William would go down to eat his supper, feeling somehow that he and the Lord between them were killing his poor, brave wife.

Nancy dreaded these martyr-days, for she had to go along to carry the jellies. Not that she minded carrying the jellies, but she hated to sit hour after hour while the minister's wife read the Bible. There was something in the way she did it that made God sound *so* unlikeable. And Nancy felt that nobody set any store by the visits but Mrs. Anderson herself, though nobody but the miller had ever come out with it and told her as much to her face.

The miller's wife had cancer of the breast. There was a queer, sad smell about the house; even the geraniums had it. Nancy would smell them to change the air in her nostrils, but nothing would take that smell away once you got inside. While the minister's wife read the Bible in a tasteless voice that hung like mist upon the room, the little yellowed claws of the miller's wife would pick in a frenzy at the quilt. One day while she was reading the miller came in, flour lying on his red face like the bloom on damson plums. He saw the picking hands upon the quilt and roared:

"What are you doing to her?"

With a look of chill dignity, Mrs. Anderson replied:

"I'm reading the Lord's Word."

"To hell with the Lord—and you!"

And his eyes between their flour-hung lashes blazed as he put them to the door.

But such treatment was rarely met with. More often there was a flutter of excitement at their approach, especially among the poorer ones. And these were the ones Mrs. Anderson enjoyed the most.

They would start by visiting old Annie Toochie and her sore feet. Summer and winter Annie wore the minister's old galoshes slashed at suitable places to accommodate her most painful bunions. She was always pleased when the minister's wife arrived, saying:

"Well, Annie, and how's your feet?"

She would detain her artfully, asking explanations of this passage in the Bible and then that. For the longer she kept the minister's wife the more she could brag to the neighbours about the length of her visit.

Then there was the wife of Willie Watt who worked in the sand-hole. She was glad and more than glad to see them, especially if Nancy had a big-looking bundle under her arm. For Mrs. Watt had fourteen children and was always in need of old clothes.

In twenty years she had never worn a garment that was bought for herself. The velvet blouse was the one the publican's wife had discarded when she began to put on weight after the doctor recommended a glass of hot porter at bed-time. And the cashmere skirt was the one poor Mrs. Menzies was wearing when she fell down dead of the dropsy. But, though she got coats and skirts and blouses in good repair, nobody ever gave her corsets till the busks were broken. This gave her an unfortunate-looking front, so it was never possible to tell when another Watt was to be expected.

They would do the one-sided street house by house, calling on Miss Cruckshank, who was a lady born and far past all reason with never doing a hand's-turn for herself. Her soft white cheeks hung down in points, so that the bottom of her face had a scalloped appearance.

On the table in her parlour there was an ostrich egg sitting in a big sugar-bowl. It was said that this egg had been brought to her from foreign parts by her sailor sweetheart, and was in a way a pledge between them that he would come back to marry her.

But fifty years had passed and he had not come back. The egg was just where she had put it the very day he gave it to her. She dusted it herself. Indeed, it was her day's work. When she hired a lassie to do her cleaning she would say:

"You're to do everything but dust the egg. Never let your hands light on that."

After Miss Cruckshank they would make a brief visit at Jean Taylor's to inquire about her sick laddie. But this was never a happy visit, for the minister's wife was always trying to get a close look at Jean's hair. Rumour said that she combed it with a lead comb to hide the grey in it, but Mrs. Anderson could not be sure if this were true because she never could see it near a light. And Jean was not minded to let her see it in the light. So the two of them would talk and manoeuvre back and forth, each with her eye on the other, till finally the visit would come to an end and they would be out on the sidewalk, with Mrs. Anderson no wiser than she was before.

But now they would cross to the other side where there were no houses, and look away down the slow sloping river-bank to the fast-moving water, still dappled with bubbles from its dance upon the mill-wheel, and to the high larch-trees upon the other bank.

Never must their eyes acknowledge what stood at the other side of the street. Never must they seem to see the woman standing in the doorway, hands on broad hips, nor hear her husky laughter.

No use to stop here and leave tracts or words of comfort. No use to bow the head in prayer for this erring sister. Even the Lord could do nothing for

"Divot[1] Meg."

She had been barely into her teens when she won the name Divot Meg, though then it had been innocent enough, and fairly enough earned. At potato-gathering time, when every man was clearing a place in his back-yard to pile the winter potatoes, Meg would come down the street leading a reluctant donkey with a cart and crying:

"Divots, divots for sale."

She came so handily that hardly a man would cut his own divots, but would wait to buy them from Divot Meg.

But that was a far day now. Meg was no more the easy-blushing buxom lass that led a lazy donkey. She was thirty or more, and no better looking for the added years. But as for that, she had never been a marvel for beauty. Her square teeth were spaced too wide apart. The tip of her nose had the look of having been pressed back with a very determined thumb so that her nostrils stared you in the face. Her coarse, curling hair was like the bright rust that comes on iron gates, and her eyes were the red eyes you see in very white rabbits. But there had been that about her which made men turn to look, and, looking, wish to follow. So it could pass for a certainty that all good women were born to say ill of her, as she was born to merit all their slandering.

If Mrs. Anderson passed, looking away to spare her eyes the sight of that careless, godless face, it was no more than others did. And Divot Meg laughed at their passing, and on occasions made vulgar noises after them. Especially the righteous ones. She had a word for everybody, sometimes a half-good-natured taunt for the good-looking ones, not wholly devoid of admiration. Though a new dress or a becoming hat on a pretty head would bring such a volley of lewd advice that few had the courage to pass that way wearing anything out of the ordinary.

She was a roaring challenge that was never stilled. Pitouie could not forget her if it would. And she could not be ousted from the town, for she owned every grey stone of the sordid house which was her stronghold.

This house was called the "White Ship." Why, nobody knew. It had always been called that, years before she owned it, though there was nothing about it to suggest the name. Nothing white at any rate. It was a gaunt three-storey building with a blue slate roof and a flat grey face. It had many small and dirty windows, most of which were broken and stuffed with rags, or pasted over with stiff brown paper. For this was no home for "Selected gentlemen" or even for "Selected ladies." This was the transient home of knights and ladies of the open road, wayfarers of the King's Highway. They came at sundown, and were gone with the sunrise. Each day brought new faces. Though there were some who came year after year, and these Divot Meg welcomed like a mother.

In the summer-time they never came. The lee-side of a hedge or a hay-rick would serve them as well. But in the winter, or when it rained, they would gather in the "tinker's kitchen" of the White Ship, huddled about the coal range that filled one end of the long, draughty room.

Their bundles of food, begged or stolen, would be unhooked from the long sticks that carried them and spread out for inspection and comment. Half a pork pie from Menzies' Farm, but the taste of that is spoiled when Tinker Tom tells that Menzies' pigs died of the yellow pocks. Seedcake, very dry, that was from the "wee-wifie" at the toll bar. She was not minded to give him anything, but he had stuck his foot in the door and she had thought better of it. Two eggs; well, he chanced to see them in a hedge. Potatoes; but everybody has potatoes. They are easiest to get. You just go up to where the divots cover them. Standing, looking about you as innocent as you please, you work your foot under a divot and scrape out as many as you want. Then quickly bend and scoop them into your bag, and away you go. Five sausages; no telling where he got them. A bowl of potted-head; had to stack peats for an hour to get that, but it is worth it. Another has a finnan-haddock, lifted deftly off a hake hanging at the door, and stuffed swiftly up the back of his jacket in the flash of time it took the good-wife to look back into the house and answer his query about the time.

But some have brought food, good steaks and fresh bread. And oh, the scramble and fighting there will be over the frying-pan, and who shall use it first. Once in a fight over it one woman had torn another's eye out. It lay upon her cheek like nothing in the world but a peeled boiled egg until the veterinary came and popped it back in again.

The man who took the front bedroom with the wooden bedstead was entitled to use the frying-pan first. He had other privileges also of a more intimate nature, but these were less prized now than formerly, for Divot Meg was not so young as she once was. However, the first use of the frying-pan was still coveted, and considered worth the extra penny.

When the company was worthy of it, Divot Meg would join them in the late evening as they sat cross-legged upon the floor; each man with his belongings safely held in the cage made by his legs, his back against the wall, while the occasional lady of the road held hers tied in a spotted handkerchief in her lap. There were rarely any women, but often there would be a pimpled slender boy, who would dress up and sing bawdy songs in a high female voice. Or Divot Meg would sing and dance a hornpipe in her shift.

But it was when the "Cauld Rice Piper" came that you heard music to warm your blood, no matter how many cold hedge-sides had chilled it.

He must have been fairly daft about rice, for there was nothing but rice in his oilskin bag, boiled rice, devilled rice, raw rice, and rice pudding. He never warmed it up, but ate it as it was, his oilskin bag in front of him, his bagpipes tied upon his back so that the pipes stood up behind his head like drunken horns.

Then, there was the "Rose-eyes" with his never-to-be-forgotten Cockney accent and his multitude of body-lice. Most of the guests had lice, but there was a belief among them about the lice that the Rose-eyes bred. It was thought that they grew and lived beneath his skin, and only came out to look about for a new skin to live under. So they made him sit off on the other side of the room, and drew a ring of paraffin oil on the wooden floor around him so that his lice would not spread. But they loved to hear him sing "When the roses come again," and asked for it over and over, though his dismal, bottomless coughing would often strangle the words and bring them to a gasping stop. There was a wistful melancholy even in the Cockney way he mangled the words:

"W'en the rose-eyes come ah-gyne-er,
W'en the rose-eyes come ah-gyne-er,
I will meetu, I will greetu,
W'en the rose-eyes come ah-gyne-er."

But it was the "Braes O'Mar" who was the greatest favourite with them. Indeed, all Pitouie loved the Braes O'Mar. Whenever he set foot across the toll-bar bridge all the children ran to meet him crying his name—a name they had given him because his first song was always, "The Standard on the Braes o' Mar."

His suit of fisherman's blue frieze was double-breasted and fastened with shiny brass buttons. A bright tartan cravat swathed his neck. Upon his head he wore a blue Glengarry bonnet, and no matter what the weather, his boots shone with black respectability. Under his arm was his octagonal concertina, and in his hand a bright yellow staff, for his leg was stiff.

He would take his stand to sing when the children had gathered about him as thick as bees. But first with his staff he would draw a circle about himself.

Outside this circle the children must stand, and *inside* the circle the pennies must fall. Then he would hang the staff upon his arm. Out would come the concertina and away would go the tune, lilting upon the air, till the good-wives came running to their doors, leaving the potatoes to boil down to soup while they stood listening. And he had a way with him of appearing to give up and walk on if the pennies did not fall fast enough.

129

But they never let him go for lack of a penny, for he would artfully hold the favourite tune until the last. Then at long length, when he was sure that there were no more pennies to be had, he would give them the tune they were waiting for, the favourite of all:

"Oh, she won my heart by sitting and knitting,
The time that I sat smoking and spitting,
And ever since then my heart's gone aflitting,
For Nanny that lived next door."

Divot Meg also was very partial to the Braes O'Mar, and gave him the front bedroom with the wooden bed at no extra charge. Once he had brought a concertina to Divot Meg's oldest laddie, but the laddie showed it to Divot Meg's sick man, and *he* tore it apart with his hands and teeth. Divot Meg said it was because the music bothered him. And perhaps that *was* the real reason.

And then occasionally there would come a silent man with close-shaved head. He would stay a week or maybe two or three, until his hair grew out. They would share their food with him, but not from friendliness.

The yearly fair brought many strange guests. The man with the electric shock machine would come and bring his wife, who was fairly riddled with electricity, they said, and could stick her tongue on a forty-volt current with the same ease that a kitten puts its tongue in milk.

And there was the Punch and Judy man, and the one-armed man who ran the heavy-hammer machine. Even Ramos, the "world-famous pin-cushion king," had come to spend a night once when business was bad.

You could stick a pin in any part of him and never draw a drop of blood. But it cost sixpence a pin, so it was not so popular as other amusements that cost less and lasted longer. Divot Meg had a life-sized poster of him with pins sticking out of every muscle like spines on a porcupine. It was pasted on her bedroom wall. She was so proud of it and showed it so often that rumour said Ramos was the father of her little Jimmy. But when the school-children took little Jimmy and stuck pins in him he bled like sixty, so they had no proof of the relationship.

At fair time every corner would be filled. Divot Meg would move her bedridden man from his own bed in the back of the house downstairs to the room where the five children slept. She would hoist him on her back and carry him down the two long flights, asking no one's help. Whether the ride hurt him or not, no one knew. Nothing but his eyes spoke, and they cried only "Why? Why?" They had been crying that for ten years.

A small sore upon his tongue made by his clay pipe had turned into cancer, and now he had no tongue.

What did he think, lying up there in the back room? Was it true that not one of the five children that called him father was fathered by him? What burned behind those eyes that screamed a question in the face of God?

Whatever it was, Divot Meg was afraid of him. Her eyes would never meet his screaming eyes that reached for hers and tried to make her look him in the face. She carried him the thin gruel which was all the food his tortured throat could swallow, but she looked past him at the wall, or over him at the picture of King Edward which hung above his head. At first he would strike at her, and she would carry his bruises on her face and arms for weeks at a time.

Now he was too weak for that, but his eyes terrified her more than any lifted hand. To drive the terror out of her mind, and maybe to avenge herself for that terror, she would carouse with the men from the fair till early morning, and then, courageous with whisky, she would go to her sick man's room and, standing in the doorway, cry out her drunken wish that he might be six feet below the grass before another day.

But it was seldom she had the heart for this. More often she was haunting the doctor's house, harrowing him with threats and pleading that he find some way to cure her man.

On this particular day when Nancy and Mrs. Anderson passed she was standing in the street door watching. As they came out of Jean Taylor's she cried to Nancy:

"Hey, bairn, come here a minute."

Mrs. Anderson made a move that refused to let her go, but the command in Divot Meg's voice was stronger, and Nancy turned to face her, leaving Mrs. Anderson to cross the road alone.

Divot Meg looked her over with a half-amused curiosity and laughed.

"There's nothing of Willie Weams in *your* face, bairn."

As Mrs. Anderson stopped and looked back she added: "*That* holy bitch! . . . If you tire of her, come here to me. . . . Better be after her now. . . . I just wanted to look at your face."

"Did you know my mother?"

There was such frank friendliness in Nancy's face that Divot Meg lost some of her bridling arrogance.

"Aye. I knew Bella Pringle," she answered cryptically.

"She was bonnie, wasn't she?"

Nancy was looking into her eyes, pleading a kind word about her mother.

"Bonnie enough . . . but you'll be bonnier."

They were both conscious of Mrs. Anderson waiting in bristling

131

indignation at the other side of the road.

"Away you go, bairn," Divot Meg ordered. "She'll flay you alive."

Nancy would have lingered, but Divot Meg left her, slamming the door of the White Ship upon her as if her sudden interest had as suddenly died out.

The charitable labours of the minister's wife ended in a bilious attack which lasted three days. Old Mrs. Anderson vowed it was the venom in her backing up in her system. She celebrated her daughter-in-law's down-lying by descending to the dining-room at meal-times, and her chortling inquiries about the invalid's health could be clearly heard in the darkened bedroom where lay the minister's wife, turned saffron with anger and gall.

Nancy was tortured between the two of them, pulled from the one to the other in a verbal tug-of-war. First the old woman would insist that this was the very day she must have her hair washed. Barely would Nancy get begun on that when the peevish ringing of the minister's wife's bell would call her below. She would start to answer it, but the old woman would detain her, crying with gleeful relish: "Never mind her . . . waiting won't hurt her."

But a minute later Mary would be crying from the foot of the stairs: "The mistress is wanting you . . . are you deaf?"

And away Nancy would fly over the protests of the old woman. But no more would she reach the musty-smelling, dark bedroom where a sweetish whining came from the rumpled bed, than the old woman's voice would come lustily down over the banister, carrying a challenge that was not meant for Nancy's ears alone:

"Am *I* to get my death of cold in the head while you bother with *her* havers? . . . If she'd keep her prayers to herself . . . if she'd keep her long nose out of the affairs of others, and put less in her belly . . ."

Here her voice would be drowned as the minister's wife querulously commanded Nancy to shut the door. But that would not be the end of it. Before Nancy would get the bolster shaken up and put back beneath the invalid's head, the door would open as if a gale had struck it, and the old woman, standing well back in the passage, holding her nose queasily, would cry:

"Come out, bairn, before you're suffocated. Foch! What a stink. An ill-skin is hard to sweeten."

This would force the minister's wife from her bed to shut the door resoundingly. She would turn the key in it and creep back into her bed, saying:

"Her mind is going, poor thing. . . . William speaks of putting her away . . . to some place (smiling weakly) . . . But I hate to think of that."

Something in Nancy would curl up cold with fear at the slinking threat in the words. She would try to make peace between them, softening as best she could the missiles that flew from one to the other. But these two would never be reconciled as long as life would last. Deep in the marrow of their souls they were enemies, sworn to do each other to death. They never came to loud words in front of William, but the javelins of hate wrapped in velvet flew softly past his head day after day as the battle went on and on.

For three days Nancy had tried to escape from the house, for she was beset with thoughts of the Whistling Boy and yearning to see him again. But at every turn she was thwarted. If she offered to run quickly to the druggist's to buy Seidlitz Powders, it fell out that there were a lot of Seidlitz Powders in the house. If she thought of buying embrocation, that too was useless, for "William was going on a visit near the druggist's and would bring it on the way back." Nothing availed her. If she so much as reached out her hand for her hat, someone would cry:

"Where are you going?"

And she would have to say:

"Nowhere, I was just going to try it on."

By the evening of the third day she had come to the place where she was ready to march boldly down the stairs and out at the front door no matter who tried to stop her.

All that kept her from doing this was the wish to have on her new dress when next she met him. But this could not be for a week or more, and in that time he might have stopped thinking of her, if, indeed, he had thought of her at all.

That was the torturous thought. Had he thought of her at all, or had he forgotten her, just as he had forgotten her the other night when he sat down to play the organ? Would he think of her again at all until something happened to remind him of her? He had been kind and penitent when they walked home. He had shortened his steps so that she did not have to run panting at his side, and at parting he had said:

"Come into the shop to-morrow, won't you?" How gladly she had promised! But had he said it because he really wanted to see her again, or only as a reward for her blowing, as an apology for his forgetfulness?

In either case, she had not gone. That was a comforting thing to remember if she found that he had forgotten her. At least it would look as if she also had forgotten him.

But perhaps he was looking for her every day and wondering why she did not come. If only she could be assured of that, she could bear not to see him for another week. She could wait till she had her new dress to impress him with.

But no, she could not bear to wait. She had no hope to impress him, but only to warm herself at his triumphant gleaming, to stand a little way aside and watch the wonder of him. Oh, the melting way he held his head. . . . Oh, the glamour of his forward-looking face! She could not wait another day, another hour!

It was not late, only nine o'clock. The druggist's shop kept open until ten. He would be there standing behind the counter in front of the important glass bottles with gilded labels written in Latin, which he could read.

If they heard her go, or missed her, she would be scolded to-morrow. But to-night she would see him!

She blew out the light of the rose-glass lamp. Silver fingers of moonlight came in at the high turret windows, and a few pale stars huddled close to the window-panes. She felt her way in their wan light toward her bedroom door, but before she could reach it there burst upon the quiet night a joyful madrigal, shaking its heart with a purling gladness, sweeping the huddling stars higher in the heavens, and brightening the jade-pale face of the moon.

It was the Whistling Boy! He was at the garden's end calling to her. She stood tremulous in unbelieving delight.

Yes. It really was the Whistling Boy, and he must have come for her. The pain of her longing for him relaxed in the ease of this. She drew herself up a little pridefully, and there was the ghost of a coquettish tilt to her head.

So he was reaching for her now. Maybe he needed her after all, not only for his playing, since he came so early. No, it could not be for his playing, it must be that he was thinking of her, wanting to see her.

But he had waited three days before coming, and *she* had blown all night for him. Now, when the fancy took him he came whistling for her. Did he think that she would run to him at the first calling? She thought of her eager trotting by his side, of her blistered hands and aching back, and pride grew where the yearning ache had been. She tossed her head:

"Whistle! Go on whistling. I'll never come to you."

She flounced about the room pretending to scorn him, pretending indifference to his calling. But in the deeps of her female soul she was saying:

"Now I can bear to wait till I get my new dress before I see him! He wants me! He needs me! He's calling me!"

"Now I can bear not to see him. I can bear not to see him as long as it hurts him not to see me."

And she took exultant postures before the mirror, in the moonlight, like some vain wraith in a triumphal dance.

Sobering a little, she climbed on the high bookcase and stared down through the turret windows at the garden's end, searching some dark movement which would show her where he stood.

But the high long hedge made one black wall which shrouded smaller shadows, only from its darkness rose the melodious fountain still commandingly.

She stood stretched upon tiptoe watching and listening, her heart strengthening against him with every moment that he lingered.

As he went from one tune to another, a tang of doubt, a hint of sadness crept into the notes, and then, quite suddenly, he stopped. She held her breath. Waiting! He must, he would begin another tune. But silence had taken back the night again.

Her eyes strained into the darkness searching the moonlit road beyond the hedge. Soon she saw him moving slowly down the road away from her, and fading at last into the hungry black beyond.

She climbed down slowly. A small ache nibbled at the edge of her heart. She sought to quiet it with inward boasting of the way he had come crying for her, and the slow moving of his feet as he went empty away, and, filled by this, she fell asleep at last with a prideful smile upon her mouth.

"DEAR NANCY PRINGLE,—I'm away to Edinburgh on the night's train. I came and whistled to you. I'm sorry you didn't hear me. I wanted to tell you that I'm not to bother with druggisting any more, but am going back to study music. It may turn out that I'll be away to France or Germany by Martinmas. I have everything to pack yet, so no more at present.

"Yrs truly,

"HARVEY BRUNE."

The letter smelled of carbolic acid and was stained at one corner. Even as she turned it uncertainly in her hands she wondered who had bought the carbolic acid and if the Whistling Boy had spilled it on the counter.

Harvey Brune! The Whistling Boy! She would run now and ask him what he meant by the letter. But no, she could not run and ask him, for the letter said: "I'm away to Edinburgh on the night's train."

He was away to Edinburgh. No, no, he could not be away to Edinburgh! She had heard him whistling last night. Calling to her. . . .

Calling to her . . . to say good-bye. That was why he had come whistling. And she had let him go without a word. "Away to Edinburgh," maybe never to come back! "Away to France and Germany." Away from Pitouie and the druggisting. Away from the waterfall that looked like Italy. Away from her.

"I have everything to pack yet." All his twelve pairs of socks without a darn in one of them and every one of his fourteen shirts with the name embroidered in fine thread, all to pack. Not a smidge or a hair of him left behind, not a sound of his whistling, not a lift of his head, not a sight of his forward-looking face. All of him packed and away to Edinburgh. Away to France and Germany! Away from Pitouie! Away from Pitouie!

"So no more at present." So no more at present, that might mean that he would write again. It *must* mean that he would write again. He had not told her yet how it came about that he could leave the druggisting. He would be sure to tell her that. And if he got an organ of his own, he would want her to know it.

If only he had stayed a little longer that he could see her in her new dress! But when he came back . . . He had said nothing about coming back. . . . Of course he would! A body could not come to Pitouie and then never come back. Birds came back, and flowers came back. Birds came back to lay again in their old nests. Flowers came back because they had left remnants of themselves in the ground. . . . But why should he come back? He had left no nest, no remnant . . . and yet . . . and yet . . .

She put the letter in the walnut box and turned the key upon it. Now once more the walnut box was the core of her life, now once more it was her destination. At nightfall she ran home to it, and in the days it waited for her secretly.

---

1 Divot: a large grassy sod of earth, used to cover piles of potatoes to keep off the frost in winter.

BOOK II

Watching for a letter from the Whistling Boy changed with time from a piercing expectation to a bearable waiting. Always the face of her heart was turned that way, looking to see the letter come. As the years went by, sometimes her heart forgot the name of its longing. But still it looked, turned always one way, in a nameless waiting.

At times his name would stab her from the pages of a newspaper, or his picture would flash out, leaving her limp and wounded, but even that, his fame and his remoteness, even that also became something which could be borne.

She collected all of them, every line of type which told about his genius. All lay in the walnut box with his letter; little thorns for ever stabbing her, till their half-numbed pain became at last the muted tune which was her soul.

All the currents of her growth inclined one way as a plant that leans toward the light. Everything she did was done for him, all her studying. Long hours spent with Mr. Robertson in the big front bedroom at Miss Clark's. Whole summer evenings, facing the big mahogany dresser with lions' claws for feet and ten glass knobs, to say nothing of the four little knobs on the small drawers where Mr. Robertson kept his collars and handkerchiefs and his four ties.

The top knob on the right with the bubble in the glass was the one which reminded you that:

"*Raison* takes *avoir; avoir tort; avoir faim; avoir froid; avoir chaud.*"

Did *he* memorise French by knobs! No! He would never need to. Knowledge would just come and light on him. Greek and Latin and French. And German too. He would speak German. Later, she must learn that also. But now this:

"*Non, monsieur, je ne peux pas le dénouer, parce que j'ai l'onglée aux doigts.*"

"*Non!* Say it with your nose! There's no such sound in French as the one you're making. *Non! Non!*"

"*Non!*"

The nasal ones were hard. But the throaty *r*'s she could do well.

And sometimes, glowering genially from under his furry eyebrows, Mr Robertson would compliment her upon these.

And music, music! She must know something about music. *He* was learning so much with all the world laid out before him. At the back of all her thoughts was this one, spurring her on. Preparing herself. Preparing herself.

Preparing herself for what? For him to come back and claim her? No. It was a frailer dream than that. . . . For him to come back. For him to come back and glance her way. For him to come back. . . . It ended there. She could not go beyond. This only was a certainty, he would come back.

She was growing a woman now, and men's eyes lingered upon her as she passed. In the eyes of most of them she saw a thing that made her angry and afraid. It was as if they said: "So *this* is Bella Pringle's bairn," and something deep in them winked slyly. She knew that they did not look like this at Lettie Taylor, the doctor's daughter, about whose father there was no mystery. It made her keep away from boys of her own age, and hurry past the older men with downcast eyes. Or if she met one alone and his eyes made free with the tender rise of her breasts beneath the blue print of her too narrow frock, she would blaze at him with angry defensive eyes till often he would redden and turn away. But even as she did this she was ashamed that it was necessary, for if men respected her she would not need to defend herself against their eyes.

If she knew that she was a Fassefern and not the child of Willie Weams she could face any look. But what was there to tell her? If she were a Fassefern, would it not show in her and command respect?

Or was the world able to put a name upon her, and then by its very thoughts, raise her up or pull her down to fit that name? Was she to be lowered to the level of Willie Weams because Pitouie secretly gave her his name? Or could she by holding herself a Fassefern defy their eyes to look at her without respect?

At times she wondered if it was not all a thing of her imagining. Perhaps men looked at her as they looked at other girls grown near to womanhood. Or did she invite their eyes by something in herself?

She was afraid of this new state, and bewildered by strange impulses that rose in herself. Wild blind energy which had no focus or outlet. A driving curiosity with nothing to fasten upon.

In the midst of this William Webster, a brother of the minister's wife, came for a visit to the rectory.

In colour he was the same tallowish blond as his sister. His eyes were round and the colour of clay. They were not set deeply enough in their sockets. Sometimes Nancy would tell herself that they would drop out if he looked down. She would do this during prayers, and shudder at the thought that when he looked up there would be nothing but the empty sockets looking back at her. His teeth were strangely irregular in size. The two upper centre ones were large, and came together in a right angle, the ones flanking these at either side were very small, and pointed as a grain of rice. The eye-teeth were long like the teeth of a dog. His smile was more repulsive than his frown. There was something in the way that he looked at her that made Nancy think of fungus and toadstools. She hated to look at him, but she could not keep from doing it. In his look was a covert leer as if he knew some dark thing about her.

One day she met him accidentally in the long passage that led from the library to the foot of the stairs. A sense of something eerie assailed her as he walked toward her. She was afraid of the meeting, yet she did not want to avoid it. Something about him lured her to *know*, as a dark cave might call her to explore it, even while its darkness frightened her. So she went toward him.

He barred her way, as she knew he would. She pretended surprise, and he laughed contemptuously, seizing her bare forearm in his long cold hand. Nancy glanced round, fearing someone might see.

"Scared we're caught?" he taunted. "Come to my room, then. Nobody comes there."

She wrenched her arm away and ran past him, the blood surging to her face. What was it? What was this? He's ugly, ugly, ugly. She would never see him again. His room! Nobody comes there! What would he do if she went? What did he mean to her? And dimly she knew that some day she would find out. Find out what? She did not know. But some darkly throbbing pulse demanded the answer. Her heart kept crying ugly, ugly, ugly. She avoided him, pretending she was ill to excuse her from attending prayers. But she was ever conscious of his presence in the house. Each to-morrow was focused on him as on something that would "happen."

She tried to speak of it to old Mrs. Anderson:

"Isn't there something queer about Mr. Webster—about his face? I don't like to look at it. Yet I *have* to look."

"It's adenoids," Mrs. Anderson answered with conviction.

"That *I* have?"

"No, bless you. *He* has them. So has *she*. Halfwitted, that's what it does to them."

But Nancy knew that was not the explanation.

The night before he was to leave, she was on her way to her room, carrying the bright copper coalscuttle and a glass of milk, when she saw him standing near her tower-room door. Here it was! Whatever it was! She hated him! She hated him! It was his head she hated. It was his smile. It was the way he looked at her she hated. Why did she hate him so?

She went toward him with feet that hurried forward while her heart hung back.

When she came near, he took the coal-scuttle from her and carried it up the narrow stairs to her room. He had been there already. The lamp was lighted and the wick turned very low. She followed him up and set the milk on the table. He swung the wooden bar across the door.

"Don't do that," she said.

"We don't want them coming in."

"Why not?"

"*You* know."

"I don't."

He laughed. "How old are you?" he asked.

"Seventeen. How old are you?"

"Twenty. Have you ever kissed a fellow?"

"No!"

"No?"

"No!"

"You're going to kiss me." He made a movement toward her which she avoided by stepping round the table.

"I'm *not*, you're ugly. I *hate* you."

"What did you let me come for?" he sneered.

"I didn't let you come. You came."

"Huh, that's the way the girls talk. They always blame the fellow."

She did not answer for a moment. His words gave her a sense of guilt, as if she were drawn into some sin common to the world.

"Get out of here," she ordered.

"You don't want me to go."

She made no attempt to deny it, but stood at the other side of the table, waiting. It was true that she did not want him to go. Something would be unfinished. Some clash that must come would be postponed. She must find out why he sneered, why he watched her, why she had to think of him, why she hated him so.

It was his face she hated, the sneer upon his face. It was as if he *knew* that she had to think of him, and despised her for it.

"Well, better kiss me." He reached and caught her hand, pulling her round to him insolently. She struck him viciously in the face. He groaned as if in ecstasy, and swept her into his arms, pressing her hard against him. She struck at him again. A part of her demanded that she keep striking him. But something deeper knew that her blows were useless, wanted

140

them to be useless. Something primitive in her wanted him to hold her. She twined her fingers in his hair and pulled it savagely. He panted, but gripped her tighter.

She fought him more feebly as his arms locked about her more tightly. She had a fancy that there were two of her, a white prim one that fought and pretended, and a black savage one rolling up like a warm sea on a hot still night. The white one struggling because it *ought* to struggle, pushing with feeble silly hands, the black one heedless of it, sweeping up in long languorous waves.

She had forgotten him. He was no longer a man. He was a force, the force of the world surging over her, mingling with her dark self. The beating of his heart was the sound of the earth, his breath was warm wind upon the sea. Her silly hands would fight no more, the prim white one was conquered.

"Come over to the bed."

The words crashed through the isolation in which she swung, shattering it into a thousand shivering pieces. He had spoken! He had a voice! He had a face! He was a man! The man she hated. The white one rose and screamed in terror.

"Don't scream—damned fool!" he hissed, trying to get his hand upon her mouth to silence her. She screamed again piercingly, staring in horror at his ugly face. Someone below answered her. There was the sound of a chair knocked over, and footsteps.

"My God! They're coming." His eyes popped idiotically, and his lower lip gaped down incredulous. He loosened his hold, and she sank against the table, a great weakness sweeping down her thighs. His loose face stiffened. He slid swiftly to the door, swung the bar, and was gone. Nancy clung to the table, staring at the black opening of the door. She could not connect herself with what had passed or what was going to happen. Her soul had gone jangling off into a void while her body hung like an empty snake-skin. Thoughts tried to form themselves, but could not.

The minister, ludicrous in his striped flannelette nightshirt, arrived in the doorway, brandishing a large umbrella. Nancy's thoughts rushed back and found a focus. She must answer him, tell him why she screamed.

"It's nothing. I thought I saw a ghost." She wondered why she lied, even as she said the words.

"I heard footsteps."

"It was me running. I went down the hall. I thought I saw something moving. I screamed and ran back."

She listened to her explanation in astonishment. It came from some part of her that was calm and alert while all the rest of her was adrift. She smiled faintly, thinking: "That is the instinct of self-preservation. All animals have it."

Seeing her smile, the minister became conscious of his nightshirt. He raised the great umbrella and held it in front of him like a screen, conversing with her over the top. His wife was crying shrilly as she mounted the stairs to know what had happened. She reached his side, clutching her pale blue nun's-veiling dressing-gown about her meagre hips, peering with eyes that could not see without her glasses, her hair hanging in listless drab wisps upon her neck. As she looked at them, Nancy thought irrelevantly: "God is love," and she laughed out loud. Mrs. Anderson stepped behind the umbrella also. Nancy laughed again. She laughed and laughed, louder and louder, and the two in the door stared at her over the spoked rim of the umbrella.

"Hysterical," explained the minister. "She thought she saw a ghost."

"*There!*" cried Mrs. Anderson triumphantly. "Her liver's upset. Too much cream. Just what I've been saying."

She felt delighted and justified by the "ghost." It proved beyond doubt that Nancy must eat her porridge with blue inoffensive milk from now on.

"And more than that, you must be sure to take calomel in the morning. This should be a lesson to your mother as well," she added to her husband.

"It's nothing but cream that makes her knee so stiff. I've told her so again and again, but of course she never listens to what *I* have to say." She sighed deeply, then smiled with benevolent forgiveness. "Well, she's old, and I suppose old people get like that——"

When they had finally twittered their way downstairs and left her alone, Nancy went swiftly to the mirror to look at herself. She expected to see a new strange face there, a face with wise eyes, a face that understood the thing that she had only felt. But the seaweed-coloured eyes stared back from under their flying eyebrows, stared back, questioning.

She sat a long time watching the pearly oval of her face, but it gave back nothing of reproach or wisdom. Clearly it knew no more than she. She leaned toward it and said firmly:

"That was not love."

And then after a pause she added:

"Love is of the spirit."

But the face looked back unscarred by wisdom or self-reproach. She had a need to feel self-loathing so that she might be purged by regret, but she felt nothing of this. It was as if she had passed through a phantom fire that left no marks.

"I have no conscience," she said, but neither conviction nor regret followed on this.

"I'm going to be like my mother. I'm weak." This statement brought no responding echo except surprise at her own apathy. She was depressingly devoid of emotion. Curiosity and hatred and guilt were asleep. If that was the love between a man and a woman, it could not attract her again. If it was sin, she felt no guilt. It mattered nothing to her if she saw him again or did not see him.

She was sleepy. She yawned widely and took her untouched body and her no longer curious soul to bed, and slept.

She met William Webster next day by chance in the garden. He had on the clothes which he wore when he arrived, and was waiting for the grocer's gig to take him to the station. His black patent-leather portmanteau stood between his feet, a funereal-looking bag, which somehow conveyed that all its contents were ill-smelling.

He was going away. But it was not this alone which gave Nancy the courage to look at him. It was the certain knowledge that his dominion over her was broken. She knew now that there was nothing in him she had to fear. She looked at him, and saw that there was no longer anything darkly mysterious about his shuffling, side-looking face. He was just an ill-grown, not very clean, and rather stupid youth who could not meet her eyes, but kept burying his gaze in the rhododendron bushes at either side. Now that he could not look at her and sneer, accusing her of dark sins, now that his eyes fumbled before hers, she knew that she had to fear, not him, not anyone, but some betraying instinct in herself.

He had looked at her with eyes that denied her respect, with eyes that named her for an evil thing, and evil had come out of her to answer his look. But why? She knew that her heart was not evil. Yet at his bidding she had betrayed her heart and believed evil of it. She was her own betrayer then, her own accuser. . . .

William Webster was waiting nervously for something that she would say, but Nancy had forgotten him. She hurried away, leaving him without a word, not because he mattered—he was no more than a log that she had tripped upon—but because she wanted to, needed to, see Andrew Morrison, the librarian of Pitouie. He could tell her what she wanted to know. She had planned all day to speak to him. And now, with a book to exchange for Mrs. Anderson as an excuse, she hastened along to the town hall where the dusty lower hall served Pitouie as a public library.

He was alone when she arrived. She could see his face, a white glimmer at the far end of the murky room, as he sat towering behind the great library table.

If he smiled she would ask him, but not otherwise. It was hard to speak with Andrew Morrison unless he smiled, and even then it was not easy. Walking up the long room toward him, she felt, as always, a sense of awe. For he was a figure to inspire awe. Seated behind the big table, he dominated the dingy long room with its windows hung with cobwebs, and its wooden benches piled up intricately at one end, waiting for a political meeting or a wedding supper to unravel them again. He dominated it, making it his throne-room, and the high seat behind the table, his throne.

His noble head was set upon the torso of a giant. So might Charlemagne have looked upon his throne. So might Caesar have looked in the day of his glory. Surely a man built to tower above other men. Surely a man meant to lead them.

There was beauty past beauty in the fine planes of his face, there was strength past the feeble strength of men. But at times his pain-moulded mouth had a terrifying bitterness, as of a wrong past all bearing, and his wide, slow-moving, grey eyes looked out with the anguish of Christ crucified.

But for Nancy, now and then, the iron left his face, and when they were alone sometimes his laugh was not a painful thing to hear.

He was smiling when she reached the table. She could see that it was a day for talking. But whether it was a day for asking what she wanted to know . . .

She seated herself precariously on the edge of the table.

"A bench is more ladylike," he suggested, expecting to be ignored.

"I've come asking questions," she said, obeying his suggestion about the bench and seating herself at a short distance from him with her knees a little self-conscious and prim.

He coloured. She should have laughed at his mention of the bench. Her change of seat strained something between them. It hinted at a growing difference in her, a difference which made him afraid of her.

"What is it?" he asked, trying to put her back in the guise of a small child asking questions. "The distance between earth and the sun? . . . The life history of Yeats? . . . The love-life of the dragonfly?"

"Worse than that," she laughed.

"Nothing more out of the Bible! . . . I refuse!"

"It isn't exactly out of the Bible."

"The way to candle eggs? Have worms got eyes? How long is the Ganges?"

"This is serious." She looked at him gravely. Her cheeks flushed as she stammered in a nervous rush, "It's very serious. I want to know about love. . . . What *is* love?"

It seemed to Andrew Morrison that he heard the distant drumming of hoofs, the hoofs of a long-expected foe. For a moment it seemed that he must cry out at her in a vicious voice, saying:

"Why ask *me*? What should *I* know of love?"

But her eyes were on his face, earnestly waiting for his answer.

She looked so childlike seated on the bench, her feet toeing inward a little in her seriousness. His bitterness passed, and with it his fear of her.

He laughed, cradling his head against the high back of his chair.

"What is love?" He smiled, turning his thought over deliciously before he answered:

"Someone has said that 'love is a curious blending of benevolence and delight.'"

"But is there nothing else? Couldn't one feel something that was like hate? . . . Not sweet, yet it attracts?"

"Desire."

"And *that* would be a wicked thing?"

"I wish it could be disposed of as easily as that. However"—his eyes held the shadow of a twinkle and his pain-carved lips carried a silent chuckle—"desire, or even lust, is what we call it when it is felt by someone else. When it is experienced by ourselves we dignify it by the name of passion, or even love."

Nancy moved restlessly. His flights of cynicism always made her uncomfortable. They conveyed to her strangely a sense of having wronged him.

"Why are you interested in love?" The faint twinkle was still in his eye, but beside it had come the defensive look again, as if he would guard himself from something that she could do to him.

"I'm not. It's desire I was thinking about."

"Oh!" He looked down at the table to shield his eyes from her.

"I wanted to know . . . I was wondering if children who are born . . . I mean children whose fathers and mothers aren't married, if *they* inherit wicked feelings more than other people?"

He was quiet, regarding the grain of the wood upon the table before he answered. When he spoke he had ceased to be afraid of something that she could do to him. She was only a little girl. His eyes were friendly as he said:

"No, except that people with unbridled desires are apt to hand on unbridled desires to their children."

"Was it unbridled desire that made my mother go away with the medicine-man?"

"I suspect it was. That, and poor taste." Quite safe from her now, he expanded with enjoyment, pausing to roll the next tasty snack upon his tongue, savouring the full flavour of its arrogance before he gave it with mellow eloquence to her waiting ears:

"The thing we call sin is a privilege which should be allowed only to aristocrats. The lower class is vulgar, and the middle class has a conscience. To be acceptable, sin must be without vulgarity or regret."

Nancy sighed. He was being very unsatisfactory. But she pressed on to her point, granting him only a pale recognition of his wit.

"What is meant by 'for I was shapen in wickedness, and in sin hath my mother conceived me.' I mean," she stammered, "is it always a sin to be ashamed of?"

He smiled drolly, as he did when she questioned him about the Scriptures.

"It means that the Church takes a very depressing view of the act of procreation."

"But is it wicked in marriage as well as out?"

He chortled. And, with one eyebrow whimsically cocked as if to say: "I'm being very, very amusing if not quite accurate," he replied:

"As *I* understand the teaching of the Church, the act of procreation is most sinful when most enjoyable."

Nancy saw that it was useless to talk to him to-day. She knew this mood. Anything she might say would merely serve him as a spring-board to leap into space.

He was not really talking to her. She was just a visible thing to address. When he was like this, she fancied that he saw about her hosts of kindred minds that flashed back at him, answering the words that flew half-understood about her head.

For weeks he would go his dusty way, seeming a part of Pitouie, talking in its tongue, brief of speech, and sober. Then, startlingly, he would become this other person, drunk with epigrams, hurling piquant blasphemies upon the air.

In this mood he would neither help nor listen, he baffled her. She felt omitted from something, as if he had hidden springs of wine at which he drank secretly, alone.

She might as well go home. She pushed the book she had brought for exchange along the table toward him, saying:

"I'll have to go. Old Mrs. Anderson would like something in big print about pirates."

At her words bitterness flickered back to settle about his mouth like a scar.

The book-shelves lay across the room! To reach them he must leave his high seat and walk. Walk!

Seated behind the massive table he was Cæsar or Alexander. Seated behind the generous table he was Plato or Nietzsche. Seated behind the kindly table he was a god, a king. Seated behind the table he was a man!

But when he left the high seat and crossed the room to find the book, he would be only the torso of a man, grotesquely walking on thigh-bones. Grotesquely trailing two little wooden coffins in which lay his dead-born legs. Propelling himself apelike with arms that touched the floor. His head would barely reach the table over which he now towered.

To stand up was tragedy! Tragedy meted out in small corrosive grains day after day. To be librarian of Pitouie, finding books about "pirates in big print"! This was the end of all his high dreaming, to live for ever in Pitouie, and to know that he would never have the courage to leave it again.

Once he had left it. The memory of that time lay upon him like a burning. He could feel its full pain even now. No sting of it was lessened for the years that had passed. No dimming of the revelation that he was "different," that he was something to stare at and comment upon. Only in Pitouie could he go unmarked. Only in Pitouie.

At nineteen he had won the bursary and was the highest rated scholar of his class in all the length of Scotland. He, Andrew Morrison, had won the bursary and was away south to Aberdeen, and the University!

So filled was he with all this that the staring eyes of Aberdeen could not pierce him.

"I've won the bursary! And I'm here in Aberdeen! Well may you stare!"

He walked along narrow bustling Broad Street to the University, swinging legs that were long and lithe, legs that responded to the high singing of his heart, though they were but legs of his imagining. He took a seat well at the back of the empty classroom and sat waiting, paper and pencil on the desk before him, his proud heart shouting hosannas up and down its red canals.

Soon bright-cheeked lads swung into seats about him with awkward shyness. Lads as fresh to the city as he. Lads as eager to learn.

"I'm a part of this! I'm a part of all this," sang the hosanna of his heart.

A slender lad slid into the seat beside him, and with bashful friendliness pushed a bag of lemon drops along the desk. Andrew took a few, but could not put them in his mouth. He had never been the one to chew peppermints in church, nor could he in this more sacred place suck a lemon drop. But to show that he prized them he took the clean handkerchief from his breast-pocket and wrapped them in a corner of it. He wanted some clearer way to show his friendliness. He thought of the three well-sharpened pencils which rested in his inside breastpocket with a fold of cardboard around them to protect their points. His companion had produced a little stub of a pencil with no point to speak of and was trying it out on the pad of paper in front of him. Andrew drew one of his prized pencils from his pocket and held it out to him. The lad took it, saying:

"Thank you, sir!" The "sir" slipped out, a clear tribute to Andrew's superior height and dignity. For as he sat there, he dwarfed the others, and many admiring eyes were turned upon him.

"Thank you, sir." The words ran in a warm stream through Andrew's veins. "Thank you, sir. Thank you, sir. Thank you, sir." It was a proud day. It was easy to see that he could have friends and to spare. He felt himself the taller for their admiration, and looked around with a new ease.

The professor came in and took his place behind the lectern.

Throughout the lecture Andrew quivered with the very ardour of his listening. No word passed him by, each found its abiding-place in his eager brain.

When the lecture had finished he sat in idolatrous silence, his eyes clinging to the bantering face of the professor as he harried this student and that with his laughter-edged tongue. But there was a kindness in his harrying, and always he comforted the student with a crumb of praise before he took the starry circle of applause to wear upon his head like an easy-won crown. Never was there such a tongue! Andrew Morrison shook with a new-found rapture. From this fountain he was privileged to drink. Even he, Andrew Morrison. What greater thing could come to him? . . .

The flashing face behind the lectern was bent upon him . . . was asking a question . . . was singling him out to make the answer. High rose his heart; his voice, proud as a cathedral bell, swung the answer over the heads of the class, across the room.

Back came the sharp chiselled voice of the professor:

"Be good enough to stand up, sir!"

Andrew Morrison could not move.

A drawn sword, it came again:

"Stand up, sir!"

The rustling about him was stilled like a breath caught in expectation. Hundreds of startled faces strained to see. The eyes behind the lectern glared angrily.

Shame swept over him in an avalanche.

"Upon your feet, you impudent loafer!"

Andrew Morrison obeyed.

His head was barely visible above the desk. A gasp rose on the air. Surely this was insult!

With a furious cry the professor reached for his pointer, and rushed, a white-faced vengeance, up the aisle.

"Upon your feet," he screamed, lashing Andrew Morrison about the head as he still seemed not to obey.

"Upon your feet!"

Andrew said no word. It was not anger that looked out from his eyes as the pointer fell in singing blows about his head, it was not even pain, it was only the puzzled crying of a new-born shame.

"Out of here. Out of my classroom. You impudent dog! Stand up! Get out!"

Andrew Morrison moved into the aisle, the wooden boxes clattering loudly.

The pointer quivered in the air again, but did not fall. The professor's hand trembled in the air for a moment, a dying thing crying for mercy. Mumbling a dazed word, he fell to the floor.

Andrew Morrison walked down the aisle past the fainting body of the professor, past the staring faces of his fellow students. Out of the classroom, out of the University, out of Aberdeen, out of the glory of his life, back to Pitouie, never to leave it again.

Nancy had asked him to stand up. Every day now it became more difficult to stand up before her. This was the thing that she could do to him. She could make him love her. She could add a thousandfold to his pain. But he would not let her. No use for her to stand slight and round against the light of the window, no use to look at him earnestly, with seaweed eyes. No use! Love her! How could he love her! He was not a man! One half of him was dead, one half of him already coffined. He laughed loudly. Nancy could not bear the sound of it. It hurt. As if all this bitter laughing flew from his throat to fasten about her own, choking her.

"About pirates in big print."

He swung himself to the floor. The wooden boxes made a cruel clatter. He called her attention to them.

"In just a moment. First let me arrange my private graveyard." He straightened the boxes behind him, laughing. "Really, I ought to get a neat little tombstone for each: 'In loving memory of my dear departed right leg,' only it *hasn't* departed. Most men bury their dead, while *I*, as you see, carry mine round with me."

His eyes dared her to look sorry or kind, dared her not to smile.

She held her face calm until he turned away and went trailing his boxes across the dusty floor. The old accustomed grief for him racked her throat, but above that and stronger than that was a new anger against him. Always and for ever he would give her this sense that she had failed him; but now she knew that he had failed her, that he had always failed her. She wanted to walk quickly across the floor after him, crying:

"What though you are lame on the outside: I am lame on the inside, and you will not help me!"

But what would be the use of that? He could not see her lameness because he saw only his own lameness. It seemed that you went for ever through the world crying, "See my wounded heart! What shall I do with my wounded heart?" And the world, deaf with its own pain, heard you not, but cried back bitterly:

"See my wounded heart! What shall I do with my wounded heart?"

She could get no help from him. He was deaf with his own pain. If she waited till he came back across the floor, trailing the boxes behind him, looking at her as he came with the sting of a whiplash in his smile, she would surely scream in his face:

"God made you lame—I did not do it!"

So she ran from the room, not waiting for the book, and as she ran she thought:

"I'm caring only for myself; I'm running away from his pain."

But still she ran on and felt no guilt. It seemed to her that she had shaken off for ever the grief and guilt for his deformity. A grief which she had carried for years and a guilt which somehow he had compelled her to carry.

Her feet turned not toward home, but, as if prompted by a secret voice, they hurried toward the bridge which opened on the Three Ways.

One was the avenue which led to Castle Burkley, one was the old coach road leading to Callochie. But the third led up the brae to the kirk and past the wood with the waterfall that looked like Italy. And this was the road she took.

It came to her to find the very spot upon the moss-grown dyke where she had gone into the wood with the Whistling Boy, to follow the path that she had followed as he trod before her over the crackling leaves, to find him again as she had found him whistling against the waterfall. It seemed that he never could have left that spot, but that he was for ever there, waiting for her to come to him.

She searched the green and grey face of the dyke, calling memory to help her as she searched, but before she had found the spot she saw Divot Meg coming down the brae, a great birn of sticks swaying precariously upon her bent back. Behind her came little Jimmy with a smaller load, but otherwise she was alone.

When the women of Pitouie went out after a high wind to gather fallen branches for kindling, it was usual for them to go in a body, making a high day of it; the young ones singing songs together, and the old ones gossiping or telling lusty tales of their youth, so that the woods crackled with the toothless lewd laughter of the old dames and with the loud singing of the young ones.

But Divot Meg was never part of this. She gathered her kindling where the crowd was least likely to go. Nancy, seeing her, hesitated, palpitating with fear of Divot's Meg's tongue, yet drawn to her as she always had been drawn to her. She stood still awaiting her approach, and as she drew near she put out a timid hand, asking her to stop.

But Divot Meg was not minded to stop. She hitched her bundle higher on her back so that her pink sweating face had to bend lower, and passed Nancy, crying back a word to little Jimmy to urge him on. Nancy, hardly knowing why she did it, or what she wished to say, ran after her, crying:

"Hey."

Divot Meg stopped and swung the bundle from her back to the road. Little Jimmy stopped also, complaining unreasonably that the thorns in his birn were jabbing his back; unreasonably, because, if his father were Ramos the pin-cushion king, he should be able to let thorns jab him without complaint. Divot Meg lifted a sharp foot at him, ordering him away. He hurried whimpering down the brae, leaving Nancy and Divot Meg to confront each other alone.

The woman sat down upon her birn, wide-hipped and groaning. The branches cracked sharply beneath her weight.

"Well?"

She was wiping the sweat from her face with her bare arm, which was dappled like a plover's egg with large brown freckles, and looking up at Nancy half tauntingly.

Now that she had stopped her, Nancy hardly knew what to say. She could only stand and look. Divot Meg's hair, wet with her sweat, curled in small rust-coloured rings upon her forehead and behind her ears. Her bare throat was rosy with her exertion. Her heavy bosom rose and fell deeply. She was lush with life still. Nancy felt this. Felt that out of all Pitouie, this woman lived, this woman was neither at the beginning of life, nor at the end of it, but was still standing with firm planted feet, boisterously laughing in its very midst.

"Well?" Divot Meg laughed tormentingly. "Tired of the holy bitch up at the Manse?"

"I don't mind her," Nancy blushed diffidently, "and I like old Mrs. Anderson."

"Getting to be quite a lady, aren't you?" This with a loud laugh. "Your mother would be proud of you."

"I often wanted to come and ask you more about my mother."

"Never ask *me*."

"You don't—didn't like my mother?"

151

"I never had reason."

"Did she—did you quarrel with her?"

"That's an old story."

"What was it about?"

"A man—two of them."

Divot Meg laughed boisterously. Whatever the quarrel had been, there was no real rancour left, and Nancy laughed with her.

"I'd like to know about the men," Nancy ventured.

"Oh, there is nothing to tell."

"Was—did you know Ramsey Gordon of Fassefern?"

"He was one of them."

"And the other one?"

"Willie Weams."

Nancy shuddered.

"You couldn't—nobody could love a man like that."

"Like Willie Weams? I'm telling you Willie Weams was a lusty lad in his day." Divot Meg laughed softly, as if at some almost tender recollection, and sat dreaming with the smile still upon her face.

Nancy felt herself near to a discovery. She prayed that Divot Meg would not get up and walk away.

"Was he your sweetheart or my mother's?" she ventured.

Divot Meg seemed to have gone back to some distant day, her face looked tender and girlish beneath the damp red tendrils of her hair. When Nancy spoke she sighed and a shiver passed over her as if some cruel wind of memory blew cold upon a warm dream, but perhaps it was only the twilight air upon her damp hot skin. She rose to her feet.

"Oh, please don't go," Nancy pleaded. "I've nobody to ask about anything, nobody to talk to."

Meg looked at her and laughed shortly, shaking off Nancy's delaying hand.

"The less you say to me the better for you."

She reached for her birn to swing it on her back.

Tears started to Nancy's eyes. Divot Meg saw them and dropped the birn.

"What's the matter, lassie?"

Nancy, ashamed of her tears, blinked them back and shook her head.

Divot Meg sat down on the birn again thoughtfully. After a minute she asked kindly, but not without a glimmer of humour:

"Are you in trouble?"

"No, no," Nancy gasped. "Not——It's that I wanted somebody to talk to about things."

"You're nearly seventeen, aren't you?"

Divot Meg was surveying her speculatively.

"Yes. Seventeen past."

"Are you still a maiden?"

"I think so."

"You *think* so! I never heard of a lass losing her maidenhood unbeknowns to her."

Divot Meg would have laughed, but the bewildered earnestness on Nancy's face stilled her.

"Do feelings make you lose it?"

Divot Meg laughed dryly.

"No. You'd have to go further than that. . . . What's on your mind, bairn?"

And then Nancy told her everything that happened the night before, the words tumbling over one another in her hurry to unburden her heart; of her haunting need to know why William Webster sneered, of his coming to her room, and the strange new emotion which had come to her, and of her screams which drove him away.

Divot Meg sat listening in silence. Nancy half fearfully searched the woman's face as she spoke. A smile or a look of disapproval would have brought her confession to a quick stop. But Divot Meg was merely attentive. There was neither amusement nor disapproval in her face. When Nancy had done, she said only:

"You were lucky." And made as if to rise to her feet and go her way. But Nancy stayed her with a hand held out entreatingly:

"Why was I lucky?"

Divot Meg relaxed unwillingly. She wanted to have finished with this conversation, but Nancy stood before her with pleading eyes. She answered reluctantly:

"I was only sixteen . . . but I didn't scream like you . . . worse luck." And then, with a philosophic laugh, "But maybe as well. . . . If it hadn't been Willie Weams, it would have been another."

"It was Willie Weams?"

"It was. . . . I can see him yet the first time I saw him. He came walking his stallion along the turnpike on his way to Rossorty fair. I was in the moss, casting divots by myself. I'd got the best part of a cartful cast, and was sitting down on the heap near the roadside, resting a bit. It was a day like this, warm and lazy. I hadn't much on but my shift and my wincey petticoat.

"He came up and stopped the stallion and asked me if I had a match. He wasn't pock-marked then, nor near so fat as he is now. He was bonnie enough to look at and had a lusty eye on him. I was bashful, never had much to say to men. I told him I hadn't a match. He said, 'I ken fine you have,' and said I was close-fisted. I swore that I hadn't. He said he wouldn't believe me till he put his hand in my pocket to see for himself.

"I said to him that I hadn't a pocket, which I hadn't in that petticoat. He laughed and said that he'd better come and see for himself. With that he tied the stallion to the stump of a tree and came over to me.

"We began wrestling together on the pile of divots. I wasn't angry with him. In fact, I liked him. And I fought with him and laughed till I was fairly panting. I thought I'd like to have him for my lad, and maybe marry him. I thought maybe he was thinking the same, and I didn't fight him much when he fell to kissing me. I cried later, but it wasn't because I was angry, though he hurt me, it was more because I knew that he'd got the best of me, and because he hadn't given me time to offer him what he took. I was in love with him before he left, and watched him as far as I could see him down the road, and I laughed and cried together with happiness because he was to meet me at the fair next day. . . ."

Divot Meg's face had grown strangely like a little girl's. She stopped speaking. When it seemed that she would not go on again, Nancy asked:

"Did he meet you?"

"I went into Rossorty next day looking for him. I took my divots along to sell there, though I had meant them for Pitouie folk. I soon saw that Willie Weams had told it for a fine joke. At every turn somebody laughed in my face and men were after me like bees. I left my divots in the street and ran away to hide my head. He hadn't meant anything. I was just another lassie . . ."

"He was a beast!" Nancy cried.

Divot Meg shrugged.

"Oh, I was willing enough, I suppose. And he was used to willing lassies. There is something about walking a stallion from mare to mare that gives a man a free air about such things. . . . Anyway, life was different after that. He told it over the countryside, and finally I fell into the character they gave me."

"Did you see him again?"

"That night. There was a dance. I knew I had to brazen the thing out now. So I went to the dance. He was there dancing with Bella Pringle."

"My mother!"

"They were very thick, and every time I passed he whispered something to her and they laughed; though I could see she didn't really want to laugh, but she wanted to please him.

"When the dance was at the height just at midnight, young Ramsey

Gordon from Fassefern came in to honour the occasion. Your mother was working at Fassefern Castle at this time, and there were rumours that Ramsey Gordon had an eye for her. That was enough for me. I wanted to spite her and to show Rossorty folks that I had some spirit left yet. So I walked up to Ramsey Gordon and asked him for a dance. He laughed and took my arm, and called for the lancers, and we led the lancers together, me and the young laird. That was a fine flea in Bella Pringle's ear, for she daren't so much as speak to him in public because of being a servant at the castle. He danced with me again, for I led him on to thinking that I was well experienced with men, all to have him make over me in front of Willie Weams and Bella Pringle. . . . Bella didn't get much satisfaction out of taking Willie Weams. It wasn't a week before he was through with her and telling it everywhere that he was fairly drowned with the way she cried on him, and that any man that liked salt water was welcome to her. It was the spring of the next year that your mother left Fassefern Castle. . . ."

"You think Willie Weams was my father?"

"Willie Weams, or Ramsey Gordon, what difference does that make?"

"It makes a lot to me. There is good blood in the Fasseferns. Good women, too. But Willie Weams!"

Divot Meg smiled.

"Willie Weams is not so bad."

"Do you think that I take after him?"

"Not that I can see."

"But maybe it's inside me—the resemblance. What could make me feel like I felt last night?"

"Just nature."

"But everybody isn't like that!"

"Everybody that's healthy, some time or other. It was just an accident. You were keyed up with changes in your body and he happened to be there."

"You don't think it's nasty?"

"The thing that's natural is never nasty, lassie. Never let them tell you that it is."

"But I hated him for making me feel like that."

"That was because you didn't love him."

"Does that come into love, too—good love?"

"That's more than half of it . . . at first, anyway."

"I wouldn't want that."

Divot Meg gave a dry laugh.

"It's to be hoped you get over that idea. I'd sooner see you grow up to be a clean-minded strumpet like me than a dirty-minded holy bitch like the minister's wife. God may not like either one of us, but I'll get a lot farther ben heaven than *she* ever will, mark my words on that."

"But I want to be good." Nancy was wistful, pleading for her friendship.

"You can be that without being nasty-minded about it."

"Am I nasty-minded?"

Divot Meg relented.

"No, you're a nice wee lassie. Just forget about what happened last night. Count it no more or less than a belly-ache. It won't happen to you again like that because you know what to avoid. But don't set yourself against love, and get a sour face thinking it is beneath you and too vulgar for you. Because the Lord created it for a beautiful thing many a million years before you were ever thought about. And it will be one of the best things in nature many a million of years after you are gone. And if you come to the end of your life a maiden, the maggots won't find you a bit better eating than if you had lived your life the way the Lord meant you to live it.

"You see, my lass, passion has its place in life—not the biggest place—it's the dirty-minded, virtuous women who give it the biggest place; it's an ugly sin to them, and they spend their time sniffing round it as if it were a smelly drain. But passion is neither the dirtiest thing in life, nor the biggest. It's a part of life that's beautiful, but it's a small part. So put it out of your head till it comes to you with love, and then you'll know what to do with it."

While Divot Meg was speaking Nancy had seated herself on the birn beside her. She timidly put her hand on Divot Meg's freckled forearm, clinging to her. Here at last was someone who gave her bread when she asked for bread, who answered her with wisdom, not with epigrams.

"But I'm frightened for fear I'm going to be a bad woman. People expect me to be bad because of Willie Weams and my mother. That's why I think about it. It was people knowing about you and Willie Weams that made *you* do things."

Divot Meg did not answer, but sat still, thinking. Nancy was clinging to her freckled arm as if to ensure her not leaving. Soon a strange half-smile flitted over Divot Meg's face, and her eyes held an amused twinkle in check as she said:

"Come to think of it, Willie Weams couldn't be your father."

"Couldn't he?" This in an eager gasp.

"What month were you born?"

"June. June the thirtieth."

Divot Meg appeared to ponder deeply.

"June . . . June . . . that makes . . . let me see . . . I'm pretty near sure that the fair that year was the first week in September."

"But it's always in October, isn't it?"

"As a rule. But that year it was an early harvest. . . . It was September all right. . . . And Willie Weams was sick and tired of your mother. . . . He would never go back after the fair."

"Then I'm a Fassefern."

"There's little doubt of that."

"Oh! Oh!"

"Will you be any fatter for that, do you think?" asked Divot Meg in a kindly, taunting way. She was looking at the girl with a new look of affection, as if she had recreated her. There was ironic amusement in her face as well, as if she were laughing at herself for the lie she had told to make Bella Pringle's bairn happy. "Will you get longer in the legs, think you, because you're Ramsey Gordon's bastard instead of Willie Weams's?"

"I'll be braver. They can look at me any way they like now. I'll know. . . ."

"There's one thing won't help you any with them, and that's talking to me."

"I'll do that no matter *what* they think."

"You'll do nothing of the kind. I've wasted more of my time on you now . . ."

Divot Meg roughly pushed Nancy off the birn and took hold of it. There was a sound of wheels approaching.

"Away you go ahead," Divot Meg ordered.

"I won't. I like you . . . I'm not ashamed . . ."

Round the corner came the four-horse carriage of the Lady of Burkley (the Lady of Burkley scorned a motor-car), and seated along with her ladyship was Mrs. Taylor, the doctor's wife.

To Nancy's dismay Divot Meg turned upon her with loud, taunting cries and laughter, so that the people in the carriage could not fail to hear her.

"Think you are too fine to talk to me, do you? *That* for you!" and she made a vulgar noise. "Who are you but the bastard of Ramsey Gordon, a Fassefern bastard! *That! That* for you!"

She raised a hand as if to strike Nancy. The carriage stopped with protesting cries from the ladies. The footman swung his whip at Divot Meg, driving her off. She laughed vulgarly, telling the Lady of Burkley to keep her false hair on, and advising Mrs. Taylor to find out where her man went at night, and finally she went blasphemously down the road, crying out on Nancy for a proud-born bastard that thought her tongue too fine for common use.

Nancy was crying convulsively. Thinking it was the taunting tongue of

157

Divot Meg that made her weep, the ladies made room for her in the carriage, and the footman fairly lifted her in on the palm of his hand.

"It's a scandal. A woman like that attacking a mere girl." The half-senile face of the Lady of Burkley was red with anger under her too black hair.

"She's a disgrace to Pitouie," fumed the doctor's wife.

"No! No! No!" Nancy sobbed.

"Not *you*, my dear." The Lady of Burkley's thin veined hand patted Nancy's arm reassuringly. "You're all right." Then in a curious voice, "What was *that* she said about Ramsey Gordon?"

The doctor's wife leaned forward and whispered something in the Lady of Burkley's ear. The Lady of Burkley whispered something back, and they both looked at Nancy speculatively and nodded their heads.

Nancy dried her eyes. She meant to claim her friend. She meant to tell these women what she thought of Divot Meg.

"She's a good woman," she said in a voice that dared them to contradict her.

The Lady of Burkley whispered to Mrs. Taylor; Mrs. Taylor whispered back. Then the Lady of Burkley in her uncertain, shaky voice, said soothingly:

"Of course she is, my dear. Every girl's mother is a good woman." And she nodded benevolently.

"Divot Meg is a good woman," Nancy said firmly.

Mrs. Taylor looked startled. But the Lady of Burkley, beaming like a foolish saint, nodded agreeably:

"That's right, my dear. That is the true Christian spirit."

Their complacent benevolence was overpowering Nancy. She wanted to suffer for Divot Meg's sake, to proclaim her goodness to the world. But the Lady of Burkley had found a theme which suited her doddering garrulousness.

"That's right, my dear, always be charitable. Jesus has said, 'Love your enemies. Cherish those hearts that hate you; still in your right hand carry gentle peace to silence envious tongues.' Or was it Shakespeare who said it?"

"It was Cardinal Wolsey, I think," Nancy ventured, abandoning all hope of making them listen to her story of Divot Meg.

"That's right, my dear. Of course it was Cardinal Wolsey. . . . Well, no matter, it's the right spirit, especially in the young. . . . I'm glad to see you know your Shakespeare. Now my dear dead husband always said: 'If a man has some good horses, some well reeket whisky, Shakespeare, and the Bible, he can't go far wrong.' And I think that's very true. . . . I'm glad that Shakespeare is your favourite poet . . . that is as it should be."

"But he isn't my favourite," Nancy faltered, not wishing to take credit where she did not deserve it.

"He's not!"

"No; Yeats is, just now, but I often change."

"Yeats?"

"W. B. Yeats."

"W. B. Yeats. I never heard of him."

"He's an Irishman."

"Oh, *Irish*!" as who should say, "No wonder I never heard of him, and who wants to hear of him, indeed?"

But this was a subject dear to Nancy's heart.

"He's a lyric poet. He wrote:

"I will arise and go now, and go to Innisfree,
And a small cabin build there, of clay and wattles made;
Nine bean rows will I have there, a hive for the honey bee,
And live alone in the bee-loud glade.

And I shall have some peace there. . . ."

"Indeed he *wouldn't* have peace," bridled the Lady of Burkley. "There's no peace where there's an Irishman. . . . As my husband used to say: 'Give them *one* thing, and they want another . . . offer them Home Rule and they don't want it. Tell them they can't have it, and they fight to get it!' . . . I don't doubt for a minute that the only reason he wants a cabin is because he has a fine house in town, and his wife pacing the floor wondering where he is, while he's away building a cabin of . . . what was that he built it of?"

"Clay and wattles."

"Wattles?"

"I think maybe they're something like divots."

"Why couldn't he *say* divots, then? . . . Shiftless Irish havers living in a divot house, with his wife all by her lone . . ."

"Maybe it's not divots—I think maybe it's little sticks."

". . . while he's away in this glade . . . what kind of a glade was that?"

"A 'bee-loud glade.'"

"'Bee-loud?'"

"Loud with the noise of bees."

"There he goes. Why couldn't he say loud bees and have done with it? . . . 'bee-loud.' . . . I hope you're not filling your head up with such rubbish. Tennyson is the poet for a nice girl to study."

"My Lettie can say 'The Coming and Passing of Arthur' from start to finish," said Mrs. Taylor, glad to get her tongue in edgewise.

"That's as it should be. And so could I at her age. . . ."

And they both looked at Nancy disapprovingly, but Nancy was not to be downed.

"I don't admire Tennyson much," she said courageously.

"You don't!" Mrs. Taylor and the Lady of Burkley exchanged scandalised looks. "She doesn't admire Tennyson!"

"Andrew Morrison says Tennyson is quite a mediocre poet."

"Young lady, do you realise that Queen Victoria herself appointed Tennyson to be poet laureate—I should think *that* proves whether he's a great poet or not! The dear old queen would never have so much as let this wattle Irishman set a foot in Buckingham Palace, let alone Balmoral, which she certainly liked better than any of the English palaces, and who can blame her? Englishmen are all right in their place, but there's nothing like a Scotchman, as my dear dead husband always used to say. . . ."

So the Lady of Burkley, garrulous and anile, finally brought Nancy to the door of the parsonage, and volubly told young Mrs. Anderson how they had rescued the child from the blows of Divot Meg.

It was little use for Nancy to remonstrate with them or try to tell them the true story. Her attempts were silenced with an acid:

"Your elders are speaking."

So she went up to the west gable in search of old Mrs. Anderson. But the room was empty, for Mrs. Anderson had gone for a drive with her son.

The "queer sister" at Menzies' Farm had taken three fingers off with the turnip hasher and the minister had been sent for. The drive lay along by the Martin Wood, and Mrs. Anderson had gone to take the air. Tucked under the frill of her black taffeta cape she carried her prized bottle of smelling-salts to present to the unfortunate creature, who was said to be neither man nor woman, and who now had lost three fingers, as if fate had not been cruel enough already.

As she came into the old lady's room Nancy noticed that it smelled of burning cardboard and glue, and saw that the small grate was heaped with charred and blackened papers. Apprehensive, she stirred them with the poker, turning up the charred remains to discover what had been burned. Out of a ring of golden brown a girl's young face was still visible, or there remained only a uniformed arm to tell that this had been the portrait of a soldier.

They were the cherished portraits and letters of old Mrs. Anderson's courting days. The packages which on certain days of the year she opened and read.

Nancy looked about her. The rest of the room, with its chairs unnaturally set against the wall, and its dusting of flea powder in the corners as a final insult, told her who had been there.

Still, it was unthinkable that even the minister's wife would burn the old lady's love-letters, and the portraits of her girlhood days. What possible excuse could she give for doing that!

Nancy hesitated what to do. Should she gather up all the ashes and carry them away, and so spare the old woman the sight of them? Later, when she searched for the album, she could tell her about it.

She heard the Lady of Burkley's carriage drive away crisply over the gravel below, and very soon came the fumbling, short-sighted steps of the minister's wife up the dim-lit turret staircase. Nancy sat still as she entered and did not look her way. A tremor of goose-flesh passed over her as the minister's wife started to speak.

"I've been burning everything that breeds fleas."

Nancy felt her peering at her in expectant hostility, waiting for her reply, but she said nothing.

"There's an epidemic of typhoid, the doctor says—and fleas spread it."

Still Nancy did not speak.

"If I let this room be the way that *she* would have it, we'd all rot with disease and dirt. It's a mercy that she goes out sometime so that I can burn the rubbish."

Her tone was growing more defensive every minute. It was clear enough that she felt guilty, that perhaps she was even beginning to regret what she had done. She prodded at Nancy with words, trying to make her retort. But Nancy never would be drawn into argument with her. She sat silent in childlike misery, her heels caught in the rung of the chair, her hands lying in her lap. Her silence infuriated Mrs. Anderson, who turned upon her waspishly:

"Have you nothing to do but sit nursing your hands? There's more than a dozen pair of socks to be darned. . . . It's a wonder that you wouldn't have some ambition to get out and earn your living. . . . You're old enough not to be eating the bread of charity I should think. . . ."

"I'll go any time you want me to . . . but I thought I couldn't go till I was eighteen."

"Be that as it may, you might at least try to earn your bread while you're here."

"I'll ask Mr. Anderson if he will let me go out to service."

"You'll do nothing of the kind, you trouble-making little viper . . . as long as you're needed here, you'll *stay* here. . . . Do you think we've fed and clothed you for years just to have you go out to service the minute you are able to be of some use!"

161

"I could pay you for what you've spent on me out of my wages."

"I want no more of your back-talk. . . . Away you go and darn the minister's socks."

Nancy rose, glad of the chance to go. This was no new harangue; in fact, it was so common that Nancy and Mrs. Anderson had a name for it. They called it "the bread-of-charity tirade." There were others which came in their season. All of them were designed to show that the minister's wife was a long-suffering martyr in a world of ingrates, but they were also especially designed to distract attention from some sly act of hers.

As she climbed to her own room with the darning-basket upon her arm, Nancy wondered what tirade the minister's wife would use when the burning of the letters was discovered.

Old Mrs. Anderson took the burning of her treasures with strange quietude. She stood looking at the little grate heaped with charred curled papers. She hardly needed to look closer to know what they were. Nancy, standing beside her, saw her hands tremble and clutch for a moment pitifully, before she sought a chair and sat with them entwined tightly.

"She said it was because there was an epidemic of typhoid," Nancy explained.

Mrs. Anderson nodded like someone who scarcely heard. After a while she spoke, and her voice was flat and hopeless:

"Look in the box and see if she has burned the programme for the Masons' ball . . . it's blue with a little blue pencil. . . ."

Nancy obeyed.

"It isn't here . . . there's nothing here but your marriage license."

Mrs. Anderson gave a short laugh:

"She *would* leave that."

She sat a while, silent and contemplative. Presently she rose.

"Take out my lavender silk . . . the one with the rose-point lace . . . and I'll wear my best lace cap."

"You're going out?"

"No. I'm going down to eat my supper in the bosom of my family."

There was a suppressed excitement that was almost gaiety about her as she dressed. Nothing would do but Nancy must get out the rice powder and the Florida water, and her best cameo brooch.

She wore a small lace cap upon her head. For she still followed this style on ceremonious occasions, though fashion had long since set it aside. She wore it not as an admission of her years, nor yet as sign of her respectable widowhood, she wore it as a grande dame wears a tiara, as a queen wears a crown. It sat regally upon the crisp silver waves of her hair, and beneath

162

it her black eyes were luminous.

"You're like a picture," Nancy cried admiringly. "I wish you'd wear it oftener."

"I'm going to . . . and my shot taffeta as well." There was grim mischief in the short laugh she gave.

As Nancy followed in the stately wake of the old lady's rustling gown, she had the feeling that she was about to see the first act of a play, perhaps the first act of a tragedy, for it was no light caprice that made the old woman change the habit of many years.

The minister's wife, penurious and drab, was already at her place when they came into the dining-room. William was entering from his study. At the sight of his mother coming to eat with them, he exclaimed in delighted surprise. William had always hankered for a closer bond with his mother. When he was younger he had almost courted her in his effort to be nearer to her. But she had always pushed him away. The nature that could have forgiven and adored a son who was a spirited braggart, could not love or forgive this spiritless man of God, with his respectable tepid love for his sallow-skinned wife.

"I've taken a sudden turn for the better, William," she announced. "If this keeps up, I'll have no more trays."

The minister's wife said nothing as William found his mother a seat and placed it near himself, but she seemed to grow more yellow and more peering.

She was nervously on the rack for fear the burned portraits would be mentioned. Old Mrs. Anderson knew this and flirted around the edges of the subject, asking William if he remembered this and that, and the day he had his picture taken on a cardboard elephant. The minister's wife would stiffen at each approach to the subject, holding herself ready for defence. But just as she was about to cry out, "I know what you're leading up to!" the old lady would drop the subject as lightly as if no thought of burned portraits had ever been in her mind, and the minister's wife would venture to lie back in her chair tremblingly relaxed. But not for long. The old lady would not let her rest:

"And, William, do you remember when you were fourteen, we went to Fraserhead and had our pictures taken on the merry-go-round?"

It seemed to William that he was finding his mother at last. He seemed to be finding again something that he had never really had. The picture she wove of them young and merry together, riding on cardboard elephants, comforted and pleased him. They really had been close friends then, and she had loved him. They had laughed together in those days and had had their pictures taken on merry-go-rounds. He was delighted at the thought, and in his gaiety recklessly bolted one mouthful of food after another without the requisite number of "chews."

He sensed nothing of the cross-current between the silent woman on his left and the laughing woman on his right, nor could he have understood what made his mother paint this merry picture of the solemn little boy whom she had dragged from one show-ground to another in a vain attempt to make him play.

He loved this new picture of himself, and kept turning to his wife to make her see it also. But she was hostile and sullen. Into William's mind crept the thought: "*She* never wants me to laugh, that's why I've changed . . . she's so different from my mother."

The thought grew upon him that his merry nature had been warped by this too sober companionship, that even his health had suffered by it. As he was thinking this, his wife said tartly:

"You're simply bolting your food, William. . . . I'll be up half the night bringing you hot water."

This irritated him unreasonably. He turned his back squarely upon her, giving her no answer, and continued to give all his attention to his mother and very little to mastication.

Nancy's heart was set on speaking further with Divot Meg. Her first impulse had been to tell old Mrs. Anderson all the truth of the encounter, but each year now she was withholding herself more and more from the old woman. Not from lack of affection, but because she came to see that the old lady lived in a state of timorous watchfulness for fear she would go the way of her mother. If she made any move to open her heart to her, the old lady would be watching for something behind her words, rather than listening to her words, and she would pounce on this or that, making it the text of a sermon to prove that Nancy must guard her very thoughts lest the evil in her rise up to destroy her.

At first Nancy had been terrified by this, sharing the old woman's fears. But as she grew older she found herself thoughtfully selecting the confidences she would make, not from fear of the old woman's sermons, but to spare her from anxiety, so that the relationship between them had subtly changed, and now it was Nancy who was guarding the old woman from life rather than the old lady who was guarding Nancy.

To tell her about Divot Meg would mean to tell her about William Webster, and that was unthinkable. Besides, it would not be wise to speak of Divot Meg. For, despite her kindly nature, the old lady would never be able to see Divot Meg as anything but an evil influence to be avoided, nor would she understand that, to Nancy, Divot Meg had shown something of the face of God.

Jesus might have sat upon the bottom of an upturned boat on the shores of Galilee talking to His disciples just as Divot Meg had sat upon the birn of sticks talking to her. Never before had calm truth been given to her as Divot Meg had given it. The old woman had given her truth coloured by her loving fear for her, and Andrew Morrison had given her the bitter half-truth of one who looks on life knowing that he may not live it. But Divot Meg had given her the truth as life had shown it to her, uncoloured by fear or cynicism. And to Divot Meg she must go.

Her heart yearned toward her urgently. She wanted to go to her and lean upon her breast. She wanted to cry out her friendship for her before the world. But first she must go and plead with her not to turn away.

She walked up the one-sided street in the long summer gloaming, when all was like a late day that had held its breath. Nothing moved in the tepid light. Sleepy little houses nodded side by side, and the river water slipped softly by under the larch-trees.

She reached the many-windowed, grey-faced house. It slept as peacefully as all the street. Nothing moved anywhere. She hesitated to make a sound, feeling that to knock upon the door would wound the silent night, might make it bleed. She leaned against the grey house, comforted by the touch of it, and looked up and down the quiet street.

Would Divot Meg know that she was there and come to her? Where did she sleep? Was it at the front of the house or at the back? She stood away to look at the many windows, taking each one from the top down and asking it a question. As her eyes came back to the window near the door she saw a square-fingered hand with a dappled forearm pulling together the turkey red curtains upon the window.

It was Divot Meg! Nancy went softly to the door and pecked upon it gently with her finger-nails, confident that Divot Meg would open it. She pecked again and waited. But Divot Meg must first put on her clothes. So she leaned patiently against the doorpost, watching the street and following in her mind each move that Divot Meg was making. Now her hair would be pinned up: now she would put on a petticoat over her nightgown: now a short wrapper: now her slippers—one of them is lost, she is looking for it under the bed. . . .

But still the door stood sullenly shut. Maybe Divot Meg had not seen her. That must be it. She went back to the window again and tapped with her nails upon the pane. The curtains stirred, but did not part. Someone was looking through them. It was Divot Meg, but she would not show her face.

What could she do now? Divot Meg knew that she was there, but she would not open for her. She leaned her face against the window, not looking in, but pressing in so that Divot Meg would feel her pleading. But no response came.

It came to her that if Divot Meg opened the window even a little she would push her hand in and keep it there. Even if Divot Meg brought the window down on it, that would be happiness. She longed for her to do this. The pain of it would seal the bond between them, would ease her of the sacrifice that Divot Meg had made.

Divot Meg had taken the whip-lash upon her shoulders to put her right with Pitouie. If she could bear a scar for Divot Meg, something in her breast would be comforted.

But the window did not open. Nor did the curtains stir again, but through them Nancy felt eyes upon her, friendly eyes. She tried to say something to them, and strove to read what they were saying to her, but all she knew was that they were sending her away, and she did not wish to go away. She needed Divot Meg.

Needed her for what? To tell her that she was brave enough to be friends with her in the face of all Pitouie. But Divot Meg was refusing to let her do this. She had put her right with Pitouie at the price of a whip about her neck. To insist on speaking to Divot Meg was to undo what she had done, was to throw her sacrifice back at her. It was insulting Divot Meg to refuse her sacrifice. Yes, she could see that, but why could not Divot Meg see her secretly? She could let her come in now when all Pitouie was asleep. Was it friendly of Divot Meg to hold out a hand and then to snatch it away when she needed her so much?

But why did she need Divot Meg? Did she need anybody to lean upon now? Of course she did not! That was what Divot Meg's eyes were saying to her through the window curtains: "You're a Fassefern! What help can Divot Meg be to you? What help do you need?" Divot Meg had taken away her hand because she knew that she did not need help.

She held her face close to the window to let Divot Meg see from it that she had understood. She felt the eyes upon it satisfied with what they read, and then she turned away. As she went there was a friendly feeling behind her as if Divot Meg were pushing her on with warm palms pressed against her back.

She was no longer afraid of her body, nor of her soul, nor of life as it would clash against these two, but, strong with a new strength, she went proudly down the sleeping street . . . a Fassefern walking alone.

BOOK III

Nancy was almost twenty now. For more than two years she had been assistant to Andrew Morrison at the Public Library. There were times when she felt that he had invented the position to give her something to do, and at other times she felt that he had done it so that he could have the upper hand with her, could order her life, and possess it.

There was an impassioned current between them that was not unlike hostility. It gave her a queer sense that part of him was her enemy. He had a strange way of appearing to think that she was blemished by her birth. She did not believe that he really thought this, or respected her less for it. But at times when she seemed to hold herself too high, he would say something to bring Bella Pringle before her, or hint of Willie Weams. It made her wonder sometimes if secretly he hated her.

But one day as he stepped from his chair before her, his boxes clattering on the floor, she happened to see his face wincing as he glanced at her to see if she had heard the noise, and the thought came to her: "He is my clattering boxes. When I step out proudly he clatters to remind me that I am a cripple. He does it because *his* boxes clatter to remind *him*. . . . He wants *me* to be a cripple also. . . . But I'm *not* one! I'm not a cripple!"

She still lived at the parsonage although she had been free since she was eighteen to leave it.

She longed to live alone. The old hankering for a "personal door" was still upon her. But yet she could not go. There was in the parsonage a threatening thing that boded ill for old Mrs. Anderson, a soft-footed danger that would not show its face. Nancy felt that if she left, it would come mercilessly from its hiding-place and destroy the old lady.

Old Mrs. Anderson felt this also, though she never spoke of it. But it was agreed silently between the two that Nancy should remain.

She paid for her board there by doing all the necessary things for the old lady in the evenings, and so appeased the minister's wife.

Young Mrs. Anderson had grown more and more bitter against the old woman, nor was there any limit to the lengths that the old lady would go to bait her pallid daughter-in-law. She would even endure the company of

167

her lugubrious son for hours at a time in her turret room just because she knew that his peering wife was haunting the staircase in a reek of jealousy. Indeed, she had altogether taken her son's heart. He "bore with" his wife now, carried her with patient humility as if she were a cross, but he no longer gave her that tepid affection which had passed between them for love.

The younger woman knew this, and her hatred was a stalking thing, yet the old woman continued to provoke her with a recklessness that made Nancy tremble.

She had thought of taking the old woman away from the parsonage and finding some small place in the village where her salary and the old lady's pittance would cover their needs. But it was useless to suggest this. She soon saw that the zest would be gone from the old woman's life when she could no longer bait her daughter-in-law. At the very mention of "living in peace alone" the old lady wilted in her chair and sat beaten and meek. "You'll be leaving me then, if I don't move with you?" she asked plaintively. And Nancy shook her head.

"No, I won't leave you."

"Except to marry," said the old lady very cheerily.

"Whom would I marry?" Nancy laughed. "The old sexton, or Mr. Robertson?"

"Two fine catches," chortled the old lady. "And don't be forgetting the banker."

"Eighty-two, if he's a minute."

"Or the accountant."

"And he's consumptive."

"Somebody will come along one of these days," the old lady assured her. "It's when you least expect it that love comes round the corner."

Nancy wondered if it ever would. Her love for the Whistling Boy had become the fabric of a dream. When she thought of him returning now, there was pain in the thought. It would be easier to have him stay away for ever than to have him return and not love her. Sometimes she asked nothing more of life than that it should leave her her dream of him.

One morning when she arrived at the library she found Andrew in high fettle. Had his legs been normal, he would have been pacing the floor excitedly. As it was, he sat with a leashed tumult in his white face that made her cry:

"Something has happened?"

"It has that." There was a letter lying on the table before him which he kept smoothing out with his hands, as if he expected by this process to make it larger. "It has that."

"What?"

"We have two libraries."

"No! Where?"

"This, as you see." He waved comprehensively. "And . . ." He leaned forward to impart the next momentous words with all the honour that was due them. ". . . Fassefern Castle!"

"Oh! How?" Nancy heard her own voice coming faintly out of a big hollow.

"Ramsey Gordon's will. . . ."

"He gave *us* the library?"

"He gave the castle and grounds to the people of Rossorty for a park and public library."

"But us? . . . How do we get it?"

"*I've* been appointed librarian, caretaker, general factotum, and what-not."

"Aren't there any relatives?"

"None on the right side of the blanket. . . . He's the last."

Andrew was not meeting her eyes. He was indeed refusing to see that this was her father he was talking about, that this was the home of her fathers which he so glibly spoke of as a public library. He was doing it to pierce her, and she must not let him see that he was succeeding.

"Marvellous," she managed to get out, with a suitable amount of enthusiasm. "And how shall we run both?"

"I thought we'd take them week about. You can stay here while I'm there."

"Is it . . . is it right away?"

"Oh, no! We'll have to get the books catalogued and that sort of thing. . . . Besides, the Castle is rented for four months. Yes . . . I suspect we will have to make arrangements with the tenant to go there."

"It's a year since Ramsey Gordon died, isn't it?"

"A little over. . . . Funny that he should have lain in bed fifteen years with consumption. He's about the only Fassefern to die naturally. . . . Had more courage than the others I suspect."

"I don't think it was lack of courage that made the Fasseferns kill themselves. . . . Maybe it was an excess of it," Nancy said quietly.

"Umph! . . . Well, neither you nor I know enough about them to have an opinion."

What was this determination on Andrew's part to deny her any kinship with the Fasseferns? It was almost a personal offence to him to say anything that tied her to them.

He wanted to quarrel with her again. She often felt that he was trying to bring about a clash of emotion between them, and some instinct warned her to prevent it at any cost, some instinct which told her that Andrew would be the one to suffer if it happened. So she smiled and said:

"We won't see much of each other, that way."

"I can't flatter myself that it will grieve you much," he said, his lip forming into the delicate painful twist that answered as a smile.

"You're the only friend I have, Andrew . . . the only man friend."

"Man! Mademoiselle, I thank you." He bowed, ironic and bitter.

She slipped into her place at the desk where she worked. Here he could not see her face, and she could control the angry tears that pressed against the front of her throat painfully. She was not sorry for him. She was not! She was not! It was not fair of him to be so bitter.

"I wonder if I shall be able to leave old Mrs. Anderson," she said after a while, not turning round. "Perhaps I should stay here and you go to Fassefern."

"That won't be possible. . . . There won't be much to do at Fassefern. The Rossorty people don't read much."

"I'm frightened sometimes about the old lady."

"You're neurotic about the old lady."

"Maybe," said Nancy, in a way that meant "I don't think so."

"You're not normal," he snapped viciously.

Nancy laughed: "A compliment? Or an insult?" She looked archly back over her shoulder.

Andrew laughed, and the tension between them, which had been so strained, relaxed again.

Old Mrs. Anderson would not hear of Nancy sacrificing the chance to go to Fassefern.

"That's fate," she said. "It's right for you to be there, and you're going there, left-handedly, just as you were born to it, left-handedly."

"I'm worrying about *you*, though; I'll be gone every other week for a whole week at a time."

"I can master her," asserted the old woman, not giving "her" a name since they both knew whom she meant. "I'll have Mary give me other food than what *she* intends for me."

"Do you think she would go *that* far?" Nancy was aghast at the suggestion.

"No, I don't. That's why I'm taking precautions. . . . It's the thing you think *won't* happen that you should guard against."

"She wouldn't do *that*."

"Never! Never!" agreed the old woman. "But it will make her fairly frothing to see me act as if I thought she *would*. . . . I wouldn't miss doing it for a pile of siller."

"You shouldn't stir her up all the time," Nancy reproved. "You must promise me not to provoke her the weeks that I'm away."

But the old woman laughed on a high key and promised nothing.

It was a week after this that Andrew and Nancy stood in the great hall of Fassefern Castle under the eye of the dubious housekeeper.

"I can give you rooms, of course," she admitted, "And I can give you food . . . but . . ." She stopped to struggle with the unprecedented situation. For in which rooms should she put them? And in which hall should they eat? Were they to be classed as a higher kind of servant, or must she treat them as quality? The young lady was quality from tip to toe, as anybody could see, and would fit like a finger in a silver thimble anywhere. But where would a body put a man with boxes on his legs? Should she take a kindly way with him and lead him back to the servants' hall, or must she call him "sir," since it was plain enough that he must have an education or the master would never have appointed him to take care of his books.

But before she could decide, Andrew took the matter out of her hands by saying:

"It is not our wish to disturb the tenant in any way, so if you will take us to the library, I will then be better able to tell you which rooms we will take."

So it was as "quality" she must treat them.

"Very well, sir," she said. "The library is in the west wing . . . as far as possible from the organ." She was leading them along a flagged and vaulted corridor which was broken every now and then by a sombre vaulted door. "The master never liked to be disturbed by it, when he was reading. But if he could hear the playing we have now——Still he never was one for music."

"It's a wonder he had an organ," said Andrew affably.

"Oh, that was put in before his time, sir. It's a fine organ, they say . . . and now it's blown by electricity, which is a great saving of labour."

She stopped before a door of greater size than the others. It was vaulted and studded with iron, and across it a heavy bar was swung.

"That's the main entrance to the east wing, where the young man himself is," she said. "It's never to be opened. . . . That's his orders, sir." There was warning as well as information in her tone.

"Oh, we will never bother him." Andrew assured her.

Nancy was saying nothing, hardly hearing them. A painful hush had fallen upon her ever since the gates of Fassefern Castle opened to admit them. She had felt that when the gates rolled back she would see her people, all her own people, all the past and gone Fasseferns, waiting to welcome her. But the wide yellow drive had stood empty between its smooth green lawns. The high copper beeches had held their heads haughtily skyward, and the dark rhododendron bushes, hunched upon the bright green lawn, slept in the warm spring sunlight, heeding her not.

But still her heart had gone flying up the drive before her, greeting each tree and bush with widespread arms: "Oh, my tree; oh, my bush; oh, beech-tree of my ancestors, speak to me. See, I have come home."

It was in the great hall that she found herself truly home at last. Andrew had stood alien upon the silken rugs that pulled upon his wooden boxes when he tried to walk, but under her feet they spread free and friendly for her to walk upon. The dark vaulted roof reached down its arms in welcome, and the bright marquetry panels of the walls, glinting with ivory and coloured stones, smiled warmly upon her.

"Moorish influence," Andrew had explained. "All this inlaid work . . . the architecture too . . . though it is almost Grecian in places . . . very little Gothic. . . . They were great travellers, the Fasseferns . . . smugglers too, of course . . . and pirates. . . . Much of this came from Spain after the fall of the Moorish Empire."

She wondered at him as he glibly explained everything to her. Could he not see that this was her home, that no one need explain the Fasseferns to her?

She could hear him still explaining as he walked with the housekeeper down the long corridors, while she walked far behind, as she always did so that she might not pain him by towering above him.

"Stone corridors of course . . . very Gothic here. . . . Gothic doors. . . ."

How could he go on like that? Could he not feel the Fasseferns listening to him . . . laughing at him?

The housekeeper opened the door of the library to let them enter. A pleasant smell of old books came out to meet them.

"What books! What books!" cried Andrew, moved at last, as he took a book in its thumb-print calfskin binding out of its place. "Look, Nancy . . . engravings . . . such illustrations . . . a grand family, knew books, knew art. . . ."

Moved for the moment out of his customary cynicism, he turned impulsively to the housekeeper:

"I'd like to write the history of the Fasseferns."

"What need would there be of that, sir?" she asked, feeling a little superior now that she saw his admiration.

"To tell the world about them."

172

"Everybody knows about the Fasseferns," she answered pridefully. "It's the first thing a bairn hears, and the last thing an old wife tells. . . . A Fassefern is a Fassefern! . . . What would *they* be needing with a testimonial!"

"Not a testimonial," Andrew hastened to explain. "A history. . . . You see, their history has never been written."

"Never been written!" She looked down at Andrew with a look that might well have made him shorter than he was. Something dammed up in her burst with savage pride. "Never been written, sir! . . . It's on the walls there! . . . Five hundred years of it. . . . It's in the heart of the country-side . . . It's on the rocks and in the caves. . . . Aye"—her old voice quavered despite the pride in it—"aye, and it's written on the bottom of the sea."

Nancy found her eyes glazed with tears. She wanted to put her arms round the prideful old woman's neck; she loved her for being so human, so boastful of the family she had served, but already she had become the proper servant again.

"But those things won't be interesting *you*, sir," she said. There was a tang of condescension, and Nancy loved her for this also. "So if you'll excuse me, sir, I'll be leaving you now."

"Emotional old party," he said, raising a cynical eyebrow after her, but nevertheless this did not succeed in giving him back his superiority again. He doubtless felt this, for he sought a high chair behind the big table and enthroned himself there.

"I wonder who the tenant is, who plays the organ?" Nancy said. She always felt a quickening toward anyone who played an organ. "You wrote to him, didn't you, for permission to come?"

"Yes." Andrew said nothing more. So she asked:

"What is his name?"

Before he answered her there was a pause, a pause so long that Nancy knew what name he would say, before he answered:

"Brune."

"Harvey Brune?"

"Yes."

"Why didn't you tell me? . . . How could you not tell me?"

"I didn't think of it. . . . Why would it interest you?"

Oh, she must not betray herself to Andrew. . . . But she must already have betrayed herself. . . . He must have known long ago or why had he not told her before?

She calmed her voice, holding out of it the purls of triumph that cried: "He has come back to me! He has come back to me!" and said:

"But he's a great musician now, and he used to be in Pitouie, at the druggist's shop."

She did not know if Andrew was deceived by this. He was wearing his iron face, anything might be going on behind it.

"We must meet him," she said, with a carefully conventional enthusiasm in her voice.

"Oh, I don't know why *we* should pursue him," Andrew replied coldly.

"Only because we knew him in Pitouie."

"If he had wished to remember Pitouie people, he would have said so in his letter."

"And he didn't say anything? Didn't remember *you* even?"

Andrew smiled his razor-edged smile.

"He said we could come here, on condition that we would be 'neither seen nor heard,' because he had a great deal of work to do and must have quiet and solitude."

This did not hurt her. It gave her a picture of him endlessly alone, endlessly playing, endlessly writing music, until one day when fate would bring him back to her.

"He sounds like a hermit," she laughed, liking her vision of him. But Andrew shattered this while she was still making it.

"A hermit! Women will never let *him* be a hermit," Andrew laughed. "He is the best catch in Europe. . . . He has wealth, his genius has already brought him fame, and he is handsome enough to turn their heads if he had nothing else. . . . He *has* to run away from them sometimes . . . to get some work done."

Was Andrew saying all this to hurt her, to kill the joy in her heart? But could it be true? . . . Oh, could it? . . . But of course it was true. How strange that she had not ever thought of this. Harvey had been away from her, in her thoughts, but away from her in a world as empty as the world she lived in. He had been away from her in a mist-world filled with organs and pianos and vague people without faces who clapped their hands over his music, and wrote pieces for the paper saying he was greater than Chopin.

But he had not been in a mist-world. . . . He was "the best catch in Europe" . . . "handsome enough to turn their heads. . . ."

What was this queer hurting that had come to her? She had never known it before. . . . Was this jealousy?

"Oh, God, give me back my dream. . . . Give me back my peace!"

She had been there four torturous days, and she had not seen him. She did not wish to see him. She wished more than anything that some morning the housekeeper would come and say to her in hushed tones:

"The young man himself is dead, miss: lying peacefully in his bed."

That would put everything at rest in her soul again. Dead, he would be

174

hers; but living, he was "the best catch in Europe," who *must* run away from women sometimes. . . .

It could not be borne. She was on the point of asking Andrew to let her go back to Pitouie. But what would be the good of that? She could not run away from the pain in the middle of her that was like a grinding mill. It ground so constantly that she prayed for sleep to go on and on, prayed that she might *never* wake and think of him and start the mill again. . . .

She had managed to deceive Andrew. He no longer thought that Harvey Brune was anything to her, and had stopped speaking of him. She could not have borne to let him go on. He seemed driven to prove to her that Harvey Brune was out of her reach, just as he seemed driven to prove to her that she had no kin with the Fasseferns. He seemed happiest when she was humbled as *he* was, blemished as *he* was.

She could almost always remember his reason and forgive him for hurting her, she could almost always say to herself: "It is because he suffers so." But she could not do this about Harvey. Andrew had to be stopped. And so she had stopped him. But at a questionable price. It alarmed her a little now, and shamed her.

A thing had lately been showing itself, a faint thing that almost was not there. Indeed, if you shrugged your shoulders and said "Nonsense," it disappeared altogether. It was nothing more than the lingering of Andrew's eyes in hers, a sort of holding on to them after he should have let them go. His eyes would not linger and say something, they would just linger as if this look were a prelude to a thing that must come, a thing which had not come. For she had not allowed it to come. She would snap the look off with a crisp smile, and its danger would be over.

But now to prevent his talking of Harvey she had let the look linger and had not snapped it off, but had pushed it gently away with the falling of her eyelids. This had done a strange thing to Andrew. He had ceased altogether to say things that would hurt her, had ceased even to remember Harvey Brune. His voice had a quality in it that made her want to weep for him, and want to fly from him.

All day now she was gently pushing away the lingering look with falling eyelids. It frightened and tired her. She tried not to meet his look, but even if she did not, she could still see his great grey crucified eyes lingering upon her.

It was like standing in a silken snare that had not yet sprung, but which *would* spring if she moved ever so slightly in the wrong direction. And *every* direction was the wrong direction. She dare not stay in, and she dare not spring out. . . .

They had been together constantly for four days. She must, must get away from him even if only for an hour.

"Andrew, do you mind if I go for a walk? It's so sunny . . . and it's sure to rain to-morrow." She asked it without looking at him. She was quite safe to say that, he would never ask to walk with her.

"Nancy, I've been driving you like a slave . . . I didn't think." He was full of self-reproach. "Go on, take a long walk . . . I'll finish this up."

"I will then." She smiled, but did not let him get the look he reached for, and in a fleet moment she was hurrying down the cool stone corridor . . . free.

She went out past the kennels where drowsy dogs lay with the sun upon them . . . nobody to hunt with them now. Where would they be going soon? . . . sold to somebody. . . .

She found a bridge over a dark slow-moving stream. Peering under it, she saw dark eels with white bellies, swimming about in their queer way. . . . The going of the Fasseferns would not trouble them. . . .

The road led her into a ragged wood that was different from the well-groomed wood that lined the drive. Here fallen leaves lay undisturbed beneath the ancient trees. The sun came through in coins of light between the leaves, and new green ferns spread out their feathery hands to catch its dancing gold. Yellow primroses dappled the ground, and tender moss made velvet stippling on the ash-grey bark. Squirrels slipped pertly about, examining beech-nuts, and little grey rabbits with snowy upturned tails sat down to watch her pass.

There was a scent upon the air too sweet to be the smell of primroses, it spoke of summer more than spring, a languorous scent that hung upon the warm air caressingly.

A ravine cut across the wood, narrow and deep. As she reached it, Nancy saw that it was filled with blooming hyacinths. Deceived by the warmth of their sheltered nest, they thought that June had come, and their waxen blue flowers sent forth their heavy fragrance with ardour of summer-time. Nancy sat down on the edge of this.

Her uneasiness about Andrew had faded. Very likely most of it was her imagination. Thoughts of the Whistling Boy crowded in upon her though she tried to keep them away. She told herself that she wanted never to see him, that she wanted him to go away, to go back into memory again and be only the little boy who could hurt her, only a very little now. But yet she knew that all her heart was listening, praying, hoping, *yearning* to see him, to hear him, to touch him.

What would he be like? What would be left of the boy who stood against the waterfall and whistled for her? What new things would be added to him, what dear things would be lost?

And even as she thought this, she saw the flash of white trousers between the trees and knew that he was near, that he was coming toward her. . . .

His head was bare! Of course his head would be bare; she never could have pictured him wearing a hat. He was swinging along loosely in the delightful way that young men walk before dignity sets in. His dark coat was hunched up at one side to let him bury one hand deep in his trousers pocket. How tall he was, and how brown! And oh, the way he held his head! By that one thing alone she would have known him anywhere!

She rose to her feet and stood in his path. A frown appeared upon his face at the sight of her, at the sight of *anyone* in these private woods. But as he came nearer he smiled, and his smile was diffident, almost apologetic. She was so slim and small in her pale yellow frock, standing beside the hyacinth-filled ravine, yellow primroses about her feet, that she seemed a part of the woodland, part of the flowers that grew there, and *he* seemed to be the intruder.

He stopped before her. She searched his face. How startling were his eyes, so brightly blue in his lean brown face, and how beautiful the thick blond lashes that curled away from them. He coloured under his tan, embarrassed by her gaze.

"I *knew* this wood was haunted," he laughed, trying to regain his poise. After all, *she* was the intruder; no need for him to feel diffident before her. These woods were his till autumn.

"And I know who you are," he rallied. "You're the dryad who makes the primroses bloom."

"That is quite simple," she said. "You could tell that from the colour of my frock."

"Oh, but I know other things about you too," he cried, not to be slighted like this.

"What things?" she asked, half veiling her eyes and smiling.

"Mysterious things," he said darkly.

"Oh, yes?" she chuckled. "For instance?"

"They're not things to be told off the bat like that," he objected. "If you ask me to sit down, and if you treat me with proper courtesy and respect, I may be persuaded to tell you—but *not* otherwise."

She laughed joyfully, seeing him from under half-closed eyes, seeing his face without looking at it; feeling his lean brown hands without touching them. Her heart was as light as thistledown upon the wind. She wondered at it that it did not float out of her breast and go sailing away through the trees. She laughed again, thinking of the funny sight it would make.

"May I sit down?" he coaxed.

"Oh, do," she laughed, "I'm dying to hear the 'mysterious things.'"

They sat down together on the brink of the ravine, he sitting cross-legged like a tailor, facing her, she leaning her back against a tree, her slim legs crossed in front of her.

Her eyelids were heavy with an amorous sweetness which had come upon them since she looked at him. She wanted to look at his face a long time, but she could not because her eyes would always veil themselves as if too much happiness frightened them.

"Do all dryads have fabulous hair?" he asked earnestly, his eyes upon her waving amber hair.

"Fabulous?"

"Meaning: 'passing the limits of belief.'"

How delightful he was! How sweet to have him say such things to her. Oh! Oh! She must not let him dazzle her so. She must keep back her heart till she knew more of his. She must remember that he was the best catch in Europe and *had* to run away from women to get his work done.

"You were going to tell me the 'mysterious things,'" she reminded.

"Well! First of all——" He paused to create a sense of the great importance of what he was going to say.

"Yes?" she questioned, glancing up for a second, a smile quirking irrepressibly at the corners of her mouth.

"First of all, I've met you somewhere before . . . in Germany or Italy . . . or maybe it was in my dreams."

"Dryads don't go to Germany or Italy," she murmured, her eyes on her lap.

"In my dreams then!"

"I don't think they inhabit dreams, either."

"Oh, you're wrong. They *do* . . . or at least they *will*!"

"And second of all?" she prompted, hurrying him away from dangerous ground, though she wanted to have him linger there.

"Second of all, I *know* I've met you somewhere. I've met your eyes often!"

"Often?"

"Yes. I'm *always* meeting them. I met them in the British Museum once . . ."

"Dear *me*!"

"They were in a necklace . . . a queer green necklace."

"Mildewed, I suppose," she said, with a flippancy that astonished herself.

"Please have some manners," he implored.

"Even a dryad . . ." He waved his hand to complete the protest, and went on reprovingly. "As I was saying before I was so rudely interrupted,

I saw them in a necklace . . ."

"A *queer* green necklace."

"Of wicked oriental stones, that had no name."

"Poor things!"

He refused to acknowledge this interruption.

"The next time was on a dark night. . . ." His voice rolled down ominously.

"Yes?"—breathlessly. She was pleased with herself. If she could just maintain this air of playing.

"But I don't think you're interested . . . you don't look at me," he objected.

Her eyelids fluttered up to give him a reproachful smiling glance.

"Why don't you look at me?" he asked, leaning nearer till the faint fragrance of tobacco reached her sensitive nostrils.

"What do you smoke?" she asked.

"A pipe."

She smiled. That was exactly what he ought to smoke. And it would be a very big, very crooked pipe, she knew.

"But I keep it very clean," he hastened to add.

She laughed: "I like pipes."

"What else do you like? Do you like organ music?" he asked eagerly.

"That's the music I like best. . . . But I don't like working the bellows much," she added cryptically.

"Who *would*? . . . Just as if you *could* with hands like that!" He sat forward and examined them with his eyes. "They look as if they had been carved from white jade."

She looked down at them, thinking of the time when they protruded red and chapped from the too short sleeves of her black frock, and of how she had tried to hide them from him. They lay now poised and assured in her lap.

"I play a little," he said. "Would you let me play for you some time?"

She hid a smile at his modest description of his playing.

"There are things I say best on the organ," he explained.

"The 'mysterious things,' for instance?"

"Yes. Those, and other things. . . . There seem to be so many things I have to tell you," he cried, mystified by the sudden need he felt to reveal himself to her. "Isn't it strange? I don't even know your name, but I want to tell you everything I've ever thought!"

Nancy said nothing. She had gathered a handful of little red-brown beech-nuts, and was pouring them from one hand into the other. He sat beglamoured, watching her. The air moved over them in warm scented puffs, caressing them, little squirrels came near inquisitively, and birds looked down marvelling at their stillness. But they sat silent, held in a spell of nearness.

He leaned forward and caught some of the little nuts as they poured from her hand. They were warm from her touch. He held them close between his palms. She stole a bemused look at him, and he looked back at her with eyes that were disturbed and pleading, eyes that said: "Why do you do this to me?" until her own eyes veiled themselves again to hide their rapture.

He stretched himself upon the ground near her, but not touching her, and lay looking up at her pearl-pale face, and at the firefly darting of the sun upon her amber hair, and at her straight ample brows which lifted a little at the outer corners as if about to fly.

Silence hung between them, a timeless sigh, painful in its sweetness.

She wanted to hold time for ever like this. But they were rushing toward each other like mad winds across a waste-land. Nearer and nearer. And when they met at last, would they be for ever still, for ever lost in each other, for ever found? Or would they rush on past each other, out into the wasteland, alone, once more? Oh, nothing was certain but this, that they were rushing toward each other. . . . Hold back! Hold back!

She sprang to her feet, shattering the tranced wood; betrayed birds flew up, and squirrels scurried away. He sprang to his feet also, half dazed still, and, like the birds, betrayed.

"I must go." It was a little gasp, apologetic, almost ashamed, but most of all it was the cry of a heart in flight, flying in fear from its too swiftly nearing happiness.

"But why? . . . Have I done something?"

"No! No! . . . No! No! But I must go."

"But please . . ." He caught her clenched hand and held it between his cupped palms like a little white bird in its brown nest. It struggled.

"Please tell me why you must go."

"Because . . ." She looked to right and left as if the wood might hang out a little sign telling her what to say. But no sign appeared. The disturbed birds were settling back in their places. Her plight was nothing to them.

"How shall I find you again? . . . I don't even know your name."

"I'll come here again," she said faintly.

"When?"

"I don't know."

"Won't you tell me your name?"

No, no, she could not tell him her name, not yet, not yet. She recovered her hand and held it behind her as if giving it a chance to fly away to safety. He seemed to understand this, and looked reproved and hurt.

She was less frightened now. Nothing could happen till she was ready for it. This was only the little boy she had known back in the "wood that looked like Italy." The little boy who grieved because he had no piano to play upon. She must not hurt the little boy. She smiled up at him.

"Please," he begged.

"Dryads never tell their names," she twinkled, now quite sure of herself.

"Never?"

"Never to mortals."

"And I'm *so* mortal." He sighed.

She laughed.

"Will you come to-morrow? . . . Let me play for you to-morrow . . . Will you?"

"Perhaps."

"Unless you give me more hope than that I'll track you to your lair, or your hollow tree," he threatened.

"Oh, you mustn't do that." She was dismayed as she realised how easily he could discover her if he tried. And she was not ready for that, yet.

"I will," he said firmly, "unless you promise to come to-morrow, at this same hour."

"Bully!"

"Promise!"

"I'll come."

"Thank you."

"Till to-morrow."

"Till to-morrow."

She left him, going along the chine in the direction that led away from Fassefern Castle. Soon, when she was out of sight, she would turn back, making a wide circle by the kennels and gaining the Castle through the servants' quarters.

She could not meet him next afternoon, because Andrew lingered, seemingly possessed with a devil of indecision, or as if he guessed that she had met the Whistling Boy and that she planned to meet him again.

First he ordered the trap to take him back to Pitouie at noon. Then, no, as long as he was here they had better check through the eighteenth-century plays, and he would go to Pitouie later in the day. But on second thought perhaps he had better go back at the usual hour; there might be early visitors at the Pitouie Library. It was hardly fair not to open at the customary time. But for that matter why couldn't they wait? There was no great hurry about getting their books exchanged. As far as that went, they never came anyway till late. No, never mind ordering the trap, he would stay and work a while.

While he debated back and forth, Nancy longed to cry out:

"Do one thing or the other, and put me out of this misery!"

She thought of another time years ago when she had tried for three days to escape and see him. And of how when he had come whistling for her, pride had kept her back, till at last he was gone, never to come back.

It might happen again! What madness had made her leave him without telling him her name! He might decide to leave to-day, to-night, and stay away for ever!

"I can't . . . I can't work this afternoon." The book flew out of her jerking hands.

"What's the matter?" The calm of Andrew's noble face was disturbed, but not deeply. It seemed to say that nothing much could be the matter. That nothing could happen to her that he did not know now. It irritated her; she wanted to say: "You think you know all my life, you think you own it—but you don't. Things happen to me that you don't know about." But she said:

"I don't feel well."

Oh, why was she lying? It was so stupid to lie, and would not help at all.

"Better lie down here on the couch." Andrew was tender, possessive, understanding. It heightened her irritation. So smugly understanding! Thinking he knew every depth of her!

"No! No!" she cried, with needless passion. "I *can't* lie down . . . I'm . . . I'm nervous."

Andrew smiled, his eyes lingering upon her face and saying things that were quite different from the things his tongue was saying.

"I don't wonder . . . It's this morgue of a place. . . . Look, Nancy, come back to Pitouie with me to-night."

"No! No! I'd rather stay."

"Then don't work now, lie down . . . I'll do them."

"No! . . . I'm all right . . . Come on, let's get this done."

"I'd rather you didn't work when you don't feel well, Nancy."

The possessiveness of his tone! The assurance that he knew all that was troubling her, and knew also the remedy for it. She wanted to scream piercingly; sharp penetrating cries, one after the other, cries that would split the world in two, and send it crashing into dust . . . and Andrew with it! . . . Yet she said softly:

"I'm all right, Andrew, really. Let us work."

He was reluctant. "Well, we'll finish the eighteenth-century plays." He picked up the pencil again and she took a book from the shelf.

"*Tamerlane*, by Nicholas Rowe." Where would *he* be now? It was time that he would be starting out to meet her. "*The Orphan*, by Thomas Otway." He would think her a cheap coquette . . . staying away to disappoint him, and make him more eager . . . Female trickery! "*The Man of the World*, by Charles Macklin." He would hate that sort of thing . . . or would he? Yes, he would hate that. It might be the end. "*The Country Girl*, by David Garrick." He would go there and wait. He might wait an hour or two, but when he left he would be finished with her and her cheap little female tricks. "*The West Indian*, by Richard Cumberland."

A sodden pain soaked its way into the centre of her. She let it stay there hopelessly. "*The Dramatist*, by Frederick Reynolds."

More books. More books. More books. Smelling faintly of mildew. . . . Mildew and God. . . . Why God? . . . What was it about mildew that suggested God? . . . Mildew and churches. . . . What was God? . . . A big deaf face. . . .

It must be after five. He would have left the wood by now. "*The Honey Moon*, by John Tobin. That's the last. Shall we start on the next shelves?"

"No! My word! What time is it?"

He came off the chair in a soft thud. The carpets again! She could not get used to him moving without a clatter of boxes.

"What shall we do, Nancy?" He was looking up at her with the different look that came upon his face when he was standing and had to look up at her. There was always accusation in it and a little shame. "Shall I go—or you?"

"I want to stay here," she said firmly, appearing to be preoccupied with a book so that she would not have to look down at his face. He must not see the mad thing that had started up in her again at the thought of freedom, and which was ranging up and down, screaming at him to be off with him and leave her alone.

"Well, if you don't like it . . ."

"I'll like it."

Finally, finally, he drove away!

No use for her to go now. He would be gone. But still she ran, her feet light as foam, and fleet with her need, along the gravel path past the kennels. A hundred dogs cried out, tugging at their chains or leaping at bars, "Stop her! Stop her! Stop her!" Baying voices which she left behind. . . .

There was no sign of him. No sign. The hyacinths shed their breath upon emptiness. A blue twilight hid under the trees, ready to slip out and claim the wood. No dappling gold came through the leaves. . . . Desolate!

. . . Desolate! . . .

The tree where she had sat; the place where he had stretched out near her, but not touching her; the little nuts . . . all desolate!

But no, near the tree, set in a bracket of its uprising roots, was a bouquet of primroses. They were bound together with scented bracken stems and edged with green ferns. For her! He had gathered them, left them, for her. He was not angry. He had not gone away for ever. He would come again! Sweet relief welled up her throat to glisten in her eyes.

She sat down leaning against the trees, the primroses held in her hand. Here, again in the wood, she could go over every moment of their meeting, every word that they had said, every look of his face and sound of his voice, more clearly than she could last night in the lowering secret bedroom of the Castle, or in the high-vaulted, outspoken library. Here she could smell again the faint scent of tobacco, and see the glistening gold-brown hairs upon the backs of his wrists.

It was strange that she could still see him most clearly as the little boy who whistled against the waterfall. His coming had not destroyed that picture, but only sharpened it more painfully.

He was always going to be, in some strange way, that little boy. A little boy who could hurt her, and whom she could not reach to hurt, or help. . . . No, that was not true. Here in her hands was the proof that she could reach him. . . . He had come and waited for her, and when at last he had gone away, he had left the flowers to say: "See, I have been here, and I will come again."

She would go to him now, simply, with the flowers in her hand. . . . Why need love be a game of hide-and-seek, of pretence, of coquetry. . . . Enemy tactics! Must it be always that? Could you not go to him and say: "For years I have lived for you, waited for you. Now you have come. All that there is of me is yours. You do not need to anguish and wonder if I love you. For I shall not hide from you, denying you this favour or that, then yielding them at a price, reluctantly, so that you may prize them more highly, thinking them hardly won." Why could you not do that? . . . But you could not. Something, everything told you that you could not. . . .

The blue twilight was changing the leaves from tender green to indigo, muffling the trunks in zafferic shadows; hidden things moved darkly about rustling dried leaves. Something blue stalked invisible through the wood, something grown hostile with the setting of the sun. Nancy rose to her feet afraid, as she always was afraid, when nature grew dark and she was alone with it. She ran; not going her secret way, but running between the trees, the shortest way to get out into the light. The roots grabbed at her feet with thin black fingers . . . evil trees. . . . Nature had a wicked heart in the dark. . . .

She laughed at herself when she reached the bright gravel path. It was daytime still outside the wood.

She ought to turn back because she might meet him here. Then suddenly, astonishingly, he was before her, coming toward the wood, a letter in his hand. He hurried to her, unbelieving in his joy.

"You *did* come! . . . I waited *years.* . . . You found the flowers. . . . I really didn't expect to find you. . . . I was going back to leave this," explaining the letter in his hand.

She held out her hand for it.

"No. You don't deserve it." He slipped it into his pocket. His first impulse of relief and joy gave way to resentment. She was safe within his sight again and he could afford for a moment to be angry with her.

Silently they walked together to the low bridge under which eels glided swiftly in dark water. They sat side by side on the low wall looking down at the black stream. Above the stream gnats danced, playing hide-and-seek with death. Every now and then there was a little "plop," and trembling rings of water would widen and widen and finally die away. But on and on would go the death dance of the gnats, seeming undisturbed by the "plop" which meant that a little gnat was now in the gullet of a fish.

The Boy had retreated to his deeper recesses, drawing his sunlight in after him. He was cold like the coming evening.

"Why don't you give me the letter?" she asked, knowing that he would not give it to her while he looked like that.

He barely glanced at her, answering her question with the most fleeting of chill smiles.

"But you would have left it in the wood for me, if you hadn't met me."

"Perhaps not."

"Then why did you write it?"

"Why didn't you come?"

"I did."

"Hours late!"

"I couldn't come before," she pleaded.

"Couldn't!"

"Yes . . . really that."

A half-believing shrug, then:

"At least you *did* come. . . . But perhaps only to keep your word, and knowing it was too late to find me there. . . . Or did you expect me to wait for you 'far into the night'? . . . I suppose most of them are willing to do that."

"Them?"

"Oh, the fifty other swains who languish."

"You haven't given me any reason to think that you languish," she answered, barely able to keep a purl of laughter out of her voice. It was so pleasing to have him angry like this.

"And I don't think I ever shall—I despise women who—who——"

"I *really* couldn't come before."

He hunched himself and glowered down at the dancing gnats. She wondered at how happy it made her to see him so angry with her. He had no right really to be so rude, so furious. No right, except the deep right which his heart knew, and which her own heart gave him gladly, gladly. He must have been thinking something like that, for he said in apology, yet rather as if it too were an accusation:

"I've no right to speak to you like this . . . you were quite right not to come if you didn't wish to see me again." He was looking at her now, his eyes denying what he was saying.

"But I did want to. . . . That is why I came as soon as I could."

"But suppose we hadn't happened to meet."

"I would have come to the ravine to-morrow."

This was comforting him. But he wanted to wring some sign of pain from her, so he said:

"Suppose I hadn't come any more." Enemy tactics, bitter warfare of love!

"I would have written to you," she said, pained by his words, though she knew what made him say them.

"How? You don't know my name."

"I *do* know it."

"Oh!" There was a great deal of happiness in his face now. And his pride was gone before a rushing need to know more things about her, before the need to know that she would have found him again even if he had not come back.

"What else do you know about me?" he smiled reluctantly, not to be too readily forgiving.

"Oh, many things."

"Such as . . . ?"

"That you're an orphan."

"Yes?" This in gratified surprise. "Go on."

"And a musician . . . a very great musician."

"Oh, not that." The brown of his face was confused with red, but pleased.

"Yes," she laughed, "*quite* that."

"And?"

"That you lived in Edinburgh when you were little."

"No!" he cried eagerly. "How *did* you know that? . . . We've met before. . . . We *must* have met before."

She nodded.

"Where?"

She only smiled.

"I *couldn't* have forgotten you."

"No?" she laughed.

"Was it Cannes?"

"Not on the Continent."

"London, then?"

"No."

"Say where."

"We met in a wood."

"*Naturally*," he agreed as if this were the answer he expected. "But *what* wood?"

"A wood with a waterfall that 'looked like Italy,'" she said, quoting his long-remembered words.

But he looked at her helplessly.

"You whistled tunes for me and told me about Chopin, only you pronounced it 'Shoppin'."

"*Now* I know!" he cried. "Now I know. . . . You're the little girl who blew the organ for me."

"Yes."

"At Pitouie."

"In the kirk."

"I was just . . . why, I was only seventeen."

She nodded.

"How marvellous! . . . How perfectly marvellous!" he cried.

"What is?"

"Me finding you in woods all the time! . . . Have you been in woods ever since?"

"Yes," she nodded solemnly. "I live in woods . . . beech woods."

They laughed together ringingly, joyously, gazing at each other, until from the very excess of their happiness they fell silent again.

"I remember the waterfall," he said after a while.

"But you'd quite forgotten me," she reminded him.

"Yes. How funny. I can't remember much except that you wore a black frock and it made me sorry for you."

"I got a new frock, the week after. But you'd gone by then."

"What a funny, solemn little blighter you were," he cried, laughing deliciously, his blue-white teeth gleaming in the bronze setting of his face. "Did they whack you for taking the key?"

She shook her head. She wanted to dismiss the "solemn little blighter in a black frock," push her back into oblivion, and start from yesterday in a yellow frock. But he wanted to dwell on that. It gave him somehow the superior position, and made her something more tangible, something more easily reached, than the yellow-frocked dryad who kept a tryst or did not keep it as fancy dictated.

"I came to let you know that I was going away. I whistled for you down at the hedge," he said.

"Oh, did you?" It would never do to let him know that she had heard and had not gone to him.

"How did it happen that you could leave Pitouie?"

"My guardians changed their minds and decided to let me study music."

So that was it! And she had wondered about it for six years. He might have sent her a note to tell her why, or sent her his address so that she could write to him. But she must not say this.

"You used to live in Pitouie," he remembered. "Where do you live now?"

"In Pitouie."

"But this is Rossorty. What are you doing here?"

"Working."

"Working?" in astonishment. "At what? Not catching herring."

"No," she laughed. "Nor smuggling. I'm librarian."

"At Rossorty?"

"No, at Castle Fassefern."

"You're at Fassefern? Why, I live there."

"So do I."

"No! No, really!"

"Yes. And I must stay in the east wing, because the grand musician who rents the Castle won't let a mere librarian darken his path."

"Oh! Oh!" He laughed wildly. "And I was pacing the floor last night wondering where you lived . . . and you were . . ."

"Just the other side of the barred door."

"I'll have it unbarred at once. . . . But now tell me why you did not come earlier," he demanded. "The library isn't open yet; there was nothing to prevent you."

"But I'm not the head librarian, you know, only the assistant. Andrew Morrison is in charge."

"The cripple from Pitouie?"

188

"Yes." She winced to hear Andrew described so. "And he wanted to work."

"Is he there now?"

"No, he has gone back to Pitouie."

"Very sensible of him." He got up off the bridge. "Come. Let us go back. I'll play for you till dinner-time. But," he laughed down at her, "I won't ask you to blow for me."

They went back to the organ-room after dinner.

A fire of logs burned on the low hearth under the hooded chimney and a few faint candles winked upon the organ at the far end of the long room.

They sat by the big window looking out at the black fir-trees that braced themselves with dignity against the rising wind. There were whispers of coming rain, and the moon was only a feeble ring of silver dodging the onrush of great dark boats.

"This is how I like Fassefern best," said Harvey. "A Scottish castle is meant to glower through rain and wind."

"And *they* like it best this way too . . . they feel more at home, I think."

"Who?"

"The dead Fasseferns . . . they never were used to the sun shining. . . . "

"Stormy petrels!" he laughed, including her with the words. She wondered what he had heard. After a minute she said:

"You know about me?"

"I heard talk in Pitouie, of course. I've forgotten just what. . . . Is it true?"

"Yes. . . . Ramsey Gordon was my father."

"Strange people." He smiled at her.

"Andrew thinks they were all a little mad."

"Most charming people are a little mad," he laughed.

"Am I a little mad, do you think?" she asked.

He leaned forward to see her blurred face, and they smiled in white flashes at each other in the dimness.

"Oh, quite!" he decided. "Quite delightfully mad. . . . But I hope you won't kill yourself . . . or is that an intrinsic part of the family tradition?"

"Oh, I don't think it's compulsory! Some of us have died of measles."

"How humiliating!" Then more soberly. "Why do you suppose they killed themselves?"

"I think it was because they could not bear life without beauty." She said it timidly, a little afraid that he might laugh at her. But he did not. He seemed to consider it for a moment.

"But the bride," he objected. "Life must have been beautiful to *her*."

"Yes. That was it, you see," Nancy hurried to explain. "It *was* beautiful,

189

too beautiful. . . . It was the evening before their wedding; at parting the lovers vowed that they would never look on each other with eyes that were less loving. . . .

"After he had gone she thought of that vow, and she knew that life would make them break it. . . . She knew that the highest height of beauty had been reached for them, or she feared that it had.

"She had promised to meet him at the altar next morning. . . . And he found her there in her bridal robes. . . . Her closed eyes would never look at him less lovingly."

Harvey smiled at her.

"So Celtic," he said. "The highlander must always hunt for the kernel of grief that sits at the heart of happiness."

"And there always *is* a kernel of grief," Nancy said.

"For the Celt, yes." He smiled. "Go on, I like to hear about them."

"I saw my grandfather's death. . . . I was just a child. . . . I didn't understand. . . . But it was beautiful."

"He was old, though . . . the others were so young."

"But *still* it was beautiful. He was such a beautiful old man.

"And I know now why he did it that day. . . . He was riding his white horse upon the low-road. . . . The sun was on the spray above the rose cliffs of Rossorty. . . . You know how it looks, like a rainbow-crown. . . . Perhaps he remembered that the day would come when he would not be able to ride out to see it again . . . that he would be sitting by a window helplessly, or lying on a bed, waiting. . . . Life without beauty! And he could not bear it. . . . So he turned his horse about upon the low-road, and spurred it up the cliff road between the little houses. . . . Up and up to the top, and crashed from there down into the gulch to join the other Fasseferns in the sea. . . ."

"Yes, that has grandeur," Harvey agreed.

"And there was the boy, only seventeen. . . . They found him in the rose stone fountain, his naked body silvered by the moonlight . . . a part of the night . . . and of the stillness."

"I can understand that," Harvey said fervently. "It's the one I understand best. . . . To melt himself back into the beauty of nature before life had time to touch him. . . .

"I've wanted to do that. . . . I've wanted to hold life away, and stay for ever with sound, and line, and colour . . . never to let flesh become a part of it . . . to live life denying life, so that one could keep beauty. . . ."

His words hurt her fiercely.

"But life is important," she heard herself saying. It was as if the words came without her consent, came of some necessity in her that had

190

just awakened.

"Yes, to women . . . life . . . new life, is their business."

His words set him away from her. They seemed to accuse her of some ruthless purpose in which he refused to take a part. It bewildered her and pained her. She could not speak.

The first burst of rain dashed itself against the window. They both watched it silently.

The fire leaped up, stirred by the rising wind. They turned to look at each other before it flickered down again.

"Beautiful eyes," he said. "I'm afraid of them."

"Why afraid?"

"Because I might get lost in them," he said half seriously.

"And you don't ever want to be lost?" She turned her head away as she asked the question and watched the struggling fir-trees as they fought the wind. Harvey was doing that, she felt . . . bracing himself against her. . . .

"I *must* not be lost," he said firmly, but laughing to take the seriousness from his words.

"Sometimes to be lost, is to be found." She laughed also as she spoke, denying her words any meaning.

"Not for *me*!" He jumped to his feet as if to break a snare, and took three restless paces away from her. "I'm found already . . . I'm found in my music. . . . Anywhere else I'm lost. . . ."

"Mr. Brune, I don't insist that you fall in love with me." Astonishing that she could say a thing like that, in that tone!

"You *do*," he cried. "All of you insists . . . the whole cosmos insists that I fall in love with you."

She smiled secretly out at the night. The fir-trees were bending to the wind.

"I think you're in no danger," she said coldly, hoping to hurt him.

He came back to his seat beside her. She drew far back into her chair so that the space between them was greatly widened.

A peal of thunder split the night, and for a flash each tree stood out in glistening black fringed with silver. . . . Black again, so black their eyes ached with blindness. Their hands groped and found each other. . . . His arms found and held her.

"You're not afraid, are you?" he asked. "You're not afraid?"

No! After long kisses how could she be afraid? What storm could hurt her now? What lightning kill?

She shook her head.

"Come, then. . . . I will play this . . . the storm, and you."

The lightning revealed his face to her, the face of the little boy who whistled against the waterfall.

"Let me play it for you."

He was withdrawing his arms from her. His music was calling him, calling him away. But she would go with him this time, would go with him into his music, making it her music also. She must not stand outside listening any more, she must share with him.

"Sit close to me," he said.

But she took a chair where she could see his face with the candlelight upon it. Keeping her eyes upon his face, she could not lose him, she would feel what he felt, she would follow where he led. She would never watch from the outside any more, she was going with him to his secret place . . . .

Hours later she shivered in her bed, drawing the blankets up about her piteous chin. Fighting her tears that spurted with sudden force, fighting with laughter which came in wild gusts, ending again in tears and long agonised trembling of her chilled body.

Faintly she could hear the organ still, its sound veiled by the dismal beating of rain upon the windows and by the wind howling like a hungry cat.

What folly for her to think that she could go with him to his secret place! What vanity to have sat there hour after hour thinking that he played for her! She laughed through chattering teeth, seeing again the black hole behind the kirk organ at Pitouie where she had blown for him, while he, heedless of her, played on through the night.

He was the same little boy for whom she had blistered her hands. The same little boy who would be for ever forgetting her. Downstairs he was playing still, unaware that she had gone, forgetful that she had ever been. Where he went she could not follow. She could only watch him go, and wait, desolate, for him to come back.

Who was it who said: "The artist must walk alone in his secret places"? Was it Andrew?

How she had held on, clinging to his glorified face, compelled along surging ways by the storm of his playing, believing at first that she was with him, that they were going hand in hand together.

But at last, spent, and cold, and desolate, she knew that he had gone beyond her, away into his deep-alone, where she might never follow.

She left him there wrapped in the bright gold of his farness, heedless of the cold and of the night, heedless of the storm, heedless of her leaving feet. . . .

Next morning the rain was still coming down in spears of silver against the blue panes, but lazily now, as if spent by the storm.

She had work before her, but she could not work. The library was her tomb . . . the rain was beating everlasting desolation upon her tombstone. . . .

What was Harvey doing?

The tweeny who came to light her fire in the morning volunteered the news that "the young man himself" had been up all night, "writing dots on paper, miss, as if *that* was a Christian way to be spending the night."

Had he missed her when he finally left the organ? Or was he glad that she was gone so that there was no one to prevent him from "writing dots on paper"?

She laughed at her vanity. Just as if anything could keep Harvey from doing the thing he wished to do. Certainly not Nancy Pringle, or any thought of her. . . .

She had fought off further thoughts of him, and was neatly listing the books, when he came in at the door which connected the library with a small study.

He was hunched in a blue flannel dressing-gown. There were rings of weariness beneath his eyes, which were bloodshot and heavy lidded. A roll of paper protruded from a deep pocket. He pulled it out and laid it on the table in front of her.

"You look cold," she cried.

"I'm frozen," he said. "I had some hot coffee—at least I had what they believe is coffee."

He seated himself wearily on the table and smiled at her. "In our beloved country the coffee . . ." He waved away the rest of the protest with a resigned hand.

"What is this?" she asked, timidly taking up the roll of paper. She found it hard to look at him; it seemed that he should kiss her, and that she could not find her place with him until he did this. She opened the roll, keeping her head down to hide her shyness.

"I wrote it for you." His voice was hollow with tiredness.

She looked up at him. All the glory and rapture were gone from his face, passed out of him; he looked drained.

"Harvey, shouldn't you go to bed?"

Now, why had she said that, when she should have spoken of his music? But he seemed not to mind.

"I don't want to leave you," he said.

"Lie down on the couch. . . . I'll cover you with something."

He rose obediently, a bidable little boy, willing to do whatever she wished.

She covered him with a foxskin rug, the one old Donald Gordon had used to wrap about his thin knees when he sat reading in the cold night.

"Don't go away, will you?" he asked sleepily.

"No," she assured him, "I'm going to work at the table here."

She went back to her seat and picked up the roll of papers.

"Opus Two . . . Brune," she read.

How like Harvey they were, these "dots." They clustered together in a way that spoke of him. She had not thought of this before, but of course a composer's work would be his alone, in look as well as in sound; and all these strange clusterings, this intricate arabesque, this was Harvey in music.

"Opus Two!" For whom had he written Opus One? She hurried away from that painful thought, admonishing herself. There she was, "searching for the kernel of grief," as Harvey would say. She must not do this. She must hold on to her sense of humour. She must not clutch, she must not try to possess completely.

Strange new hungers had arisen to devour her since she met Harvey again. She had things to fight, greedy clutching things whose existence in her she had never guessed.

Why had she made high tragedy of his need to play? Because she wanted his kisses more than his playing, because it wounded her that his passion for music was greater than his love for her.

She must fight against this. She must open her hand and let him go when he wished to go. And when he came back tired, she must put him to bed. Yes, she saw that this was the sanest thing that she had done. . . . Like the fishermen's wives in Rossorty, she could not go to sea with her man, she could only wait at home, and mend the nets when he came back. . . .

But it was enough. . . . It had to be enough.

It was still raining wearily. He had been sleeping almost two hours when she heard the trailing of Andrew's boxes coming along the corridor. It was impossible! Andrew could not be back so soon; he had only gone yesterday. What reason would he have for coming back to-day? But as he opened the door and stood in it, his face red with wind, and wet still, she saw why he had come. Andrew said nothing, but there was that in his face which needed no words to tell it.

Terrified that he would tell his love as he stood there, she cried out: "Andrew! Look, Andrew!"

Her cry woke Harvey, who sat up, and Andrew saw him. Nancy turned away that she might not see Andrew's face.

"Harvey was up all night . . . so he was sleeping here," she said vaguely, looking at neither of them, but out through the window.

Harvey hauled himself to his feet.

"I'm so casual about my sleeping," he yawned.

He trailed his way over to Andrew and shook hands. Nancy could picture him stooping to do this, and she knew how Andrew's face would be looking as he reached up his hand for the greeting.

"Have dinner with me to-night . . . both of you," Harvey urged.

She slid into a seat with her back to them so that she need not see them standing side by side. Andrew made some confused sound of greeting.

"I'll go and sleep somewhere," Harvey yawned again. "Excuse me . . . my yawning. . . . Good-bye till dinner-time. Good-bye, Nancy."

"Good-bye," she sang out, her tone far too casual.

The door closed after him. She heard Andrew take a seat behind her, but she did not turn to face him. His eyes were on her back, but she could not tell until she heard his voice what look was in them.

When the last sound of Harvey's free-walking feet had died away in the long corridor, Andrew spoke, and his voice was like the rain:

"Why did you do it, Nancy?"

Still she did not turn to him, but sat looking out at the tired raining. She forbore to say: "Do what?" or to take any other easy way to evade him. She knew what he meant, knew *why* he had come back to her with that look upon his face. Now she must tell him why she had let her eyes linger in his. She owed him honesty.

"I did it because you were hurting me, Andrew. . . . I did it to keep you from speaking about *him*."

She felt his eyes upon her back in puzzled anguish.

"I didn't know you knew him ,"

"It sounded as if you did, Andrew."

"I was just afraid that you might want to know him. . . ."

She said nothing; she had vaguely known that this was why he had done it.

"I've never tried to hurt you, Nancy." His voice was injured, as if he really believed what he was saying.

"Yes, you have . . . you have, Andrew."

"But not knowingly," he pleaded.

"Yes, knowingly. And you have hurt me about other things too. . . . You often hurt me."

"About what, Nancy?"

"About being a Fassefern. . . . You've never wanted me to feel that I'm a Fassefern. . . . You want me to think that Willie Weams is my father."

"That's true. . . . I've done that," he admitted after a pause.

"Why, Andrew?"

195

He laughed.

"A cripple would naturally do that if he loved someone. . . . Trying to make things equal. . . ."

She dare not turn round and look at him, she dare not say: "I'm sorry." Andrew would hate it so, to have her sorry for him. It would be better to go on blaming him for things so that he would have to defend himself. Anything was better than to let the flood in her throat get loose. Andrew must not see that she was weeping for him.

She heard a soft thud and knew that he had got off the chair.

"I'll go back to Pitouie, Nancy."

"All right." She managed to say it lightly, working a pencil on the paper before her.

"Come in on Saturday with your report. . . . I won't come back here again."

"All right, Andrew." The "Andrew" almost betrayed her by its quavering. She clenched teeth on teeth hard. If he would only go now. If he only would not speak again in that grey, rain-drenched voice. . . . Oh, Andrew, Andrew, going back with your breaking heart in the rain. . . .

"Won't you walk with me to the stables?" His words came, forced painfully past a barrier in his throat, but bitterly too, striking at her.

"It's raining, Andrew," she said, catching at this for an excuse.

"Not enough to matter."

Why must he crucify himself so? Why must he ask her to walk with him now? Never, not once in all the years that they had known each other, had she walked by his side. Both had taken care to avoid it. Nearly always he would be there first, and seated before she came. Or if he came after her, she would seem not to see him till he was upon his chair.

"It isn't raining in the corridor," he said.

The corridor! Where his boxes would clatter on the stone flags.

She stood up and turned to him. A smile tortured his mouth and his crucified eyes cried to her: "Now here we will see the final agony of Andrew Morrison; now here we will see his last humility."

She met his look, reining back her tears. Wordlessly they went into the corridor together. Never had his boxes made such a noise. Never had he walked so labouredly. With every clatter he seemed to be crying out: "See the cripple that would speak of love; hear his dead legs; hear the wooden crying of his dead, dead legs."

Why could he not spare himself this? Why could not God spare him this? God was not usually so bitter. He had given to hunchbacks a swaggering conceit and to most blemished things a vanity to sustain them. But why had He been so cruel to Andrew? Why had He left him so clear-eyed, so quiveringly able to see his own deformity?

For days ceaselessly the rain coming down, and ever and ever, for hours on end, the organ playing. And always between them the barred door.

She went over each day in her mind again, as she had been doing hour in and hour out ever since he yawned his way out of the library, and Andrew went back to Pitouie in the rain.

The first day he had gone to bed sleepy, leaving orders not to disturb him. She had hoped and hoped to dine with him. But her tray was brought to the library as usual. She looked for a message upon it. But there was none.

She drank her tart wine, blaming it for the tears that came to her eyes, and she told herself that she was glad he was sleeping, as he was sure to be. To-morrow she would pretend to be vexed with him, but she would not really be vexed. . . .

In the morning she heard the organ start at ten o'clock, and knew that he was playing over the music he had written. Very soon he would come bursting in, calling her to come and hear it. . . .

Noon came, and evening. The organ was quiet now, but still he did not come. The door stood barred.

To-day she woke to hear the music of the organ high above the raining. She opened her window wider and stood by it listening. It was victory, glory, splendour: the clash of shield on shield; the cry of a victor, the cry of a lover, the cry of a god!

She had no part in that! She closed the window to shut it out. All day she had been trying to shut it out. All day she had been trying to shut *him* out, to bar him out of her heart. . . .

Oh, torture of uncertainty! This was the hardest thing to bear, this ever-moving quicksand. Had she even the right to be angry with him? It was possible that he had forgotten their kisses, that they meant nothing at all to him. It might be that every time he was inspired he kissed the girl who had inspired him, and hurried away to the organ, forgetting her. Opus Two! He may have written twenty "opuses" and kissed a different girl for each one of them. A kiss could mean no more than that. If he had meant no more than that, then she had no right to be angry at his neglect. . . . All this love, then, was a cob-webbed dream. . . . An artist had kissed her in a moment of ecstasy . . . and in a moment had forgotten it. . . . What right had she to reproach him?

But no! She must have firmer ground beneath her feet. . . . He *did* love her . . . and his kisses had meant all that her kisses had meant. . . . He had come to her with his music. . . . He had fallen asleep, saying: "Don't go

197

away." . . . He would come again when his work was done. . . .

He was following his inspiration, not forgetting her, but remembering her, knowing that she was waiting for him, secure in that thought . . . strengthened by it. . . . She must wait for him, as the fishermen's wives waited till their men came back from sea. . . .

But then again back to the quicksand. . . . He could have sent her a note . . . only one word. . . . But what did he care! . . . Oh, she hated him, she hated him for his indifference and his cruelty. . . . A desperate anger that was more than anger rose in her as she heard the organ peal out again. . . . If she stayed she would run to that barred door and beat upon it with her clenched hands, beating them upon the iron nails till their bleeding washed away this pain. . . . She could not stay. Not a moment more. She could not listen to that hated organ . . . she would go back to Pitouie this night . . . this moment.

She was soon upon the highway walking in the rain. It beat upon her face. The wind sought its way between the buttons of her raincoat and blew upon her angry heart. Her feet, heavy with mud, dragged themselves toward Pitouie.

It would be midnight before she reached it. . . . What story could she give to explain her walking? . . . It did not matter. . . .

The anger was drenched out of her when she reached the Manse gates . . . Nothing mattered but a bed to rest upon.

She pushed her mud-laden boots off at the door and entered in her stocking feet.

There was a light on the floor above . . . left by mistake likely . . . everybody would be asleep by now. . . . She would look in and see old Mrs. Anderson before she went to bed. . . .

As she reached the top of the stairs she was startled to see the minister's wife upon her knees at the bottom of the turret staircase that led to old Mrs. Anderson's rooms.

She was groping and peering at the steps, too engrossed with what she was doing to notice Nancy.

"What have you lost? . . . Your eye-glasses?" Nancy asked, going toward her.

At the sound of her voice the minister's wife let out a scream and sprang to her feet.

"What are you sneaking about like that for . . . terrifying people!" she demanded.

"I wasn't sneaking. I just didn't want to waken anybody. . . . Have you lost something?"

"I wasn't looking for anything," she denied.

Nancy became conscious that there was a light in the spare bedroom and that voices were coming from it.

"Visitors?" she asked, surprised.

"It's *her*—she's fallen down and broken her hip."

It was the voice this was said in that was so terrifying; in some blood-chilling way it connected the fall with that blind groping on the steps. . . . Oh, why had she gone away and left the old woman? . . . She *knew* that something would happen, and now it *had* happened. . . .

"What are you staring at *me* for?" demanded young Mrs. Anderson. Both her hands were clenched as if something were in them that she wished to hide.

"Can I go in and see her?" Nancy asked.

"The doctor's there and Mrs. Boweys, the midwife . . . I suppose you can."

Nancy dropped her wet raincoat upon the landing and went into the room. She could not see the old woman, but she could hear her making little panting sounds. The doctor and Mrs. Boweys were bending over the bed. The minister was bending over it also. They completely hid what was on the bed.

Nancy's feet refused to move a step nearer, nor could she say a word.

"Who came in? Who came in?" cried the old woman. Piercingly she screamed: "Nancy!"

The others turned and saw her. She could see the flushed face of the old woman upon the pillow, and her eyes, black and glittering.

"Come here! Come and hold my hand!" she cried to Nancy, who could not get her feet to move.

"You said you didn't want your hand held," the midwife reminded her irritably.

"We're trying to set her hip," the doctor explained. "We can't get it right, but we can get it better than it is."

Still Nancy could not make a move toward the bed, or get her tongue to say a word. The minister took her and brought her round to the other side of the bed. The old woman held out a clenched fist to her:

"Hold it in both your hands," she commanded.

Nancy took it in both her hands.

"But you're not suffering much now, are you?" the doctor asked. "That medicine should have helped you."

"It isn't hurting me," the old woman answered shortly.

Her eyes were on Nancy's face, trying to say something to her, something that the others were not to know. Nancy tried to understand what it was. The clenched hand moved gently in hers and began cautiously to open. It pushed her hands round till one of them was cupped under it to catch something. It opened, and into Nancy's palm fell several small warm things. Nancy closed her hand over them as the glittering eyes warned her to.

"I won't need you now," said the old woman. "The pain's gone . . . go and rest yourself. . . . I'm sleepy."

Nancy left the room without speaking to the others. As she went out at the door the minister's wife went into the sick-room and shut the door after her.

When she was alone Nancy opened her hand to see what was in it. On her palm lay five little round lead pellets . . . shot! Where could the old woman have got that? . . . What could she need with shot? . . . And why had she given it to her so secretly? . . . Had she had it in her hand when she fell, or did she . . . ? Suddenly Nancy knew. . . . The groping!

She hurried to the turret staircase and felt along the steps. She could find nothing. She mounted them to Mrs. Anderson's room for the lamp and inspected the top steps. On the top one were several small round impressions where a foot had stepped on some round and hard objects, pressing them into the soft wood. On the next were three long strokes in the wood where the round objects had slipped under the foot that rested on them. . . . She felt about in the corner and found two more little lead things that had escaped the short-sighted eyes. . . . So that was how it had happened! . . . The old woman knew, and did not wish her to tell. . . .

Numb with sleep and weariness, she climbed to her room. With wooden fingers she dragged the clammy clothes from her body, and crept into the bed, already half asleep before she had pulled the blankets about her.

It was noon the next day before Mrs. Boweys would let her in to see the old lady. Nancy sat down near the bed, but Mrs. Anderson lay motionless with her eyes closed until Mrs. Boweys had left the room.

"Close the door," she whispered, not opening her eyes.

Nancy obeyed, and came back to her side.

"She put shot on the stair so you would slip . . . I saw the marks," Nancy said. She was holding the old woman's thin-veined hand between her own. First she would raise it to her fresh lips, then press it against her breast, trying to tell by this mute tenderness what she felt.

"I grabbed some as I fell. . . . You didn't say anything about it? Did you?"

"Not yet . . . but your son should know."

"You're *not* to tell." The old woman's voice was firmer than it had been, and she opened her eyes.

Nancy was heartened to see that a glimmer of mischief lurked in them.

"But she should be punished," Nancy protested.

"She *will* be." The old woman chuckled softly. "Better than by telling."

"I can't let you stay here at her mercy. . . . You'll *have* to move now."

The old woman rolled her head irritably:

"You're always going to extremes," she snapped.

"Extremes," cried Nancy, irritated by the old woman's unreasonableness on this score. "She's likely to poison you any day."

"No, she won't. . . . She only wanted to prevent me coming downstairs to my meals, and she's managed that."

The old woman laughed.

"I'm glad you can laugh about it," said Nancy severely. "*I* can't see the joke."

"I never thought she had the wit to do it!" laughed the old woman. She was trying to coax Nancy into seeing the funny side of it. But Nancy would not be cajoled.

"What did you do to make her do it?" she questioned.

The old lady's eyes twinkled at Nancy as if to say, "It's a pity you are such a sobersides."

"Nothing more than usual," she laughed. "Only William liked a text I picked for his sermon. . . ." She chuckled.

Nancy looked at her reproachfully, knowing that nothing but mischief could prompt the old woman to take an interest in William's sermons.

"I helped him write it . . . William thinks I'm a great inspiration to him." The old woman was shaking with mirth at some deep joke.

"You won't move, then?" Nancy asked, knowing well enough that the question was hopeless. The old woman would never move away. She loved the battle too much.

"There you go again!" she cried. "Why would I move? . . . That's the very thing she wants!"

"Then I'm going to tell your son how it happened. I can't go away and leave you with nobody to watch . . ."

"You're *not* to tell! How often have I to tell you that? . . . What good would it do to tell William that his wife tried to kill me? It won't give me a well hip, will it?"

"So you're going to let her go unpunished, and stay here so that she can *poison* you if she has a mind to. . . ."

"I'm telling you she *won't* poison me. Mercy me, bairn, can't you see that she's in a sweat of terror already for fear I know about the shot?"

"That's why she'll kill you," said Nancy stubbornly.

"She won't because I'll let her think that I don't know a thing."

Nancy said nothing. She had no faith at all in the old woman's words. She knew her too well.

After a few minutes of silence the old lady chuckled softly to herself:

"But some fine day when she least expects it, I'll say something to set her nerves jumping. . . . I'll have her on tenterhooks."

"Give it up," Nancy pleaded. "What good will it do you to torment her, if she kills you at last?"

The old lady let out a whoop of a laugh, and, looking at Nancy with wicked, dancing eyes, in a ghostly whisper she said, pointing with her thin forefinger:

"If she *does* . . . I'll come back and put my cold forefinger . . . on the back of her neck!"

This pleased her so well that she shouted with laughter, starting up the hiccoughs which always troubled her. She lay panting and purple with mirth upon the pillow, as Mrs. Boweys ran in and angrily bustled Nancy from the room.

It was Saturday. She went to see Andrew, purposely choosing the busy time in the afternoon so that she would not need to be alone with him. He would have detained her, but she said that she wished to call on Miss Clark that afternoon and must hurry away. Indeed, she *did* wish to call on Miss Clark, for by mentioning Harvey as "one of your old lodgers," she could get the comfort of talking about him. Miss Clark might even tell her things about him when he was a boy, which would bring him within the bounds of understanding, and put firmer ground beneath her feet.

Slattern young Lettie opened the door. Wiping her hands down her sides rhythmically while she spoke, she said that she did not know if Miss Clark could see anybody because she was tied to her bed with the asthma, but she would see. Nancy sat down on the slippery leather-covered sofa to wait, while Lettie, trailing her hands on the wallpaper as she went, mounted the steps to Miss Clark's room.

It was a rare thing for Miss Clark to let the asthma "tie her to her bed." Indeed, for fifteen years, ever since Mr. Robertson had come to lodge with her, she had battled it, keeping on her feet. For to stay in her bed was to deprive herself of pouring his breakfast tea, with fresh white frilling on her cuffs to "set off her hand." But *this* morning that thought had no power to move her from her bed. She had fought for her breath all the night. She was sick. And she was tired. She could not struggle against it any longer, and so she had kept her bed. Lettie from next door could attend to the lodgers, could attend to *him*, to Mr. Robertson himself. Lettie had grown handsome in a slattern way, with too much bosom and too much hip and a careless way of not caring how she displayed them. But men seemed to like that. No doubt they would think it a fine change to be waited on by a young lass, even if she was not over particular about keeping her hands clean.

No doubt *he* would like it, too. It might even be that he would not hide behind his paper saying never a word when he had Lettie to wait on him. He might even crack jokes with her, and maybe even try to kiss her.

Oh, well, she did not care. She was tired. Fifteen years of hoping and waiting, and watching over him, with nothing, not a word of praise since that first day when he had spoken of her frilled cuffs. She was tired of it. Let him go his way. What had she worn herself out for? Why did she bother with lodgers at all when she had enough to keep her? She would send them all away. Send him away, too, and take her ease, and be old, as old as she felt this morning. . . .

She lay back upon the pillow; her tired hands, edged by the frilled cuffs of her nainsook nightdress, lay listless on her breast. She would give them all notice to go on Monday, and until then Lettie could attend to them. . . .

Had Lettie remembered to put very little salt in his porridge? She was such a harebrain, very likely it was as salty as brine. . . . Would she remember to put the tea cosy on the teapot? . . .

What was all that tramping about? They could not be finished already? She strained forward to hear better. Sounded like someone coming up the stairs . . . but that was not likely, they never came back up the stairs, but went right out after they had eaten.

There was a knock on her door. Before she thought she had said, "Come in." Mr. Robertson stood scowling in the door, his morning paper clenched in his hand. He was taken aback when he saw her in the bed, and the scowl fell from his face.

"Are you sick?" he cried, with disheartened astonishment that sought to discredit the evidence of his eyes.

"I've been ailing all this year," she said, not without a secret maliciousness.

"I've never noticed," he stammered guiltily.

"Oh, I wouldn't *expect* you to notice it," she soothed, pleased at the concern in his face.

"What did you want to see me for?" she prompted, as he continued to stand helplessly clenching his paper as if it were the spar that kept him afloat upon a stormy sea.

"Oh"—he tried to recover his scowl—"it's that Lettie. . . . But if you're sick I can put up with it till you're better."

"What's the matter with Lettie?"

"Her hands . . . I've been used . . ." He caught sight of Miss Clark's hands and smiled, gratified.

"You even have frills at night."

She smiled back at him. It was worth it. Oh, it was worth it. He really *had* been conscious of the clean frills all the time. And he could not bear to let another pour his tea with dirty hands. Not even pretty young Lettie. She smiled at him tenderly.

"Sit down," she urged.

And he sought a seat near the bed.

"Will you be in bed long?" His tone was half aggrieved and half pleading. He was only thinking of himself and the way he missed the things that she did for him. She knew this. But that was what men were like, and he was no less dear to her on that account. How would he take it when she told him that she had decided not to keep lodgers any longer. She was not so sure that she meant this now, still, she said, with an underlying glee:

"I'm going to take a long rest. I've decided to give up keeping lodgers."

"I've thought of that," he agreed. "They're a great trouble, and that accountant never lets me read my paper in peace. You'd have less to do with just the one."

So he thought he was to stay on and only the others go.

"I may close the house for a while and go to the seaside."

"You mean that I'm to go?"

"Well, I couldn't very well keep just one lodger. . . . The looks of it . . ."

"But I've been here fifteen years!" he cried aggrievedly.

"It's a long time," she said, with blithe cruelty as she saw his real distress. "I haven't decided if I'll go to Rossorty or Fraserhead."

She was watching him wickedly as she spoke. He looked dumfounded by the way she washed her hands of him. She gloried in this, and lay back with a well-satisfied look on her face.

He could not stand it. To have her turn him from the door and lie there smiling about it. Something must be done.

"I've often meant to speak about it . . . It's been on the tip of my tongue a dozen times, but I thought you would rather go on the way we are!"

She could not believe her ears.

"What way did you mean?" she faltered, her breath halted in her throat. She coughed and fought desperately to regain it. He looked at her, dismayed at her agony, and feeling somehow guilty.

"But I can see that you need a holiday. . . . What I meant was . . ."

He shifted the paper over to his other hand as if to give himself more support. She lay against the pillows trembling in expectation and fear, her breath coming now as if her very will had compelled it to function again.

Nothing must stop him from saying it now that he had begun. But he seemed to be tongue-tied. After a minute he rose to his feet and said:

"Well, the air of Rossorty is said to be good for asthma."

She could not let him go like that. And yet how could she hold him?

"What was it that was on the tip of your tongue a dozen times?"

His face brightened. He took hold of the end of the bed, and from this point of vantage said:

"When people have lived in the same house for fifteen years they might as well get married."

"I think so too," she agreed breathlessly. "You could tell the other lodgers to be moving and we could have the banns cried to-morrow."

"I'll tell them." He let go of the bed-end and walked to the door. "What's your Christian name?"

"Janet."

"All right, Janet," he said, "I'll tell them. . . . I never could stand that accountant."

When the last sound of his steps could be heard no more, her tension relaxed in a long fluttering sigh. She lay back upon the pillow and closed her eyes.

But soon she sat up, coming forward in the bed until she could see herself in the long mirror. An astonishing change came upon her face; she nodded graciously at the mirror and in a crisp clear voice said the mysterious words:

"Thanks; and send it to Mrs. John Robertson." Stifling a yawn daintily to show her phantom wedding-ring, she turned away from the phantom saleswoman behind the phantom counter.

She lay back upon the pillow again as if exhausted by this effort. But once more she sat up, and now she looked alarmed. "Five o'clock!" she cried in that tone of pretended martyrdom which happy wives use. "Oh, dear, John will be simply *furious*! He can't bear to get home and not find me there." Then, with that patronising malice which she had borne all too often from complacent wives, she added: "You single women have all the best of it. Nobody to worry if you never come home." With a satisfied smirk she lay back again.

The best catch in Pitouie! And *she* had landed him. . . .

She could get the frilling by the bolt. . . .

She was debating with herself whether grey taffeta or grey satin would make the richest wedding-dress when Lettie came in to say that Miss Pringle was wanting to see her.

Nancy was in favour of grey taffeta with a grey hat to match. Secretly she wondered about the respirator. If the wedding-day was fair, the respirator could stay at home, forgotten for that once. But if it should be raining? "The bride wore a grey taffeta gown and a black respirator.". . . Or could it be covered with grey velvet for the occasion?

She could not say a word about Harvey. Miss Clark's certainty of happiness seemed to destroy her right to mention him. In the face of such secureness her frail dream vanished. When men loved you they spoke of banns and wedding-rings, they did not forget you for music.

She could not bring herself even to say his name casually; it seemed that if she did this, she would be claiming acquaintanceship with a stranger.

It was settled in her heart that she would go back to Fassefern with all her doors barred against him. She would laugh with him, she might even flirt with him. Oh, yes, she would flirt with him, her kisses had committed her to that. If she did not flirt with him, he might guess that he had hurt her.

Old Mrs. Anderson was past her worst pain, and Mrs. Boweys was to stay and care for her, so Nancy took the bus back to Fassefern on Monday morning.

She was fortified against him by days of reasoning. But she wore her green dress with the green hat that made her amber hair flame like the beech in autumn weather and made her eyes green as the moss-covered stones that lie in shadowed pools.

Still, it was for herself that she wore the green dress. She told herself this at every turn of the bus wheels, and when she stood at the big Gothic door she told herself this again. But for the last time!

He opened the door for her and pulled her in, a fury in his face.

"What have you done this for? Why did you run away?"

He pressed her hard against his breast to staunch a wound that cried its pain in his angry voice:

"Why did you go away? I came to find you yesterday and you were gone."

What could she say to this hurt man, who hurt her too with the bands of his angry arms, but such a different hurting, and so sweet? What could she say?

She said no word, but held her face in a sweet swooning for the storm of his angry kisses, his hurting kisses, his pleading kisses, his tender, his forgiving kisses.

And when he set her on her feet, at last, calmly to ask her again: "Why did you go away?" she kept a little of the wisdom that pain had taught her and smiled upon him, saying only:

"I'm back again. . . ."

This did not comfort him. He wanted security so that he could forget her. He wanted to see her bound, so that he could be free.

"I can't work, when you're so uncertain," he cried petulantly. "I'll never be *sure* now that you are waiting."

Oh, that is very fine, said her heart, that is a very fine thing, if you don't feel sure. And she smiled at him perplexingly. She was a bird perched upon a bough, but ever with wings ready for the open sky. He felt this, as she meant him to feel it.

"If you loved me, you couldn't go off like that," he reproved.

"It was only for three days," she said, as if three days had not been eternity, black with its endlessness and pain. "And, besides, I'll spend the whole day with you. . . . I won't work to-day." She was granting queenly favours, sure of herself, sure of his unsureness. "This is a day to see Rossorty with the sun upon it," she said. "We will go there."

"And take a picnic basket," he cried, grateful and eager, though his wishes had not been consulted.

"No need . . . I know a fishwife who will bake scones for us, and fry fresh herring."

They climbed bareheaded up the rose-coloured cliff between the lime-white cottages. It was a day for drying nets, and a day for mending them. Fishermen's wives with three-cornered shawls upon their heads stretched the nets upon the white walls or sat mending them in the doorways.

A sure-footed donkey, buttressed on east and west with a creel full of cabbages, zigzagged its way up the slope in front of them.

The sun caught the sea spray at the cliff-top in a fitful rainbow, and the air was sonorous with the gentle booming of the sea in the caves beneath them.

The Websters' cottage at the cliff-top was empty, its door gently swinging on its hinges. The weary-willies in its window-boxes were crystalled with the salty spray. Its doorstep, blue-clayed by some kind hand, was unblemished by footprints, as if none but ghosts walked over its threshold. They looked in, and finally went in, stepping carefully over the blue-clayed doorstep.

"Somebody must blue-clay it in memory of the Websters," Nancy said. "Nobody will live here now because the sea has taken all the Websters. They think the cottage is ill-fated."

Harvey smiled, as he always did when she said things like that.

"But *I* don't think so," she said, defending herself against his smile. "I'm going to live here when Fassefern is open to the public and I can't stay there any more."

"It's too mournful with that sea pounding under it all the time," he objected.

"Not for me, I feel at home here, and near to *them*."

"The Fasseferns, or the Websters?" he laughed.

"The Fasseferns . . . their bones lie under this. . . . Come and let me show you the smuggling caves."

They went first to the cliff's sharp edge, and, lying side by side, gazed down upon the "Rumbling Gulch" far below. The sea swirled with frothing lips about the black rocks, sharp teeth, on which the Fasseferns died.

"You see the path that runs down?" she asked him, pointing to a narrow ledge-like path on the face of the cliff. "That leads to the Fasseferns' cave. . . . There are other smuggling caves here, but only a Fassefern could guide a boat through those rocks. The sea is out far enough. . . . Would you like to go down and see the cave?"

"No, I shouldn't like it a bit," Harvey sighed, drawing back from the cliff's edge to regain his feet. "But I see that you're determined to show it to me."

"I *am*," she laughed. "I'll introduce you to my ancestors or die trying to do it."

Protesting mildly, he followed her as she guided him headlong downward by the ragged path that led to the cave.

"Jump," she called back. "It's safe enough."

"Oh, *quite*," he retorted, eyeing with disapproval the crumbling rock which was to receive him.

Her laugh, dancing like a silver ball on the face of the cliff, rose up to him:

"The Fasseferns used to come here at dead of night, when a boat was expected."

"Yes, but I'm merely a Brune," he sighed, "and I would *so* like not to break my neck."

"Oh, you won't," she flung upward, and her bright head disappeared again beneath him.

"It's all right here," she called with many silver voices. "Room for two."

He joined her on a kelp-grown ledge, and warily, step by step, they went along it into a cave, a cave with black sea for a floor, a secret, a catafalque-like cave, dripping with moist green weeds, green arms that reached sinister fingers into the air, feeling, feeling for something.

"This is right under the Websters' cottage. . . . The Websters were lookout men for the Fasseferns in smuggling days. There are probably chests of Spanish gold and jewels at the bottom of this . . . but there are Fassefern bones as well."

"I hate the smell of it," said Harvey. "It smells like a tomb."

"Well, it *is*. . . . This is the back-wash from the gulch," she explained. "It's the Fasseferns' tomb. The sea washes their bones in here to keep them close to home. . . ."

"They're welcome to it. . . . I wouldn't want it to get me, even after I'm dead."

"Oh, it wouldn't *have* you. . . . It takes only Fasseferns," she retorted. "And *we* like it. . . . I want to be here when I'm dead."

He laughed. It was a laugh of indulgent amusement at her expense, but the cave took it from his mouth, and threw it back at them multi-voiced, a hollow yet venomous laugh. Terrified for a moment, they peered into the cave's far recesses, expecting to see the green-boned ghosts who had laughed at them.

"It's just the echo," Nancy whispered.

"Not a bit of it," he said. "It's your nasty old ancestors laughing at me. I don't like them. Let's get out."

He hurried her out, hastening dangerously their steps on the kelp-slippery ledge, until they stood in the sun again, their hands and clothes green-grimed with the sea-moss of the cave.

She was glad to be out. In there it had really seemed that all the Fasseferns laughed at Harvey, disapproved of him. Almost it seemed that they wished to tell her something, to warn her. "Celtic nonsense," she reflected, following Harvey up the cliff.

Soon they were sitting at Mrs. Penny's white scrubbed table, eating fragrant scones and fried fresh herring, while Mrs. Penny herself, a ruffled Cochin China hen, clucked back and forth from table to griddle, baking new scones to set before them.

And finally they went down the cliff to the low-road, leaving Rossorty hanging upon the sky, a mirage picture, behind them, and went back to Fassefern at dusk to music. But to music in which he did not forget her now. All through his playing he kept his eyes upon her face, asking for some deep gift that she could give him. A gift that he must have before wholeness would come to him again. His eyes kept asking her, and his music kept telling her why he asked. But she had need to hear it in words, and she asked:

"That night, you said . . ."

"Whatever I said that night isn't true," he answered, his eyes begging her to believe him.

"But you said you must not be lost."

"Words."

This warmed her, so she confessed:

209

"I was jealous of your music, Harvey, that was why I ran away."

It was not wise to say this, but the need of wisdom was past, was quite past, surely.

"No need to be jealous," he said. And after a while:

"*You* are my music."

She knew this was not true, but her heart was seduced by the sweet thought that it might some day be true.

"I've done my best work for you . . . this suite . . . nothing else I've done is so good. . . . And when I finished I came to look for you."

Reproach hung in the air after his words.

How foolish her running away seemed. How childish. . . . Narrow heart that could not understand, slow heart that needed words, blind heart that must see banners flying to know that love has come.

Still, she *did* need words, guide-posts, for fear she might lose her way again, and so:

"When did you love me first? . . . What was the very first moment?"

"When I took the beech-nuts out of your hand."

Ah, but she had loved him since he stood against the waterfall whistling the Barcarolle! Some day she would tell him this, some safe day. To-day was beglamoured, but it was not safe, not yet. There was a place past all this, where she could tell him honest things, but they could not reach that place till the asking in his eyes was answered. And she was afraid of the asking in his eyes . . . not afraid, but not ready with the answer. . . . Not yet. . . . This waiting was sweet. . . . It would be sweet to wait always. . . .

So beglamoured day followed on beglamoured day, till a sharp night came, and the asking in his eyes flared to rebellion:

"No, damn it, I can't play. . . . Can't you see? . . . *Don't* do that!" He broke her hands down as they reached to his hair.

"Harvey!"

"I'm sorry, but I'm only human."

This was blaming her. And he should not be blaming her. She was not refusing . . . only, only she did not know. . . . He could break his way through to the answer in her, and she would be glad . . . but she could not find it for herself. . . . Why was he so apart and angry, so as if she had injured him?

"I'm going out." He jumped to his feet.

"May I come, Harvey?"

"God! *No*." He jerked his head up like a pained beast. The fierceness of his voice ran through her, a red thread of sweet fire, calling from some deep place the answer to his savage need.

"Harvey!"

But he was gone . . . out through the long window . . . hurrying away from her, a black slender swiftness under the clear moon.

She sat down in the deep chair by the window. Her eyes, surrendering and bemused, watched the moon-clear path for his return.

BOOK IV

The trees along the drive flamed with autumn, yellow and orange and rich dark red. No wind had come yet to shake the leaves and spread them in a glowing patchwork quilt upon the ground. They were warm with their fullest beauty still.

The summer had gone by with breathless, almost with treacherous, haste. Why need it have hurried so? Nancy thought of all the summers that had lagged, taking their time with primroses, with bluebells, with sweetbriar roses, and lingering at the long length with the heather purple upon the hills. Giving each flower its slow opening time, and its long blooming, unhurriedly. But this summer, *her* summer, where had it gone flying on swift feet?

She tried to see it day by day, to bring it back step by step as it had fled away, but it would come back only as one big haze of happiness, golden and sweet and warm, it would not be broken up and examined.

She wondered if Harvey had noticed that autumn was here. She wondered if he remembered that in only a few weeks he must leave Fassefern and she must leave it also. But to go where? To go up to Webster's cottage on the cliff-top, or away to the Continent with Harvey. Surely it would be to the Continent, for how could they part now even for a little while?

She could hear the organ. He was playing a piece of his own, a piece full of suppressed irritation, restless, almost bad-tempered: "my headache" he called it laughingly one day when she asked its name.

He was playing longer than usual this morning, an hour longer almost. She wanted to go to him, but felt a timidity about interrupting, though that was foolish. He had told her many times that she did not "interrupt," that only she out of all the world could come to him without "interrupting." "You never destroy me, you build me." He had said that over and over through the summer months. Still, she hesitated.

He had not composed anything all summer, nothing since that first week . . . but it was enough . . . *he* said it was enough. "I must have periods of lying fallow," he had said, "I'll work all the better for this, I'm absorbing."

212

He had practised, of course, hours every day, but he had not been lost in his music, he would always know when the time was up and come to her, glad to get out and walk upon the windy road with her. Glad to walk in the sun, or through bracken-scented woods, glad to sit by the fire on rainy days reading to her. These were almost the happiest days, the days when rain made silver bars enclosing them together, holding all the world away.

It was strange that she had always this timidity about interrupting him, a sort of slumbering guilt, always on the verge of awakening, no matter how he tried to reassure her. Even when he left the organ of his own accord to come with her, she found herself making great efforts to please him, as if she had somehow to make up to him for a wrong she was doing him. "It's because it isn't in me to be unreservedly happy," she would tell herself. But still she could not dispel the feeling that she was guilty toward him in proportion to her happiness, and that a day of reckoning must come. Sheer nonsense of course. How could her love hurt him?

She went to the organ-room and stood silently behind him. He played on for a moment, not knowing she was there. Her eyes travelled over him, worshipping the slim long length of him, and the upward-held head, so dear, so deeply dear.

He felt her behind him and turned round, not smiling, still with that caged look which he had when he played "my headache," but coming out of it to her quickly, and quickly answering her smile.

"You have practised a long time to-day."

"Not long enough. I can't play."

She smiled at that.

"I *must* get some honest work done."

"Do I hinder you, Harvey?" Her slumbering guilt started up in her words.

"No, darling, no . . . I'm just weak-minded." He clasped her to him, kissing her to wipe out the suggestion that she hindered him. But a minute later he looked moodily toward the organ again:

"I've got to get seriously to work. . . . All these concerts, and nothing ready."

"I'm going to Pitouie to-day to be gone for a week." She offered it hastily.

"Oh, it isn't your being here . . . it's something in myself. . . ."

"You're sure?"

He kissed her again for answer.

"I'm sorry I came . . . but I'm leaving at four. I'll go away now and let you work."

"No use! I can't concentrate in little snatches . . . and you're going. . . ."

"But it's four hours yet . . . you can be working."

"*Hours* are nothing . . . I need days . . . months."

"You'll have a whole week, anyway," she said, still accepting the blame though he did not put it upon her.

It was strange to go back to Pitouie. She seemed cut off from it by centuries of time. Nothing seemed the same, because *she* herself had changed so much.

It disturbed her not at all that Pitouie was whispering and nudging over her, and discussing Harvey and his "intentions." Pitouie's opinion could not matter to her any more, she was beyond it. But she was not beyond Divot Meg's opinion! Sometimes she was tempted to go to the White Ship and tell Divot Meg about her love, but she always put it off till she could go and say: "I've come to tell you that I'm to be married next week." This would be the easiest way to start such a conversation, and would put a dignity upon their love that it could not have without this.

She wanted to tell old Mrs. Anderson also, but she put off telling her for the same reason. Though the old woman would question her avidly about Harvey. So avidly in fact that she had to lie carefully to keep the old woman from knowing: "Yes, I see him, but only rarely. Only when we happen to run into each other in the corridors." "No, I don't think it is queer of him to be so solitary." "Well, perhaps I'm not the kind that attracts men." Mrs. Anderson was not wholly deceived by these answers, but she was silenced by them.

Mrs. Boweys, the nurse, was permanently at the parsonage now. It was thought by the village that she was there to take care of the old lady, but in truth she was taking care of the minister's wife.

A blight had fallen on young Mrs. Anderson. She lived in terror of death. Everyone was trying to kill her. When Nancy came she would whisper her fears, plucking nervously at her sleeve:

"Do you know that they're trying to poison me? . . . *She's* doing it."

Nancy would try to soothe her, pointing out that "she" could not leave her bed, being crippled for life by her fall, and could not possibly poison her. But this would only start a new terror. Clutching Nancy hard, she would whisper:

"She tries to make me fall . . . she puts shot . . ."

But at this point some dim instinct to guard herself would stop her, and she would glare at Nancy suspiciously:

"What has she been telling you about shot?" she would scream. "It's a lie, it's a lie!"

Nancy wondered if the minister guessed what lay under these ravings. But William went his way as usual, giving each bite its required number of chews at meal-times, preaching the same bilious sermons about the same flaccid God, and making his customary rounds to "comfort the sick and dying." If he knew anything he never betrayed that he knew it. His wife's behaviour was always "nervousness."

On the third day that she was back at Pitouie, Nancy went down to the library to see Andrew. She barely expected to find him there, for it was feeing market-day, and sometimes the revelry of drunken farm-hands made it wise to close the library. But he *was* there, and he was alone. She was glad of this. She missed Andrew. Every time she came down she tried to restore their old friendship, and carry it back to what it had been before they went to Fassefern. But Andrew always prevented it. He had been entrenched behind a wall of flippancy all summer. It was rarely she had an honest word with him now.

But this morning he was more the old Andrew, and willing to talk. She was glad when he said, smiling a little crookedly, but with friendly eyes:

"And must I get a new assistant in October?"

"I don't know, Andrew." She looked at him freely, hiding nothing. "Harvey is not good at planning practical things." She smiled. "We'll be married, of course, but I think *I* will have to arrange it."

"He hasn't proposed yet?" Andrew was turning a paper-cutter over and over in his hand, his eyes, directed upon it earnestly, did not lift to her face as he spoke.

"Proposed! Oh, Andrew!" she laughed teasingly. "Down on his left knee with his hand upon his heart? . . . 'Will you be mine for ever!'"

Andrew conceded a smile, but a very faint smile.

"Harvey and I understand each other . . . we don't need proposals and engagement rings."

"Nor marriage ceremonies?" Andrew's eyebrow asked the question more pertinently than his words.

"Oh, yes, marriage ceremonies in due season," she admitted, and, laughing softly, asked, "Are you trying to warn me against Harvey, Andrew?"

Andrew flushed. A flicker of annoyance passed over his face.

"Oh, no!" he denied. "Nevertheless," he added, and he smiled crookedly to take away the suggestion that he was being a moral adviser, "nevertheless, I advise you to limit his privileges till after the ceremony."

"You think that love is right or wrong because of a ceremony?"

"Oh, no, my dear. But it is wise or foolish because of a ceremony. 'Good' women make the marriage bargain first."

"This from *you*, Andrew. . . . You know that you despise calculating women."

"Still, I concede their wisdom in a world where men hold women lightly who give themselves without this barter." Andrew's voice was as cool and glinting as the edge of the paper-knife.

"Harvey doesn't hold me lightly," she cried fiercely, betraying herself into his hands.

But Andrew was the one who looked betrayed. His eyes were heavy with shame. He could not lift them to her face.

"I didn't know," he muttered. "I wouldn't have spoken . . ." He was pushing the knife along the grooves of the table with a desperate aimlessness.

"I'm not ashamed of love, Andrew," she said, compelling him to meet her proud eyes.

"No, Nancy, no," he stumbled, trying to hide from her brave face, but she would not let him hide.

"You are ashamed for me!"

"No!"

But the way he said it sank into her breast painfully.

"You think that Harvey holds me lightly!" She thrust the words, glinting like a spear, toward him.

He winced.

"No!"

But his eyes moved away, leaving her to feel that he *did* think this.

"You don't *know* Harvey. . . . He is different." A faint tone of pleading stole into her voice, although it was still proud.

Andrew's lips formed themselves to say bitter things at the mention of Harvey's name, but he held his peace and sat staring past her through the window, his eyes pale with looking hard at things they did not wish to see.

"Andrew, it isn't a tragedy." She was trying to cheer him, though her heart ached drearily.

"Will you go now, Nancy?" he asked.

"You're sending me away, Andrew?"

"He's here." She followed his glance out of the window and saw Harvey getting out of his car and coming in through the library gate.

Her drearily aching heart quickened at the sight of him. How silly of her to be depressed by Andrew. What did he know of love?

"It's Harvey," she cried unnecessarily, but unable to keep from saying it.

"So I observed," Andrew answered dryly.

"He . . . do you want to see him?"

"I can survive if I don't."

"Well, then . . . do you mind?" But she did not care if he minded. She

216

must get to Harvey at once and stand close to him so that the current which flowed from him to her could fill her with happiness again and stop this ache which Andrew had started.

She met him in the little outer room. He had his caged look, as if he might burst bars at any minute and declare something, but she was too blind with her own need for comfort to see this.

"Harvey, oh, Harvey, you came just when I needed you." She was pressing her face like a frantic child against the Donegal tweed of his coat, which smelled faintly of peat.

"What's the matter?"

"Nothing! Nothing now," she laughed gaspingly. "Andrew was being cynical about love. . . . This is silly of me."

He soothed her with mechanical tenderness, his mind still adjusting itself.

"Poor chap, I'd be cynical about most things in his place."

"He had me all ready to quaff the hemlock cup," she laughed, quite restored again.

"Poor chap, I suspect he's in love with you."

"Oh, it wasn't about that . . . and I don't think he is . . . not now."

"Well, if he ever was, you can be sure he still is. . . . It isn't very easy to stop loving you."

"Have you been trying to?"

"With no success, as you see," He bowed, chivalrously mocking, but there was a current of irritation behind his words. He took her arm and guided her out toward the car without asking if she could leave.

"Why did you come?" she cried, still marvelling at this unexpected happiness.

"I had things to say to you."

"Dreadful things, by the look of your face," she mocked up at him, her feet almost dancing in their joy to be walking by his side.

"We'll go for a drive." He was putting her unceremoniously into the car as he spoke. She laughed at his moody face. She was too happy to be troubled by it.

"Mr. Brune," she said with that polite manner of nonsense which she used when her heart was overflowing, "if you didn't look so fierce, I *might* be induced to mention that I'm rather fond of you."

"Mention away," he said, with a half-smile.

"Not with so little encouragement," she objected.

He said nothing to that. And her mood was stayed for a moment, but it burbled up again irrepressibly.

"Any slight mention that you might make of your emotions toward me would be most gratefully received, Mr. Brune."

He smiled widely at her nonsense, but hastily withdrew the smile again, as if determined to maintain a mood.

"May I dare to hope that you love me?"

"You may," he said, laughing outright despite himself and turning to her with a begrudging but surrendering face.

"You're such a little fool."

"Yes," she agreed brightly.

They drove on a while in silence.

"You know, Nancy, we can't go on like this . . . I haven't done any work all summer." He was gathering his mood back again, as if bent on putting something through.

"You were going to work all this week," she reminded him.

He moved irritably.

"I know, but I came to talk to you about that."

"What, Harvey?" Her face was turned up to him in an effort to be grave and discuss whatever clouded thing he had upon his mind. But her face would not be grave, happiness lurked in all its curves, and sighed from her parted lips.

He looked at her, and seemed to shift his ground.

"Nothing really . . . an excuse to see you."

But she saw through that.

"There *was* something."

"It's really my fault, not yours," he parried. "A musician should be a Trappist monk."

She sat a while thoughtful.

"I'll let you be a Trappist monk, Harvey."

"By desire, I mean. . . . It's no use when I don't *want* to be one."

"Did you *used* to be a 'Trappist monk'?"

"Pretty much."

"And you got more work done?"

"Yes . . . and I've got to regain my singleness of purpose . . . somehow."

"How 'singleness'?"

"I've got to stop loving you so much." He said it laughingly, though there was a fringe of accusation in the words as well.

"I shouldn't like that," she laughed uncertainly, surprised that tears wanted to come into her eyes. Silly of them! This was just a conversation. He could not stop loving her just because he decided that he should.

Their aimless driving had brought them to a place on the kirk brae road which was opposite the marketplace. Through the screen of trees the softened sound of a calliope rose up to them.

"The feeing market?" cried Harvey. "Is it the feeing market?"

Manhood had fallen away from his face, discarded like a mask that had never fitted, and he was the Whistling Boy again.

"Oh, let's go, Nancy!"

A few moments ago she would have loved this change in him, but now it hurt that he could say: "I must stop loving you so much," and in the next breath turn joyously to the feeing market, leaving her with that thrust still aching and unassuaged. How deftly he could wound, and how quickly turn away!

"You don't want to go?" he asked in disappointed tones.

"Oh, yes, I do," she hastened. And she really *did* wish to go. She liked feeing markets. But she would go more happily if he said: "I was talking rot, I couldn't stop loving you! And I don't want to stop." But she could not trouble this eager little boy with such grown-up emotions. He belonged to another time, and was not concerned with love.

They left the car by the roadway and walked up the lane which led to the market square.

As they neared the end of the lane, Divot Meg came out of the market. She had been making the rounds of the vendors' stalls and sideshows, in order to estimate how many lodgers she might expect for the night. And to advertise her lodging-house to those new wayfarers who had not yet heard of the White Ship.

Nancy could see by the lively way that her eyes dwelt on Harvey that she had heard the gossip about the two of them. She tried to smile at her, but Meg did not look her way, but passed them, still giving the tail of her eye to Harvey. Nancy was sure that she stopped to look after them, but she did not turn her head because she wanted Meg to look her fill. It made her feel happy that Meg had seen them together, and had got such a good look at Harvey.

The market was past its height when they arrived. Children had eaten and yelled through the hot hours of the day and now were subdued and fretful. Farmhands, with their early morning hilarity dying down, were inclined to be quarrelsome. Candy vendors lashed at the flies which crowded upon their wares and cried shrilly to know if the yokels had glue in their pockets or why was it so hard for them to get a penny out. The man at the heavy-hammer machine taunted in vain; nothing would make the farmhands part with a shilling to show that they could drive the marker flying to the top to ring the bell. No use for the bespangled barker to cry the wonders of the one and only mermaid in captivity. Everyone had poked at her with an inquiring finger, and all knew that her tail was only the skin of a white shark varnished to make it shine, and several had seen her stretching her legs between acts behind the sideshow tents.

The paths between the vendors' stalls were ankle-deep in paper bags and discarded gewgaws. Some of the shows were already packing up to take the road again before sunset. The "Beautiful Queen of Bareback Riders" sat on a small beer-barrel, eating a blood-pudding. From the spigot between her feet she filled a tin cup with beer and drank thirstily. No more performances to-day; she could drink all she liked.

"It wasn't like this when we were kids, was it? It used to seem grand. Didn't it?" said Harvey.

"And much bigger," said Nancy. "I used to think the feeing market was an endless fairyland going on and on for miles and miles. I never thought of it as a few stalls in the middle."

"And the bareback riders with spangles and tights; surely they weren't painted old hags too."

"I wish we hadn't come," said Nancy, a sadness creeping into her heart. There had always been a glamour in feeing markets for her as a child. Her earliest memory was mixed up with bright balloons and spangled ladies, with merry-go-rounds and loud music, and her mother, her yellow-haired mother who had left her side and disappeared in all the glitter and glory of a feeing market. Gone away perhaps to be a shining princess on a swaying elephant. . . .

Was it into this tawdry thing that she had gone, into this garish "fairyland" where "Beautiful Queens" sat on beer-barrels eating blood-pudding and scratching themselves?

"God! How can a white woman do that!" Harvey's face was pale with distaste.

Nancy looked where he was looking. A downward rushing fear almost bore her to her knees, and her ears roared like caves into which a wild sea was pounding. Memory went tearing its painful way back to the day when her mother had left her to mount just such a platform. . . . A negro medicine-man was calling his wares. On the platform by him sat a woman, a white woman, holding the bottles of medicine for the crowd to see. . . . "God, in your mercy, God, in your mercy, make it not my mother! Make it not . . ."

Was it, was it her mother? No! No! It was not, it could not be her mother. Her mother's eyes were blue and always flecked with laughter. Her mother's hair had glinted with gold and curled about her head. This woman's eyes were no colour. They were flat and glazed like the agate brooches in the watchmaker's window. . . . Round pieces of cold agate set in a face long dead. . . . Two agate tombstones guarding the secret dead. . . .

No! No! This was not her mother. . . . Her mother's hair had been something to wonder at and reach for in the sunlight. . . . This woman's hair was like cold ashes . . . broken wings about a dead face. . . .

No! It was not her mother: "Oh, God, I thank Thee, I thank Thee!"

"Let's get away from here, Nancy. . . . That woman! . . . God, how *can* women degrade themselves so!"

His arm was about her as if to make a barrier between her and such ugliness. Possessively, he steered her through the untidy tumult of the market out into the lane that was bordered with honey-suckle spilling over the walls of gardens on either side.

"Did you hate it as much as that, dear?" he said, as he saw her drained face.

"Harvey!" Oh, why did she have to tell him? Couldn't she ignore this thing that cried that he must know? It was not her mother, so why need she tell? "Harvey, you saw that woman?"

"Terrible creature. I shouldn't have let you see her. . . . Forgive me."

"Harvey, do you love me?"

He laughed:

"Must I show you here, with Mrs. Walker picking gooseberries for a pie, and pretending not to see us?"

"Just tell me."

"I love you." He looked inquiringly at her white, earnest face.

"No. . . . Don't look at me, Harvey, while I tell you this. . . . You saw that woman. . . . My mother went away with a negro medicine-man when I was six."

"Nancy!"

"Don't look at me, Harvey. . . . I thought at first that that woman was my mother. . . ."

"God!"

"No! No! She isn't my mother, but my mother did what that woman is doing. . . . So you see . . ."

"See what, dear?"

"That is the other side of me . . . the side that isn't Fassefern."

"It isn't *any* side of you. . . . It's got nothing to do with you. . . . You are all Fassefern. You are Nancy. My Nancy. . . ."

"Is that true? It doesn't make any difference?"

"How could it? I love you."

"I'm glad I told you."

"Let's forget it"

"Where do you suppose my mother is now?"

"Dead, let us hope."

"If she were alive, Harvey? If that were she . . . what then?"

"Need we bother about that, dear? It isn't a pleasant subject."

"You said it made no difference."

"It doesn't. But need we dwell on all the horrible possibilities?"

"I think I'm going to dwell on them after to-day."

"Why after to-day?"

"I never realised before how terrible it is. . . . That woman looked . . . she looked like something dead . . . yet moving."

"She's a drug addict, that's why."

"My mother might be that."

"Perhaps so." His voice was tinged with irritation, and he quickened his step as if some thought needed a hurried action to keep pace with it. Nancy walked faster also. She had the feeling that he was running away from something. Running away from her, and that she must hurry, hurry, and hold on lest he escape her altogether.

Why had she told him? He hated unpleasant things. He always hurried away from them. But it is necessary to be honest, isn't it? It would have been wrong not to tell him, wouldn't it?

"Were you sorry that I told you, Harvey?"

"No, of course not."

"I *had* to tell you. Hadn't I?"

"Why *had* to?"

"It would have been deceiving you if I hadn't. Wouldn't it?"

"I don't think so."

"But you would have told *me* if it had been your mother. Wouldn't you?"

"I wouldn't have remembered it," he said.

And she knew that this was the truth. Harvey would have forgotten it. Harvey would never remember anything that caused him pain. If grief came to him he would go to his organ and drown it in floods and floods of music until all trace of it, all memory of it, was for ever wiped away, and it existed at last only as a nameless thread of pain in a tapestry of sound.

She was sorry now that she had forced this knowledge upon him. She must learn that Harvey was not to be leaned upon. He could love with her, dream with her, play with her, laugh with her, but he could not, and would not, sorrow with her. She must do that alone.

"Will you come to the parsonage for dinner?" she asked, as they reached the place on the street where his blue car stood waiting.

"No, I can't; I must go back to Fassefern . . . I must write the end of the third movement."

He was holding the door open for her. "Hop in . . . I have to work hard when you're not there, so that I can play when you *are*." He smiled at her, and she felt that he was smiling because he had been able to put it so nicely. He was smiling because he could hurry away from her and the thought of her mother, and yet leave her pleased with his reason for going.

They reached the parsonage gates. She forbore to ask him again to stay, and jumped out quickly, not waiting for him to help her.

"All right, I'll see you the day after to-morrow," she said, quite gaily. He held her hand. He seemed grateful to her for being gay.

"Don't be longer than that," he urged.

"No! . . . Get a lot of work done."

"I will." He climbed back into the car. "Au revoir, darling."

"Au revoir."

He slipped in the clutch and was off. She lingered in the gate, watching. Would he look back? Would he? Would he? It was so important that he should remember to look back to-day. The bend of the road . . . now! No! He was gone. He had not looked back . . .

He was glad, glad to get away from a girl who had a mother like that, and who insisted on remembering her, insisted on talking about her . . .

She turned in at the gate. She was tired, tired. Oh, if Harvey's arms would only be a shelter . . . But that would never be. They were arms to demand, arms to thrill, but never, never arms to comfort. . . .

At dusk the Tinker's Kitchen in the White Ship was heavy with the mixed odours of fried herring, fried steaks, and fried sausage. Kale was boiling at the back of the stove with a ham-bone in it. And above all other smells there rose the pungent smell of boiling turnips. Hungry vendors sat about waiting for the frying-pan. Divot Meg, a sharp-tongued justice, stood by to see that there was fair play, and that no customer slipped ahead and took another's turn, also that each wiped out the frying-pan with the newspaper which was put there for the purpose.

It had been a poor market, and some grumbled about the price of the beds. Others decided to move on that night to the next town after having eaten. A row started between the Heavy-Hammer Machine Man and the owner of the Hurdy-Gurdy. The Hurdy-Gurdy Man's monkey made a blunder past excuse on the back of the Heavy-Hammer Machine Man's neck. He threw the chattering creature at its owner in his fury. They were at each other's throats in a minute. But Divot Meg, making good use of her feet, had them separated in no time.

"This is a place for ladies and gentlemen, I'll have you know. Anybody that's got fighting to do can do it on the street," she yelled, as she deftly lashed out with her feet, managing by years of practice to land them on the most painful places.

This quieted, a hullabaloo started in the lobby. The Home-Made Candy Wifie was screaming:

"I'll not be housed with a nigger, I'm telling you . . . I'm a lady born and bred."

Divot Meg pushed her way out to the lobby, her fists and feet ready to settle whatever they might encounter. The Negro Medicine-Man and his white woman had come in. The Home-Made Candy Wifie was barring their way, and crying out that if such dung were to be housed here, she was going to leave. The white woman was taking no part in the argument, but was trying in a sort of stupor to seat herself upon the floor. But the negro was holding her up on one side and the Home-Made Candy Wifie was kicking her up on the other.

Divot Meg threw the Candy type out of the way:

"No black men here," she told the negro. "Your woman can stay if she likes, but you'll have to find other quarters."

"Let's move on, Snowey," said the negro to the woman.

But she had managed at last to slide to the floor, and was sitting with legs stretched out before her, back against the yellow ochred wall.

"I'm staying here," she announced thickly.

"I'm going on," he warned her.

"Go on, then," she retorted sullenly.

He kicked her on the hip: "Get up, you scabby slut!"

She paid no attention to the kick, but settled down, seeming about to sleep.

"Here!" The negro drew a small package of something from his pocket and threw it into the woman's lap. Her hands seized upon fit rapaciously and thrust it into her bodice. It was startling to see her move so quickly in the midst of her half-sleep.

"Come on now, Snowey. You can take it as we go," he urged.

"I'm staying here!" she yelled, with amazing vigour. "Do you hear me, you stinking coal-bag. I'm staying here!"

He raised his foot to kick her again, but Divot Meg pushed him toward the door.

"No more of that," she warned. "Make your feet your friend now, before I get the police."

But he would not be pushed from the door. He shoved past her and got the woman by the shoulders.

"Come on." He tried to pull her to her feet.

"Then give it back," he cried as she resisted him. He tried to reach in her bodice, but she rolled out of his grasp and with unlooked-for speed rose to her feet and ran up the rickety stairs to the floor above. The negro would have followed her, but Divot Meg dragged him down and pushed him backward out of the door, where he fell blasphemously on the pavement. She swung the bar across the door to keep him out, and ran upstairs after the woman.

The door of her sick man's room was open. The negro's woman was standing in it, crying:

"My God, Sandy Tocher, you're no' dead yet."

The negro's woman advanced into the queer-smelling room and sat on the sick man's bed. He sat, spectre-like, looking at her, his silent mouth open in a soundless crying.

Divot Meg followed her in.

"How comes it that you know my man?" she demanded, looking at the woman's toothless face for some sign to know her by.

The woman was snuffing something that looked like sugar up her nose.

"Why wouldn't I know him?" she grumbled. "It's losing my teeth makes me look so bad. . . . That damned nigger pulled them . . . the first nigger, I mean, the one that sold Jujah for painless teeth. . . . When trade was bad, and nobody else would volunteer, he pulled one of my teeth. I had to look as if it didn't hurt me so that they would buy his medicine. . . . I left him. . . . But this one's just as bad. . . . Have some? . . ." She pushed the white powder at the frail silent ghost, and laughed shrilly. Her eyes were brightening.

"Who are you?" Divot Meg demanded, but she could have answered the question herself.

"You haven't changed much, Meg . . . still the same ugly bitch that Willie Weams jilted." The woman laughed, "And small blame to him."

"Bella Pringle! So you're back again."

"For good. . . . I never let on to the nigger that I came from here. . . . He would never have come if he'd known it." She laughed wildly in a short gust, then stopped. "Is my mother living?"

"No."

"And my lassie?"

"She's living."

"Married?"

"Not yet."

"All the better. I need somebody to take care of me."

"You're going to let her know?"

"Let her know what?"

"That you're her mother?"

"Don't you suppose I have a mother's feelings?"

"You've taken quite a while to remember them."

"Taunting me! Taunting me!" cried Bella, and she started to whimper. "You're taunting me because I've had a lot of bad luck and lost my teeth. . . . But my lassie will love me just the same."

"Your lassie's grown up to be a fine lady with an education. . . . She runs the library with Andrew Morrison."

"That cripple that used to trail his legs. . . . I thought he was training for a doctor. . . . And *he's* living with my lassie!"

"No, he's working with her. She lives at the parsonage."

"With the minister?"

"And his wife."

"I'm going to see her. . . . She won't taunt her poor mother." Snuffing up more of the stuff that was white like sugar, she put the rest of it in her bodice and stood up.

"Wait, Bella," said Meg, pushing her into a chair. "Let's have a drink together. . . . You can't leave like this. . . . We haven't celebrated your coming back."

"I'm going right to my lassie," said Bella determinedly, and made for the door.

Meg followed her, shutting her man's door after them.

"Bella, come in here," she urged. "Come in here and let me lend you a better-looking hat."

"Away," said Bella, pushing off her hand. "My lassie will like me the way I am."

"You'd look none the worse for a comb through your hair, though, and a clean face."

"What's the matter with my face?" Bella demanded belligerently.

"Come in here and look at it," said Meg, opening her bedroom door.

Bella went in after her, and peered curiously in the small square mirror which hung on the wall.

"God damn that black b——," she said, rolling back her lips to stare at her toothless gums. "I'd not look so bad but for my teeth."

"You look fine. It's just that you're tired and dirty with the market dirt. . . . Sit down, I'll get some water to wash you, and a drink of whisky."

"I will, then," Bella consented, sitting down in a chair. "We've been on the road ten days. It's hard to get a place to sleep on account of his black skin, so it's been a hedge or a hay-rick every night . . . and up at daylight and on again. . . . But I'm finished with it. . . . From now on I'll bask in the sun and lie in a bed. . . . I'll be no black b——'s fancy woman."

"What name was that the nigger called you by?" asked Meg.

"Just a fancy name," said Bella shortly.

"Did you go by his name?" Meg persisted.

"I never went by *any* name. I was just his woman."

"But I suppose he knew your real name all right. He would never have taken up with you without knowing your name."

Bella laughed, "I've had a dozen names since I left Pitouie. . . . I was just Snowey to him . . . just Snowey."

"A queer kind of name. . . . How did you come by it?"

"What the hell is that to you?" said Bella, suddenly irritated.

"Oh, nothing, nothing. No offence meant, Bella," Meg said. She fumbled in a kist behind the bed, finally bringing out a bottle of whisky, which she set on the table.

"No offence meant; I was just interested. . . . Open this and take a mouthful while I get the water, then we'll have a drink together."

Bella laughed, a shrill, uncalled-for laugh, a laugh that sounded as if she had no knowledge of its cause, or control of its duration. It snapped off again as suddenly as it had begun.

When Meg came back with a wooden washtub filled with hot water, Bella was pulling her clothes off, and groaning with relief as the busks of her heavy corsets sprang open. She seemed to have forgotten her hurry to go.

"That's right, Bella, take off your shoes and all, and put your feet in this tub . . . there's nothing so resting as getting your feet in warm water."

"Away, away!" Bella's eyes were glittering. "There's nothing that rests you like this. . . ." She held out the little packet. "Take some, if you're a friend of mine. Take some," she commanded. "But you're *not* a friend of mine, you red-headed, easy-to-get bitch, you never were a friend of mine."

"I'll show you if I'm a friend of yours," cried Meg. "Give me some of it, whatever it is. I'll take this with you . . . and you drink whisky with me. Turn about's fair play."

"Turn and turn about," shrilled Bella piercingly. "Turn and turn about. . . . Hold your hand, Meg."

Meg held her palm out. And Bella, jerking and squealing in unreasonable glee, shook some of the white powder on to it, screaming:

"Snuff it up! Snuff it up!"

Meg raised both her palms to her nose, carefully sliding the empty palm over the one that held the powder, and snuffed loudly and greedily, while Bella slapped her hips and laughed in a high key.

"There!" cried Meg. "Now you take a drink with me. Turn and turn about."

"Turn and turn about," screamed Bella.

"Put your feet in the water while we drink," advised Meg.

227

And Bella with a suddenness that took Meg's breath away jumped into the water, shoes and all, and sat with a hard clap on the bottom of the tub, sending the water splashing on all sides. But she carefully held her hand with the packet of powder high above her head.

"Whoops adaisy," she yelled, thumping the side of the tub with her free hand. "Look at the canary in her bath, Meg! Look at the canary! Tweet, tweet!"

"Drink this with me," said Meg, handing her a glass of whisky. "Here's to Bella Pringle, the bonniest lassie in Pitouie."

"I was *that*, I was *that*!" cried Bella. "You never could hold a candle to me for looks, Meg, though the men liked you the best."

"Who cares about men?" cried Meg. "Drink up, Bella. To hell with men!"

"To hell with them, black or white," screamed Bella, and drank the whisky, gulping it ferociously as if she hated it, but wanted to get it past her throat as soon as possible.

"Come, sit up on the chair, Bella." She slipped her hands under Bella's arms and hoisted her up to the chair.

"I'll take your shoes off and dry them."

"You're a good friend to me, Meg."

"Now put your feet back in the warm water . . . that's the lass."

"You're a good friend, Meg, you're a good friend to me."

"Havers!" said Meg. "Didn't we grow up together?"

"We did that. . . . That was the happy time, Meg." Bella was talking in a lower key now. The splash in the warm water had made her sleepy. She lay back in the chair while Meg kneeled on the floor, washing her legs.

"Whatever became of Willie Weams?" she asked after Meg had dried her legs and pulled away the tub.

"He's still on the road. I saw him last year with a stallion at Callochie." Bella laughed sleepily and yawned:

"My God, I'm tireder than a man that has stood the thrashing machine all day."

"Look, Bella, why don't you go to bed here and get a good sleep."

"But I'm going to see my lassie."

"Well, she's neither sugar nor salt; she won't melt before morning."

"Give me my boots." Bella was ugly with obstinacy again.

"They're as wet as sponges. . . . I'll tell you what, Bella. You go to bed and I'll go and bring your lassie here. It will look better . . . and you can see her all by yourself here without the minister to interfere."

"That's right, Meg. That's right. Bring her here to see her poor sick mother," mourned Bella whimperingly.

"Fine. Into bed with you, and I'll give you my best nightgown to wear."

Bella moved reluctantly about, taking off the remainder of her dripping clothes. She laid the little package of powder down on the table, but snatched it up again every time that Meg came near it. Meg appeared not to see this, and Bella finally slipped it under the oilcloth on the table when she thought that Meg was not looking.

"Now, lie there. I'll go down and make you a nice toddy to take the ache out of your bones before I go for your lassie."

She put a clean pillow-slip upon the pillow and pushed it under Bella's head as she spoke.

"You're a good friend to me, Meg, you're a good friend. I'll never forget this."

"Never mind that," said Meg. "I'll bring the toddy now."

When she came back with it steaming hot in a Toby-jug without a lid, Bella seemed to be asleep. The little mound under the oilcloth on the table was no longer there. Meg glanced covertly about, trying to see where Bella had put it, but there was no sign of it anywhere. Bella was lying with one hand under the pillow. She had not heard her come in.

"All right, Bella, sit up and drink this."

But she had to shake her to get her awake. From the way she clutched at the pillow as she came to, Meg could see that the package was under her head.

She poured the toddy into two glasses, using a steel shoe-horn to keep the glass from cracking. Bella lolled, half awake, against the head of the bed and watched her.

"I never thought that you and me would be friends, Meg. Do you mind on Willie Weams at the Rossorty dance the night that he bragged about taking your maidenhead?"

"I mind fine," said Meg dryly. "Take a drink of this." She handed one glass to Bella and took the other, seating herself upon the bed. "I mind Willie Weams fine. . . . But I'll warrant he was too late to take *your* maidenhead, Bella."

"He was that," laughed Bella toothlessly, rolling her head against the top of the bed. "He was that. Ramsey Gordon had been there before him."

"Tell me, Bella, which of the two is your lassie's father? You were very close-mouthed about that. . . . Was it Willie Weams?"

"I never could be sure, Meg."

"You'll better not tell your lassie that," Meg advised.

"What for wouldn't I?" demanded Bella, getting angry again. "Is she setting up to preach at her own mother?"

"Oh, no," Meg soothed. "But I've heard she sets a lot of store on having

Fassefern blood."

"Well . . . just let her so much as give me a cross look and I'll tell her she's a bairn of Willie Weams. . . . That will settle *her* pride for her . . . I'll have the whip-hand of *that* hussy, mark my words!"

"You will that," Meg agreed.

"I will that, Meg. . . . Let her so much as question me . . . I'll settle her."

Bella had sat up and was brandishing her almost empty glass. Meg slipped her hand under the pillow and got the package of powder, concealing it in the pocket of her black apron.

"Let me fill your glass, Bella. . . . I want some more myself. . . . That's fine toddy; isn't it?"

"Fine toddy. . . . I'll settle *her* . . . prideful bitch, living at the parsonage and her poor mother tramping the roads!"

Meg stood with her back to the bed. She half filled Bella's glass with hot water and whisky. Then she emptied the white powder from her apron pocket into it and stirred it with the shoe-horn.

"Bairns have no gratitude . . . the more you do for them, the less thanks you get."

"That's right, Bella," Meg agreed soothingly. "Drink this. . . ." And she gave her the whisky in which the white powder was dissolved.

"Where's yours? I'll no drink by myself . . . I'm a lady, I'll have you know."

"You are that," Meg agreed, taking her glass. "You always were a lady, Bella. Here's to the days o' auld lang syne, Bella, when we were bairns together. . . . Make it a good drink, that's a grand toast."

"It is that."

Meg watched her with narrowed eyes as she gulped the drink.

"My God, Meg, that's bitter stuff."

"It's strong, that's all. . . . Once again. Here's to us as bairns, Bella."

Once more they drank.

"My God, that's bitter."

"Just strong, that's all."

"Strong, my God, Meg."

Bella fell back asleep, snoring thickly. Meg took the glass from her hand and set it on the table, and beside it she laid the paper which had contained the white powders. Some of the crystals still clung to it. Meg wetted her finger and applied some of them to her tongue. She made a wry face and spat, wiping her tongue with the corner of her apron.

Bella was making a smothering sound in her throat. It was like snoring, but was more muffled. Meg looked down at her a minute and then left the room, walking quickly, as if she had something to do that had best be done with speed.

She entered her sick man's room and took the pillow from behind him. He was sitting up uncomfortably in the middle of the bed, all of him rigid, as if he were saying: "I have to stay in this bed, but I refuse to be comfortable in it." He watched Meg take the pillow with a silent question in his eyes. She said nothing, but threw it under her arm and went out, shutting his door behind her.

She paused on the landing between the two rooms long enough to listen to the medley of sounds that rose, borne upon a wave of smells from the Tinker's Kitchen below. Then she went into the room where Bella lay, locking the door with a preciseness that seemed part of a well-ordered plan.

She laid the pillow on the bed and sat down upon a chair to take off her shoes. This done, she mounted upon the bed. Bella was lying on her back, her hands above her head. Meg took them down and put them at first straight by her sides. She thought better of this and got off the bed again.

From the kist she took a sheet which she tore in strips and folded.

Bella was breathing in queer spasms, very loudly, as if something had fallen into her throat and was rattling there. At times she would stop breathing altogether. Meg went and looked at her when the silence had lasted unusually long. She had just put out her hand to feel her heart and see if it was still beating when the breathing started up again, so she went back to preparing the sheet.

From the fancy blue pin-cushion on her dressing-table she took a number of safety-pins. She took one end of the sheet and made a neat cuff for Bella's wrist, pinning it with the safety-pins so that it fitted snugly but did not pinch. She pulled the sheet down under the bed, bringing it up at the opposite side, and with the other end of the sheet she made another neat and snug-fitting cuff for Bella's other wrist. In this way the arms were held without any force that could mark them. Next she took her own high shoes and laced them tightly on Bella's feet. These she bound securely to the bars at the foot of the bed.

She got back on the bed again and sat on Bella with a knee pressed securely under each of her armpits. She took the pillow and pushed it firmly down upon the sleeping grey face and held it there. The figure tried to roll under Meg's heavy weight. The arms pulled at their restraining bands, the knees at Meg's back tried to rise, the head strained back.

But Meg bore down, down. . . .

Sweat rolled off her face and trickled in a stream between her breasts. A wild determination glared in her eyes as the head under the pillow struggled, struggled. . . .

A rage, a mad rage, came upon her, a passionate need to quiet the struggling thing under the pillow. . . .

She clenched her teeth, groaning through them, and held, and held. . . .

When it lay still at last, she lifted the pillow. Her arms were trembling now that their tenseness was relaxed.

She jumped off the bed and took the small square mirror from the wall and held it over the grey face. No mist gathered on its surface.

She hung the mirror back on the wall again.

Bella's face was flattened. Her nose was pressed back unnaturally. Meg took it gently between her fingers and moulded it into shape again. She closed the open mouth and softly worked the eyeballs under their lids to make them more peaceful in sleep. She unpinned the sheet from about the wrists. They showed no marks. She took the shoes from the bound feet, and covered Bella with a blanket.

Everything was returned to its place, the safety-pins to the blue ornamental cushion, the sheet to the bottom of the kist, the shoes to her own feet. She took the pillow under her arm.

Bella lay restfully upon the bed. She was almost beautiful in the new rigour that had come to her loose face.

Meg looked round the room to make sure that she had not forgotten anything, before she went out and closed the door.

No sooner had she safely reached the landing, with the quiet thing lying behind her and a closed door between her and it, than a shivering took her.

She hurried into her man's room and threw the pillow on the bed.

"I've killed her, Sandy. I've killed her." She heard a throat that was not her own screaming the words.

"It's true enough," the throat cried, as Sandy shrank from her, cringing against the head of the bed. "It's true enough. She's dead. I smothered her."

Her knees took on a shaking that had nothing to do with the rest of her, and she sat down heavily in a chair.

By the way that Sandy was staring at her she knew that the screaming must have come from her own throat.

She had told him! That was the last thing in the world that she should have done! But it was too late now to worry about it. His eyes were screaming an accusation at her, and his empty mouth was racked open with the words that streamed from it silently. She could hardly believe that she read them aright. But she knew that look, and knew what he meant when he wore it. She sneered:

"Not for the reason *you* think."

Strength was coming back to her knees now. She got up and went to the bed, and, standing over him, she cried:

"I've no call to be jealous of *that* toothless drab. . . . Willie Weams would think shame to wipe his feet upon her. . . ."

His eyes called her a liar. She picked up the pillow and flung it in his face, laughing as he cowered away from it.

"I did it for a reason you'll never guess. But what the hell care I what you think? . . . Think what you like and be damned to you."

She started for the door, but turned round again and came back to the bedside.

"Mind *this*, if you tell it to a soul, I'll kill you. . . . Cower, damn you, cower away. . . . And never think *I'll* swing for killing you. . . . You'll be dead without a mark on you, like *she* is."

She was calm again, and glad that she had done it. But it ate at her that he should think she did it for jealousy of Bella Pringle, and she knew that he would never believe the real reason.

"Well, *whatever* you think about it, keep it to yourself," she warned, regarding him contemptuously.

"Hell!" she laughed as he huddled in fear against the bars at the top of the bed. "You'd never have the courage to tell. . . . You've never had courage for anything, Sandy . . . not even when you were well. . . .

"You knew I liked Willie Weams when I married you. . . . But you were too weak-gutted to bring up his name and thrash it out with me. . . . If you'd taken a grip of my throat, if you'd taken a rope's end to my back, if you'd let me see that you would be master, and I would love you or you'd break my back for me. . . .

"But you mealy-mouthed about, letting me make a fool out of you at every turn . . . till for very devilment and just to see how far you'd let me go, I carried on with anything in breeks that came my way, right under your nose. . . .

"You were able-bodied then, and more than a match for any man in Pitouie. But did you lift a finger? . . . Never!

"If you'd thrashed Willie Weams when he came back making eyes at me . . . if you'd taken my head and banged it against a stone wall . . . I'd have come to love you in time . . . and I'd have been true to you, Sandy.

"Oh, sneer if you like, sneer away. It's the truth, just the same. . . . Oh, I know what you think of me . . . you married me because you wanted to lie with me, but you didn't believe that I was good. . . . I was never a pure lassie in your eyes . . . but just the same I *was* a pure lassie, and a good lassie. . . . There was no evil thought in my head when I first met Willie Weams. . . . No, nor *after* I met him, though I let on that I was free with men just to keep folks from laughing at me. . . . But *you* never thought of me as

233

a good lassie . . . never once . . . you wanted me for your body's pleasure, and you married me, not because you respected me, as I thought at the time, but because you hadn't the courage to take me, like Willie Weams. . . . But you never respected me . . . and a lassie has a right to be respected. . . . It makes the world of difference to a lassie."

She stopped, aware that he was calling her a stinking liar and a dirty trull. She wondered at herself that she wasted words on him, but she must win him round to silence if she could.

She went nearer to the bed and took a new tone.

"Sandy," she said, "the nigger never knew Bella Pringle's name. Nobody will be the wiser that yon is Bella Pringle lying dead. . . . Nobody will ever be the wiser that she came back. . . . She'll be buried as a stranger. . . . Nobody will be the worse."

A look that could not be measured for its malice and its fear glittered in the sick man's staring eyes. Meg, who rarely looked in his face, looked at him now, and *saw her enemy*.

She seized him by the bare bones that were his shoulders and shook him, crying:

"You'll tell, will you! Just try! Just you write *that* on the sheet!"

She straightened up, releasing him:

"Mind what I've told you," she said, and her voice was more controlled. "Say that I murdered the woman if you like . . . I'll swing for it if need be. . . . But tell that her name is Bella Pringle . . ."

This was the wrong tone to take. She must find some way to soften him.

"Sandy," she said, and looked at him, holding his secretive yet loud-crying eyes with her own, searching for some sign of friendliness or understanding in their hate-seething blackness. But she found none.

"You're like an essence from hell . . . sitting there hating me," she said, hardening hopelessly, knowing that no words would win him. "I shudder when I pass your door because I feel the hate you're feeling . . . and I hear the things your tongue will never say . . . I'm terrified of your glowering face! . . . But you tell that it's Bella Pringle lying there . . . tell *that*, and see what comes to you!"

She stood off regarding him, trying to fathom what her words did inside his silent blackness. But there was no change in the steady venom of his eyes.

"Well," she said at last, "rot there."

And she left him staring skeleton-like and yellowed, his eyes reaching after her like poisoned fangs.

That night Nancy dreamed that she was a little girl again, being pulled by

234

the arm through the feeing market. At one moment her yellow-haired mother was holding her by the arm, and at the next she had left her and was mounting the platform beside the medicine-man. But no sooner had he reached it than her hair changed from gold to ashen grey, her blue eyes died in their sockets, and from her open mouth her teeth dropped one by one, bloodless, gleaming white upon the platform at her feet. . . . The little girl that was Nancy screamed in fright and woke. . . .

She lay thinking of the woman. Trying to fit what she remembered of her mother's face into the gaunt old face of the woman on the platform. There was no resemblance, and yet she could not put from her the thought that a bond lay between her and this woman. Perhaps it was only that her mother also had gone away with a medicine-man.

If it were her mother, what would she do? Would she have the courage to claim her and introduce her to Harvey? Harvey would hate that. Harvey would hate the fact that she was lying awake now, brooding upon it, trying to connect the woman with herself. Yet she was not trying to connect the woman with herself. She was trying to be sure that the woman was nothing to her.

She must go to her and find out. She would be staying at the White Ship. But even if she had gone on to the next town, Divot Meg would be able to tell her if the woman were her mother.

This would not be Harvey's way. He would walk away from this unpleasant thing, denying it, refusing it a right to exist, and even destroying its existence by forgetting it. He had an escape from everything. He could escape into a world of sound where nothing could follow that he did not wish to follow. But she could not do that. It was not for her to walk away from painful things. Something drove her to walk toward them and stare them in the face. Something made her claim them and carry them, as if all dark and hurting things were kin to her. And yet she feared such things more than Harvey feared them, and shuddered at the thought of their kinship, and so great was her fear that she dare not walk away, leaving them behind her back. She must know. She must know. To walk upright still, she must know that this woman was not her mother. . . .

She rose early so that she would not need to explain where she was going, and went to the White Ship. Divot Meg's red-haired laddie opened the door to her, but seemed uncertain whether to step aside and let her in or close the door upon her at once. She prevented this by pushing the door open and stepping inside. The lobby, with its yellow ochred walls and floor partly covered with oddments of oilcloth, was empty except for the little boy who gaped bewilderedly at her. The house was quiet, strangely quiet, and the air was hung with blue smelly smoke.

Nancy hesitated what to do. Now that she was here she realised that the market people would long since have gone on to the next town. The blue and smelly smoke which hung in the lobby was a belated evidence of their early breakfasts. But since she had come, she would speak with Divot Meg and tell her what she feared.

It was years since that night when she had stood at Divot Meg's bedroom window and communed with her through the turkey-red curtain. But she still felt near to her, still felt that Divot Meg was watching her. It was not just curiosity that had made her look so hard and long at Harvey yesterday. Nancy knew this with a warm certainty.

"Where is your mother?" she asked the red-haired laddie. He fumbled bashfully with the door-knob, which he still held in his hand, as if that fact would prevent the visitor from feeling that she was inside to stay.

"Is she in the back of the house?" asked Nancy, preparing to go into the dim-lit back hall to look for Meg.

"She's up the stairs," the laddie finally admitted.

Nancy walked up the stairs, which had once been painted a dark Indian-red. Little patches of linoleum adhered to the steps, held there by nails that were polished with many feet.

As she reached the dim square landing at the top of the stairs, Divot Meg and Doctor Taylor came out of one of the rooms. Divot Meg gave her a with-held look, and the doctor looked at her in surprise.

"Good morning, Miss Pringle." His words asked a question which she found herself indirectly answering as she turned to Divot Meg.

"I came to speak with you about . . ."

"In just a moment, miss," Divot Meg interrupted. "We've had a death in the house."

"Your man?" asked Nancy, dismayed that she should have brought her troubles here at such a time.

"No, miss. It's a strange woman. She came here with the negro medicine-man."

"Who . . . who is she?"

Nancy heard her own voice thin and panting, asking the question.

"An Englishwoman, you said?" the doctor asked Meg.

"Well, she had an Englishy sort of voice, and she spoke about Devonshire and clotted cream," said Meg.

"Ah, yes, ah, yes. From Devonshire, no doubt. And the man, the negro? . . . There were no hard words between them . . . no quarrel?"

"As I told you, he wanted her to go on with him, but she was tired and said she'd come on to Callochie the next day. . . . I never let black people stay in the house, so he had to look for quarters somewhere else."

"And her name?" the doctor was asking as if the question were no more than a formula.

Nancy hung against the wall of the landing, spent with dread.

The other two ignored her. The doctor was anxious to get the facts and be on his way to his morning round, and Meg, half hostile, had turned her back upon her.

"The only name I heard him call her was 'Snowey,' a queer kind of name," said Meg. "She was none of the regulars that come every year. I'd never seen her before."

"I see. And you found her dead when you went to call her this morning?"

"It was like this. I like to have the people out of the house by eight o'clock, unless they mean to pay another day's rent. . . . The last of them had gone, and she hadn't put in an appearance yet, so I went up and rapped on her door. . . . But she said never a word, so I pushed it open, and there she lay just as you saw her. . . ."

"Quite peacefully. Died in her sleep. . . ."

"I suppose so. As I told you, I had a drink of whisky with her early in the evening and took her a tub of water to wash herself."

"Umph!" the doctor nodded. "She must have taken the drug after you left."

"Would that kill her?" asked Meg astonishedly.

"Well, in *her* condition it might . . . in fact, as you see, it *did*." The doctor laughed cheerfully. "System rotten with the drug, heart bad, lungs congested . . . one dose too much and . . . pouf! . . . Well, I must be getting on. . . . Lots of grippe in the town. . . . I'll send the undertaker."

"There won't be an inquest?" The words seemed to slip out of Divot Meg's mouth unbeknown to her.

The doctor laughed. "No need for that. It's as plain as day. . . . No, no. . . . Well, good-bye."

"Doctor," Divot Meg clutched his arm as he was about to go down the stairs. "My sick man, Doctor . . . haven't you anything to ease him? Couldn't you take a look at him?"

"I will if you insist," said the doctor reluctantly. "But what's the use? It's a wonder that he lives . . . malnutrition, you know. . . . Food is what he needs, and he can't swallow it."

"He manages the gruel if I get it extra thin. . . . Couldn't you give me something strengthening to put in it?"

"He needs meat and vegetables. . . . I'll go and look at him."

"Doctor"—Divot Meg seemed suddenly to regret having spoken about her man. For a moment it looked as if she would prevent him from entering the room—"he's out of his head, I think," she whispered. "He imagines things."

"Very likely. . . . Not unusual. Well, I'll see what he looks like."

He went into the room, leaving Nancy and Divot Meg together in the dim-lit landing.

Nancy went close to Divot Meg and whispered:

"I came because I was afraid it was my mother."

"Who, miss?" said Divot Meg coldly.

Nancy had expected her to melt out of this precise, slightly sycophantic being into the broad-hipped, warm-breasted Meg whom she had met on the kirk brae as soon as the doctor was gone. But instead she found herself looking into a pair of eyes that refused to know her, that denied all past knowledge of her.

"Who is your mother, miss?"

"Miss!" Could it be her well-cut suit and silk stockings that made Divot Meg call her "miss." Oh, no! Divot Meg could not, must not be impressed by such things. Nancy could not bear it. She cried imploringly:

"Don't you remember me? . . . Don't you remember on the kirk brae road? . . . Don't you remember the night that I came to your window?"

"My window, miss?"

Oh, why was Divot Meg doing this? Why was she looking at her as if she had never known her before? Could she really have forgotten the little girl who begged for advice, the little girl to whom she had given courage and comfort?

"I'm Bella Pringle's lassie," she cried passionately, reaching out her hands. "You remember Bella Pringle?"

"Oh, yes, miss. She had a bairn to Ramsey Gordon of Fassefern," said Meg crisply, stroking her apron down with an air that said, "What has that to do with me?"

"I'm that bairn," said Nancy, her hands falling to her sides hopelessly.

Divot Meg curtsied with the right amount of deference from one in her station of life to one of the gentry, and said: "Yes, miss."

And she looked impatiently toward her sick man's door as if she were wishing that this strange visitor would make an end to her senseless talking and leave her free to follow the doctor.

But Nancy made one more desperate try.

"Tell me," she begged, "have you ever seen the woman who is lying dead? Is she Bella Pringle?"

"Bella Pringle?" Divot Meg looked at Nancy and spoke quietly, as one who states a truth too certain for any questioning. "I went to school with Bella Pringle. I would know her, dead or living."

It was impossible to doubt her. But, indeed, she had not doubted her.

It was all nonsense to think the woman was her mother. . . . And nonsense to think that Divot Meg was her friend. Divot Meg had forgotten her, had never given her a thought in all these years. Everything, all her supposed friendship, was just imagination, the sick imagination of a lonely child. Tears struggled in her throat.

She groped for the banister and hurried from the death-haunted landing down the stairs and out into the living street.

The sun was on the mill-stream that flowed beside the larch-trees. Buttercups upon the water, floating on outspread saucers of green, tugged at their frail chains.

Nancy ran down the long bank and sat at the water's edge watching the lazy buttercups through a glimmer of tears.

A thing that was dear to her had died. Maybe it had never lived. A friendly hand behind her back was gone. Had never even been. . . . "Yes, miss." "No, miss." . . . She would laugh at herself later for feeling so bereft. But now it hurt. She had glorified Divot Meg, made her a saint, and a martyr, and a gallant warrior. But Divot Meg could not remember her.

She had believed that even God would not be able to overawe Divot Meg. She had pictured her standing, hands on broad hips, before the throne of God, saying:

"As you can see, I did the best I could. But if you're determined to give me hell-fire for it, let me tell you before I roast that I've small respect for your judgment."

And now Divot Meg had been impressed and curtsying to a ten-guinea suit.

Nancy laughed at herself. She was for ever making gods out of clay.

She reached out and pulled the floating buttercups toward her. They would look pretty on the dining-room table if she could find a shallow wide dish to float them in. . . .

Monday would soon be here, and she could go to Fassefern again . . . and Harvey . . . and Harvey!

All the way to Fassefern Nancy found herself forming the words with which she would ask Harvey about their marriage. If she dismissed this thought, trying to centre her mind on the fishwife in front of her who smelled of smoked haddock, or the shepherd at her side who smelled of sheep dip, she would find herself back again saying, "Harvey, shall we be married here in Fassefern before you leave?"

Or perhaps *he* would be the one to ask the question and she would joyfully reply, "Yes." But she knew that this latter was only a game she was playing to make herself feel happy. Harvey would not bring up the subject of their marriage. An instinct told her this, though she had never admitted it to herself before this day.

She saw now that she had not dared to let herself admit it. That she had been flying from fear of admitting it all the summer. But now that Andrew's words had shown her this fear, she must turn and walk toward it. She could not bear it behind her back. She must know.

As the 'bus neared Fassefern, a lorry of manly-looking luggage passed, going in the direction of the railway station. Nancy saw it vaguely through the cloud of her thoughts. Not until it was well past did her brain leap to wonder: who would have such trunks, such buckled bags of cow-hide? Who in Rossorty? Who at Fassefern? Who at Fassefern would have such wise, such travelled luggage? . . . Harvey's luggage!

But it could not be Harvey's luggage. He was not going for three weeks yet. *They* were not going for three weeks yet. Why must her heart rush downward so unreasonably?

She knew it was not Harvey's luggage. But her mouth was suddenly puckered and dry as if she had been drinking Burgundy. It stayed so even when she entered at the big Gothic door and heard the organ playing. . . .

The music was faint . . . very faint. The organ-room door must be closed. . . .

The vaulted door between the wings was closed also. The bar was swung across it. . . .

She would like to say: "He is practising . . . of course, it was not his luggage," and go quietly to the library and her work; destroying her fear by refusing to believe in it. Instead, she swung the bar away and went along the corridor to the organ-room. Whatever hurting thing waited for her there, she must face it.

The playing stopped. He turned slowly toward her. How strange that she had never noticed that strained-back look at the corners of his eyebrows! He looked trapped! He looked as if he were seized by the back of the neck and held. How wary his eyes were!

Would he mention his luggage? She knew now that it was his luggage. The strained-back look told her. But even as she thought this, the look disappeared, and he smiled.

"You're back!"

"Yes."

He came toward her to take her in his arms.

"What's the matter?" he asked.

Her eyes were hostile, holding him off. How could he send his luggage away, and stand there smiling at her, telling her nothing?

"What is it, dearest?"

She had the feeling that she was putting a knife-point to the tender hollow of his neck where his soft shirt fell away.

"You are leaving to-day," said the knife, pressing close to the hollow.

"What makes you think I am leaving?" He felt the knife and pushed it away.

"I saw your luggage." She had the knife back at his throat again.

He flushed angrily, and his eyes became hostile also.

"I'm not going till to-morrow . . . I meant to tell you this evening."

"Why?"

"Why what?" he demanded sharply, feeling justified because her tone was so possessive.

"Why are you going so soon?"

"I've got to get some work done."

These were not new words. But there were new things behind them, new resolutions, new resolutions full of pain for her. She could retreat from them even now. By lowering the knife and saying, "Yes, I understand, I think you should go away and work," she could keep from uncovering them. But retreat was no longer possible; she must know. So this hateful asking must go on.

"You haven't said anything about our marriage since spring."

"My dear, I can hardly discuss marriage on the eve of leaving." He was trying to be sweetly reasonable, and was begging her to be sweetly reasonable also. . . . He was hating this so. He did so hate ugly, logical words. . . . He did so hate being called to account. . . . But she could not spare him, nor herself. The truth was her desperate need.

"You mean, you don't wish to discuss it!"

His smile seemed to pat her on the head.

"You wouldn't be happy if you married me, Nancy."

"Why not?"

"I'm not good enough for you, dear."

Ah, that would be a charming escape for him!

"You mean that you have stopped loving me?"

"I'll never do that, Nancy."

Oh, his eyes when he said that! If she ran to his arms now, he would be hers again. Hers again . . . but unwillingly hers. . . . No, she must not look at his eyes. It was better to look away and say hard words, words that called out the truth.

"Why, then?" she asked, keeping from her voice the sound of her inward weeping.

"I'm not a man who should marry."

"It's a little late to decide *that* . . . isn't it?"

241

The knife pierced the hollow that time! She had never seen him blush before. . . . But this was not fair of her. . . . She had not bartered for marriage when she gave herself. . . . She had no right to blame him.

"I didn't mean that, Harvey. . . . If you don't want to marry me . . . it's all right."

"I *do* want to."

"Then why not?"

"For the reason I said . . . I can't be married to you . . . and music."

Why was it that this sounded such a frail excuse to her? Was it because she had no soul for music? She pondered it a while. And Harvey stood studying the toes of his stout shoes critically one after the other in a painful, careful way.

"Could you be married to anyone else . . . and music?" she asked.

"Possibly . . . a nice fat *hausfrau.*"

"I could be that."

"Not fat," he joked, lifting his eyes to hers, smiling, coaxing her to stop this painful questioning and let them laugh together again. But she could not make her lips smile.

"I could be a *hausfrau,*" she persisted, wondering at the calm force with which she refused to let him escape.

"You couldn't be anything but a siren." He said it with the air that it was a compliment, but also as if it excused all that he might do.

"Harvey, I could. . . . It's you . . . I never . . . Harvey, who made me a siren?" The sound of weeping welled into her cry.

"*Dearest*, you're not crying?" He sprang to her side. The arms with which he held her were trembling. He was sick of this sorry hurting.

No. She was not crying. She would not cry. It would not be fair to cry. She would win if she could . . . without that. She saw now that he had come to Pitouie to tell her this. No weakness must prevent him this time. She drew away from the trembling shelter of his arms.

"What do you mean, Harvey?"

"I mean, dear, that music is *my* life . . . and love is *your* life."

"So you take my life from me."

"Nancy!" His eyes reproached her.

"I won't say any more. . . . You'll . . . I'll . . . She felt the tears rising, so she walked away from him to the chair by the window, and stood there.

"We had to face it sooner or later," he said, regaining some of his purpose now that she had left his side.

"Yes?" She did not look at him.

"Well, can't you see that we had?" He was very positive now. But his positiveness did not create any certainty in her. She wished almost that she could accept this reason, giving it the value he gave it. But it just would not be a sufficient reason in her eyes.

"Is music the real, the only reason, Harvey?"

"What bigger reason could I have?"

"You could feel that you do not love me enough to be tied to me."

He did not answer. She turned round to look at him. He seemed to have detached himself from this difficult scene and to have floated away, following the drift of his eyes as they soared out through the window. But she pulled him back.

"Harvey, will you be honest with me?"

"I have been."

"The music doesn't seem enough to me."

"That is because you don't understand. . . . I didn't want to love you in the first place, you know. . . . I knew it would upset my work."

"That was what you meant by saying you were 'afraid'?"

"Yes."

"But was it love you were afraid of . . . or was it marriage? . . . Being tied?"

"I suppose I wanted to keep my freedom, also." He said it defensively, his eyes saying: "You are forcing this out of me, and it's very tactless of you."

"Freedom to do what?"

"Adventure . . . I suppose I didn't want to 'close my horizons' so soon."

"Yes," she whispered. "I believe in that reason more."

"But that is bound up with my music also," he protested. "Adventure inspires me."

"And a wife would not."

"No, a wife would not."

"I see. . . . That is all right, then. . . . I . . ."

"And now I suppose you hate me?"

"No," in a smothered voice. "No, I could never hate you."

"I'm sorry."

"Don't . . . don't be that. . . . I'm not, for anything."

The space between them quivered. It was something to leap across and so stop this nightmare. It was something to fly from and try to forget, but it was not anything to be borne, even for another moment.

"I'll go then," she said.

"Nancy! I can't bear it."

He had her in his arms.

"Forget all this that I've been saying. . . . It isn't true. . . . I *do* love you enough for anything. . . . We'll be married . . . I want to . . . really, dear,

I want to. . . . I don't know what made me talk such rot. . . . Let's go and be married now."

"Before you get panic-stricken and want to back out again?"

"Nancy."

"Forgive me! . . . No, Harvey, I don't want to."

"You're just hurt."

"No! No! I couldn't marry you, now."

"Well, perhaps not *now*," he said, giving the "now" a new meaning. "But when I come back."

He was so pleading, so eager to have all this painfulness stopped. He was willing to marry her, willing to imprison himself for life, just to have it stopped. She had made it so hard for him. But now she had the truth at last, and she could be merciful. . . . She would help him to get away painlessly.

"Perhaps," she said.

He smiled, grateful for this, believing that he would come back for her.

"Next spring, darling. . . . We will go to Rome. . . . You will love Rome, Nancy."

Oh, yes, she would love Rome. . . . How was she going to live through another day of this? . . .

"I won't go to-morrow. . . . I'll stay another week."

He was being generous now. She could have another week of him since she was willing to let him escape at last! . . . But, no! No! She could not do this for a week . . . her heart must be allowed to break to-morrow. . . . It could not wait a week.

"No, you must go to-morrow. . . . Think of your work . . . the concerts."

"That's true," he admitted.

"You *must* go. . . . Spring will soon come." She said it jauntily. Was it too jauntily?

"I'll write you every week."

"No!" It was a cry of pain. Oh, no, he could not do that to her. She would die once for him, and stay dead for ever. But he could not kill her over and over. "No, don't write. . . . Come back for me when you want me."

Nancy pushed against the wind step by step, overcoming it. Her body liked this fight, needed it. By the time she reached Webster's cottage at the cliff-top her body would be spent, it would be calm, and it would sleep.

Her mind was moving in its own paths, heedless of her struggling body. Phrases from Andrew's letter kept coming up in it.

"Divot Meg's man sent a note to the doctor"; "The Hurdy-Gurdy Man's wife knew that she was Bella Pringle"; "Divot Meg's man said Meg killed her, but he's out of his mind, besides the doctor saw the body"; "I wouldn't give it a thought";

"She's dead and gone. Just forget it."

Just forget it! Just forget it! She's dead and gone! Just forget it!

Her galoshes were saying this over and over as she pulled them out of the mud and set them down into it again: *Just forget it! Just forget it! She's dead and gone! Just forget it!* Funny that her galoshes were all that mourned: "And when she heard that her mother was dead, her galoshes wept bitterly."

She tried to feel something besides relief that the woman was dead; and thankfulness that Harvey had gone without knowing. She said things like: "Your poor mother came home to die," or "After all, she loved you, her dying feet brought her back to you." But this only made the galoshes cry more loudly, almost triumphantly: *Just forget it! Just forget it. She's dead and gone. Just forget it!*

The tossing fir-trees slapped her with handfuls of rain, and the wind plucked spitefully at her mackintosh. It was an evening to be sorrowful, but nothing would rouse her tacit heart or make it feel grief.

The woman was not any part of her. The woman was dead and could not claim to be any part of her. She was all Fassefern, having kin with no one else. She was alone with them. Their books in her hands by day, and their bones in the sea beneath her by night.

Harvey had gone, Divot Meg had gone; Andrew and Mrs. Anderson had fallen away from her. She had nothing but the Fasseferns . . . and the summer that was past . . . love given without barter . . . given in beauty. But her heart was quiet; it asked nothing more. . . .

Yes. She had one other thing. She smiled, thinking of it. Of all her dreams, this childish dream had come true at last; she had her "personal door." She had a home that was *her* home. A door to lock upon the world.

It was a long way from Fassefern to Webster's cottage at the cliff-top. But she needed the walk, and the wind, and the rain. She needed the struggle up the cliff, and finally and most deeply she needed her "personal door."

She had taken the Websters' cottage for her own. The "ben" which had been their "best room" she used for a bedroom. And the "but" which had been the Websters' kitchen—although there was a box-bed in it—she used for a living-room.

She had moved out the box-bed, and in its place she put book-shelves painted yellow to match the yellow ochred walls. Candlesticks of black bog-oak with red candles stood on the shelves against the yellow walls, and between them was her red and white china cow attended by a cowherd in bright blue coat and yellow trousers.

She covered the cold slate floor with a rag rug in blue and rich orange red. On the windows she hung muslin curtains tinted yellow. She yellowed the hearth with sandstone, leaving the crane, with its soot-hung chain, just as it was when the Websters had boiled their broth there.

At one side of the fireplace she had a willow basket painted blue to hold the peats, and on the other a blue painted box filled with fir-cones to burn on special nights. She gathered pewter plates and bright dishes in blue and red to fill the back of the old oak dresser. A round oak table held a dented pewter lamp which she polished till it kept up a constant winking at the shining pewter plates.

It was a glowing room. Thinking of it, she hurried her steps, turning off the low-road up the cliff. Climbing against the wind with a certain joy in its biting cold, knowing that Mrs. Penny would have lighted the fire. The pewter lamp would be winking cheerily in the red radiance of the burning peats.

She was breathless when she reached her own door, at the cliff's very summit. She went in upon a gale of wind, gasping as she fought the door to make it shut again.

The room was welcoming and warm, as she knew it would be. She surveyed it, as she always did, with pride, and a quiet kind of happiness that it was hers.

Life was complete about her, a cloud-coloured ball rolling on and on changelessly. Nothing could come through its vapour walls to pierce her. . . . Sorrow was lying dead, and joy had forgotten her name. . . .

No! No! Joy had *not* forgotten her name! . . . This was from Harvey! This letter lying so meekly by the pewter lamp, and never calling to her when she opened the door! How could it be there and not call her name? How could it not leap up calling to her? . . . Paris! He was in Paris! . . . And this was to say: "Come to Paris and marry me, for I can't live without you." Or it might be: "Come to Paris, for I can't live without you." But what did that matter? It was "Come to Paris—come to me," that it said.

Oh, why must her fingers bungle now!

"DEAREST NANCY,—You said I was never to write to you, but I must, because I do truly love you, my dear, and you must believe this always. I can't get you out of my mind, not that I want to, but I feel more and more that I had no right to do what I did.

"I want to feel that you are in a happier environment. It isn't good for you to be in that cottage, so morbid and unhealthy.

"I have more money than I know what to do with, so I have made some of it over to you. You will be able to travel and have a motor and servants, and meet interesting people.

"You can always reach me through my bankers, who will also be your bankers now.

"I am working very hard. Next month I go to Warsaw to pay homage to the heart of Chopin, which lies in the Church of the Holy Cross.

"I shall be more at peace about you when I know that you have left Rossorty.

"With all my love, "HARVEY."

"I shall be more at peace!" Oh, yes, he would be completely at peace about her, now that he had paid her off. . . .

No! No! She must not go mad yet. There must be some other way to think of it. Harvey could not do this to her. He could not make a dirty traffic of their love. . . .

She laughed screamingly. He has paid me off. . . . But he cannot marry me. . . . "Good women make a bargain first!"

She must not laugh like this. She must be calm. She *must* be calm. A horse was galloping in her brain, a white horse with blood upon its sides. . . .

She must be very quiet—people would hear her. . . .

She must think of it quietly. . . . Harvey meant to be kind. . . . He felt that he had wronged her. . . .

Would he have felt that he had wronged Lady Nancy Gordon by taking her love? . . . Would he have paid *her*? . . . Would he have sent money to a Fassefern? . . . No!

She was not a Fassefern! . . . She had never been a Fassefern! . . . She was Willie Weams's bastard. . . .

Nothing was left to her . . . the Fasseferns were gone . . . the beauty of her love was gone. . . . Nothing was left but Willie Weams and the nigger's fancy woman. . . .

Nothing! Nothing!

Nothing left but a trull who must be paid!

O God!

O God, with your big deaf face, hear me! . . . Must I be this? . . . Must I be this? . . .

She pulled upon the door. It swung in upon the gale, helping her. . . .

The wind took her feet upon its swift palms and bore them to the cliff-top . . . and past the cliff-top.

But as they left the firm rock, flying wingless on the blue, it came to her piercingly to think:

"Would Willie Weams's bastard die for this? It is a Fassefern who dies!"

And as the sharp black teeth of the sea came up to meet her, she smiled.

POETRY

POETRY

A small number of poems survive, which Lorna appears to have written at times of emotional crisis during her life – in particular after the birth of her son to William de Mille, and when seriously ill. Only the first, 'Broken', was published, in *Woman's Home Companion* 51 (July 1924). 'If ever I rise up again' was written in 1928, during her illness, while 'Bereft', unpublished and possibly unfinished, responds to changes in her relationship with William de Mille. The final fragment is an unsent reply to William after the birth of their son.

BROKEN

Broken I am because I love,
But do not pity me;
A branch I was that grew above,
Now stricken from the tree.

A branch I was, with running sap
That warmed to every spring,
And ardent buds that would unwrap –
A glad, but songless thing.

Echoes I have of songbirds now;
Song where I once was mute;
For Sorrow's hand that broke the bough
Has fashioned it a flute.

UNTITLED

If ever I rise up again and walk the busy street,
If ever I rise up at dawn with eager, lightsome feet,
If ever I can breast the wind or bide the lashing rain,
Or feel the sea upon my face and meet my friends again,
Oh, if that day will ever come, when I can walk on grass
And smell the mouldy smell of earth and watch a bird fly past,
I'll be a better girl – maybe. But maybe I'll be worse.
It isn't in me to be good except inside a hearse.

BEREFT

Let each burgeoning happy tree,
Think of the Cross on Calvary.
Take the seasons, one by one –
Tell them Spring and Summer are done.
Still the Wind. Hush the Sea,
Let the Moon set the tide's heart free.
Stay the rivers – hide the sun.
Let the Day and the Night be one.
Take the faith of Simple Folk,
Make for my soul a goaded yoke.
Take from me hope – then let me be –
For the arms of my lover are gone from me.

Freeze the rivers, dim the sun,
Let the day and night be one.
Take the babe and dig my plot,
If my heart yearns and yours does not.

LETTERS

LETTERS

The following pages offer a brief selection of Lorna Moon's lively letters. Written some time after the birth of her son in 1922, the letters date from 1925 when Lorna was in Hollywood and show her in negotiation with publishers and editors, asserting her very definite opinions on how her work should be marketed. They also depict her own awareness of developments in her writing as she engages with broader and more melodramatic topics than village life in Drumorty. In each exchange she is clear and uncompromising in this sense of her own direction

Her correspondents include Hewitt Hanson Howland (1863–1944), who left Bobbs-Merrill, her publishers, to edit *Century Magazine* in August 1925, and an assistant to the publishers, Anne Johnston, but the bulk of the letters are to David Laurance Chambers (1879–1963), the Bobbs-Merrill publisher. These letters combine a warm response to his flattering comments on her work with a determination to defend the nature and characteristics of her writing. They sustain, too, an enjoyably flirtatious fantasy about the nature of their relationship, which saw Lorna playing out seduction, jealousy and (genuine) sadness when he too falls ill. In these letters Lorna also expresses extremely frank criticisms of social attitudes to sexuality and the effects of such prudery on women. Above all the letters are characterised by their resilience, humour and a refusal to allow herself to conform to the role of invalid.

To Hewitt Hanson Howland
Written from El Capitan, 633 3/4 So. Westlake, Los Angeles, 30 April 1925

Dear Mr Howland:

I'm a terrible woman – I'm afflicted with a kind of scribendi-batophobia or something about answering letters (unless they are love letters). I will doubtless end my days penniless and friendless for this reason – and serves me jolly well right!

But the thing that has kept me from answering you before, is something that I had to be reasonably sure of before I COULD answer you. In the last eight or ten months I have been going through a sort of mental change of life. I'm coming out of it a different person from the one who wrote 'Drumorty'.

Notice 'The Courting of Sally Ann'. It was written last May. It is the last of the truly Drumortish tales of Drumorty. Then look at 'Wantin a Hand'; it was written in July after the land began to slide. I have nothing to say against it, except that it is a golf suit made of silver-cloth. The manner doesn't suit the matter. The style is fine, so is the story, but they don't belong to each other. The truth is I am through with Drumorty in that vein. Other things are crowding in on me demanding to be written. I have taken myself by the shoulders and said: 'But you *can't* be through with Drumorty because the publisher says that thirty thousand words is only half enough. Here is a story about a haggis, and there is one about a funeral, and here's another.' But it is all useless, the stuff I have written under this method DOESNT PLEASE ME, and so it is of no significance at all to me who else may be pleased by it. I have said my say about Drumorty. I'm not going to drool and slaver through thirty thousand words of filler because the book seller says an author must say his say in sixty thousand words. The tales of Drumorty will be published as they are or not published, it's all one to me. They should be published on very wide margin paper with big print anyway, there isn't an extra word in one of them anywhere. As you can see I'm irritated. I am, because an up-and-coming very efficient publishing house has just written to say: 'Now is the time for you to get out the novel of Hollywood we asked you to write last spring. Snap into it and let us have the copy by fall etc.' Just as if I were a penny in the slot machine into which a publisher put a nickel saying: 'Novel of Hollywood please' and out it would come. How does any one know the moment when I should write a novel of Hollywood? Will you tell me how publishers 'get that way'? That's that!

Now about the 'naughty novel'.[1] It isn't naughty at all, that is why it will doubtless be suppressed if published. It is just a sincere effort to show what the men in a woman's life bring to her, and take from her. It is the sex life of a woman from sixteen to thirty five. It's the inside of a woman written from the inside.

The other is a Drumorty novel[2] but not the Drumorty of the 'tales'. It is the story of three women. The first beautiful and a great musician but lacking the strong fiber of character and force to use her genius. So she fumbles it, wastes her life in petty loves, has a love child to the minister, who is thrown out of his church. She dies a drunken outcast after having fallen with the child and injured its back. The child has the genius and moral fiber and works, but when she goes to the city for her debut – that is the finish of hope, the public won't accept genius with a hump back. She comes back, another failure. A handsome young gardener falls in love with her music. They marry. She dies giving birth to a daughter. The daughter has *everything*, the beauty of the grandmother, the genius and power of her mother, she WINS. It is the story of how much fumbling and failure there is when genius hasn't the other things to carry its flag forward.

You can see from the above that I'm 'not a good buy', and why I can't sign the contract.

Oh thank you so much for the novel *Prisoners*, I liked it so much.
very sincerely
LORNA MOON

---

1. *Dark Star*.
2. *The Three MacPhersons*, never published.

To Hewitt Hanson Howland
Written from Hotel Plaza, Union Square, San Francisco, 9 May 1925

Dear Mr Howland:
I'm so glad that you agree that I shouldn't tack an annex on to my little brown egg.

I saw your Mr Curtis before leaving L.A. and told him the changes I wanted in the contract.[1]

Here they are briefly:

1. that I retain all dramatic and moving picture rights.

2. that I be paid on first book, ten per cent on first five thousand copies, twelve and a half per cent on next five thousand, and fifteen per cent on all over that.

3. on second book twelve and a half on first five thousand and fifteen per cent on all over that. Contract for third book to be drawn on a basis decided by sale of first two books.

By 'serialization' do you mean first magazine serialization rights? I would want to sell the first magazine rights on the novel myself as I did the stories.

That's all, if you agree, its a go.

I like the title Doorways in Drumorty very much, it looks and sounds well.

I wish I COULD change the Rosehearty story into a Drumorty one. But you see Drumorty is an agricultural village while Rosehearty is a fishing village. If I took the sea out of Feckless Maggie Ann there wouldn't be any story and of course I couldn't bring the sea to Drumorty in ONE story and omit it in all the others. And anyway, you see, the fishing people and the land people in Scotland don't mix, they are widely separated in their sympathies, even their blood isn't the same. The fisher folks are mostly Celtic, they come from Orkney and Shetland etc. and follow the herring around the coast, they have no dealings with the land folk except to sell them fish. Maggie Ann is a true Celtic, a Drumorty lass would never have rushed up the scaup[2] to kill herself in a frenzy, nor would a Drumorty Danny have carried the flagon or sat by the grave to smoke his evening pipe. I see these two kinds of people as so apart from each other that I'd know myself for a fakir if I tried to make them seem one. Some day we will publish Hearts in Rosehearty, and steal Maggie Ann out of the Drumorty book and put her where she belongs.

Oh, your copy of The Courting of Sally Ann is not complete, if you'll return it I'll fill in the lacking portion.

Mightent it be a good idea to have Aley[3] approach Barrie[4] about a preface while he is over there? But not, for God sake if you think somebody is going to say that I 'write like Barrie'. I once said that I'd always wanted to write 'as WELL as Barrie', and of course 'well' became 'like'. I don't write at all like Barrie. Do I?

Address me here.

Faithfully yours,

LORNA MOON

---

1. This is the *Doorways* contract, as becomes clear later in the letter.
2. 'scaup': head(land).
3. Maxwell Aley, Managing Editor *Century Magazine* 1922 and at Bobbs-Merrill 1925.
4. J. M. Barrie.

THE COLLECTED WORKS OF LORNA MOON

To David Laurance Chambers, Bobbs-Merrill publishers
20 August 1928

Dear Mr Chambers
have your wire today which makes me very happy. The book[1] is already twenty five thousand words longer than what you have read. I think it will run to ninety thousand. I'll be finished with the actual writing in two weeks. But I'm such a 'persnickity bodie', that I'll probably spend a few weeks more finding fault with it.

My friend Frances Marion plans a campaign of publicity amongst reviewers. She will get Elizabeth Marbury and Wershein to whoop it up. Also William Randolf Hearst will give it a sendoff[2]. So, with your doing your share, and Vance[3] doing his we ought to sell a couple of copies despite the fact that it's a pretty good novel.

There's one thing I'd like to say – In fact there are several – but the main one is this. I have learned, by dealing with the public through movies, that nothing Scotch attracts them except in bottles. We have to disguise a movie of the scene if it is Scotland. So, no plaid jackets please. No thistles, no heather, no Barrie blah. (As you see I have thrown out dialect.) If you call me anything, besides a piece of 'fromage', call me a British novelist – lay off Scotland.

Next, this novel is today – the girl was born in 1910 or there about – so lets have a nice modern jacket – something that stays in peoples minds, a woodcut – or when I'm feeling peppy I'll tell you a list of jackets that I think are successful – I may be 'all wet' but I've been obliged to study what people react to in order to be successful in movies.

Do you think it would be advisable for me to write a preface about the complete omission of dialect? You see I have come to the conclusion that it is never justified. Indeed if it *is* correct to write in dialect then *all* conversation should be in dialect, since there is nobody, not even the Oxford Don who pronounces English according to the dictionary. I use the idiom common to Scottish people but I see no reason to stress their mispronunciation which is all dialect is. Ne'est ce pas?

It is possible though that the reviewers may want to show how clever they are by pointing out that Divot Meg would say 'dinna' for 'dont', and 'ken' for 'know' etc. A preface would jump them on this. Or do you think that it is not necessary.

I trust that you are chewing your fingers and getting hangnails in your anxiety to know the rest of the story.
LORNA

1. *Dark Star*
2. Frances Marion was a highly successful writer for MGM and a close friend. Elizabeth Marbury was an influential theatrical agent. William Randolph Hearst, the American newspaper magnate, owned a chain of newspapers across the country. The reference to 'Wershein' [sic] has not been traced.
3. Arthur T. Vance, editor of *Pictorial Review*.

To David Laurance Chambers
Written from Graciosa, 30 August 1928

Dear Mr Chambers:
Your charming letter has made me very happy.

I whooped with delight over your remark that I 'handled the dialect' well. Because this shows me that I did what I tried to do: that is: create the impression that the characters spoke in dialect while keeping strictly to English. Do you know that in the whole book there are only six scotch expressions and only two of those are used in conversation? The six are: 'bairn': 'kirk' 'brae': 'mycerties': 'kist': 'havers':[10] and one other which I forget at the moment.

But it is no wonder that I tricked you, because, I also put it over on a Scotch professor, just over! When he had read the thing he said: 'Yon's a grand book. Yon's a Scotch book.' (which you know is simply wild praise from a Scot). I said: 'You didn't miss the dialect?' He misunderstood me, thinking I meant, 'you could understand the dialect', and answered: '*miss* it, would I be forgetting my mother tongue in a twae month think ye?'

'But you know,' I said, 'there are only six Scotch expressions in the book. The whole thing is written in English.'

'Niver! Niver!' he cried 'I woulda seen it at a glance!'

'But I'm telling you' I urged

'Oh maybe the lassie, she was educated, but Divot Meg was Scotch as peat – '

When he re-read Divot Meg, he was fairly winded:

'I couldna hae believed it!' he cried.

And that is the answer! I use the idiom and *they* supply the pronunciation. If the reader knows the Scotch pronunciation he will supply it himself without realizing it. If he doesn't he will think he is reading English as spoken by the Scot and never be a bit the wiser. So I think there is no need for a preface. Do you?

The book is twelve thousand words short of being finished.

Yours
LORNA

---

1. 'bairn': child; 'kirk': church; 'brae': hillside; 'mycerties': take my word for it; 'kist': chest; 'havers': nonsense.

LETTERS

To David Laurance Chambers
Written from Graciosa, 31 August 1928

Mercy me, Man!

I seem to be forever writing to you. But this dialect thing will have to be settled once and for all. I'll have no readers muttering off on the horizon that Divot Meg is too well spoken for them. So lead them out for me and stand them in a row, while I show them the error of their ways, or die in the attempt.

Setting altogether aside the question of whether it is ever justified to spell words as mispronounced by characters (loosely called 'writing in dialect'), let me settle this question for them quite apart from that.

Firstly (as the minister says), 'Have I ever said that Pitouie was south of the Grampian Mountains?'

Ask them that! It won't mean a thing to them! But it means a whole lot when it comes to Scottish speech. Beetle your brows sternly at them when you ask this question (oh, that I were there to do it myself!).

'Grampians! Grampians?' they will say vaguely.

'*Yes*' you will say witheringly. 'Pitouie is on the border of the Grampians.' (Drumorty is in the lowland – Pitouie borders the highlands.)

Now I will make them bite the dust. (If you haven't any dust handy, send out for a shovelful before you line them up.)

Then (this comes before the dust-biting) you will say loftily, 'Do you know that there is a different race of people living north of the Grampian Mountains?. . . The 'unconquered Scot' in fact. . . who is *no* Scot at all, but a Celt, whose native tongue is Gaelic. And furthermore it is only in the last hundred years that he has learned to speak English at all, English schools having been forced upon him by law. So since the present inhabitant of the Scottish North learned his English from an ancestor who learned it from a school teacher, he speaks it with great purity, so that it is admitted that in Inverness the English is purer than anywhere else on the British Isles. And if Divot Meg lived on the border of the Grampians, she would speak just as she does in Dark Star, and if she lived *north* of them, she might speak a whole lot better.'

Dust biting is now in order!

Now let me lick them from the other angle, viz: the justification or not of omitting mispronunciation.

Would they expect me when writing a novel of well educated American people to spell the word 'been' as they pronounce it, or 'can't' as they pronounce it. I should be then writing 'bin' 'bin' all day long. I have listened to a President of the U.S.A. 'binning' for an hour on end. But if I

263

were to write a book about him, I shouldn't think he was 'out of character' if I forgot to spell it the way he said it. Would the readers think he was? If not, is one then compelled to record the mispronunciation of Scottish peasants or negroes, but not the mispronunciation of American presidents? How come?

This mispronunciation thing has not got a leg to stand on.

I am a stickler for using the idiom of a people, and the form in which they make a sentence. But to write 'y'', 'yi', 'yar', 'ye', 'yous' for 'you' according to location; and 'o' for 'of', and 'bin' for 'been', and 'canna' for 'cannot', is just a lot of tripe. The writer who can't get his effects without that should go back to selling, whatever it was he *was* selling, before he bought a pencil.

If all the readers have wilted by now, give them some ice-cream, and tell them that all is forgiven.

But if a few should yet be 'muttering' just wire me, and I will go to even greater lengths – I've barely got started yet. The above is my answer to all comers on this dialect thing – we may start a fight when the book comes out, which would be good.

Thanks for the promise of the Robert Nathan book. Tell me about him. He and Mussolini and Commander Byrd[1] are my three weaknesses in the male line.

If I were Cleopatra, I'd send an army to collect them for me.

Bitter aloes put on the finger ends prevent hangnails – mittens are also a help.

Yours very devotedly (this includes the readers, God bless 'em[2])
LORNA MOON

---

1. Robert Nathan: a prolific novelist, also published by Bobbs-Merrill in the 1920s; Benito Mussolini: Italian fascist dictator; Commander Byrd: presumably Richard Byrd, who made the first aeroplane flight over the North Pole in 1926 and over the South Pole in 1929.
2. 'The readers' here are members of the publisher's staff, who according to Chambers, 'thought Divot Meg's speech just a little too well spoken to be in character': letter from David Laurance Chambers, 27 August 1928.

LETTERS

Dear Mr Chambers
et moi aussi! How I should like to publish immediately. And if Vance is trying to make Dark Star into an Elsie Book,[1] publish right away is just what we will do. We'll see what he wants. It's just a matter of money with me. You see I counted on the serial money[2] to keep me a year while I wrote another book.

If we publish Dark Star now, I would have to do movie work, perhaps at considerable risk to my health, and I wouldn't get another book written. I'm just in the state of health now that I can go backwards, or forward to health depending on what I do. The serial money would give me peace of mind which is the biggest part in getting me well.

Your suggestion about writing Vance something to his measure would be all right if he would take a short story for the thousand he gave me. But I couldn't face writing a book with that end in view. After all I'm not Hans Anderson. Maybe I can mortgage the old homestead, give Vance a short story for his thousand, and trust to God that the book goes and the movie people want the screen rights. I'll wire you when I see what Vance says about changing the expressions. I want to change the 'cheese' one because I learned that this is a vulgar expression in America among low men. I didn't know this – my virtuous women friends told me! (Isn't that delicious!) But what do you think about 'maidenhead' – frankly I think it is a beautiful word. It is certainly the word Divot Meg would use. I remember as a little girl going into the kitchen where a kitchen lass was serving a shepherd a bowl of brose. He caught her by the hand and said: 'Tell me Bella hae you still got your maidenhead.' 'I have that,' she retorted. 'Eh weel,' he sighed 'Never tell it. Never let the world ken you've been so ill-liked.' They are a lusty people. Words don't frighten them. I shall feel like a fool putting prissy words into Divot Meg's mouth. What about it? Shall I just change the 'cheese' thing and let the rest go?

Do you think maidenhead would wound their tender ears less?

Tell me how much you think such expressions would hurt the sale of the book. God help me, these maiden-ladies will end by convincing me that I have written an obscene book.

I'll wire you what I decide about Vance. There's a reckless streak in my heart which makes me hope that his requests are too ridiculous to grant. Then there will be nothing to do but publish now!

I wish you weren't so far away.
LORNA MOON

1. 'Elsie Book': this appears to be a reference to the 'Elsie Dinsmore' series of sentimental novels, written from the late 1860s by Martha Finley, in which the heroine Elsie struggles through trials, fortified by her religious beliefs.
2. $10,000.

To David Laurance Chambers
5 or 6 January 1929

Dear Laurance Chambers

as I wired you a minute ago I'm trying to get comments for the jacket, I don't know what you will think of this, but anyhow – I like very much the part of the blurb which catalogues the things in it. I mean the part which says: 'Here are so and so a brothel worthy of Hogarth, a Tongueless man etc. – this seems to me good sales talk – it gives the reader images – the things I don't like are dead words like 'strength, delicacy, beauty', they are over-used till they have lost the small savor they had, all books bear them. They convey nothing to the reader.

I don't like the part which says she 'belongs to the Scottish heroines of literature and that Scott, Stevenson, Barrie would have understood her – because they *wouldn't* – (Thank God!) and a comment like that relegates the book to the musty old shelves where women wore rats in their hair and became 'fallen'. Nancy is 1929. Barrie the dear old 'whimsical' bastard wouldn't understand her at all. And besides that any mention of Scotland on the jacket is in my opinion fatal.

If we don't get the comments in time I think the jacket as I edited it is not bad at all. I must confess that it is a formidable task for an author to sit down and tell the world that she has written a swell book – modesty cramps my style.

Now about the chapters – it seems that we are both so amenable! Your argument that the book would look 'heavy' had weight with me. You know this end of the business better than I do, and while I think that good spaces left between each little division is sufficient breaking up, still I don't want to cramp the salesmen's efforts by insisting on this. I see the story as progressing in books, within each book there are thought divisions, but they don't really make chapters as I understand the word. Also I shall always write my books in this peculiar way. I had to get this technic in order to be able to write a novel at all. And then again, open the book, start at the beginning of any division and I bet my boots you will want to go on. This is because a thought pushed, I wrote it as it came, without effort at the old chapter form. But still for all of this, don't be influenced to change your first plan if you think a more usual and recognized method will help the sales. If you add anything to the edited jacket following the line: 'But this is Nancy's story and not to be broken on the wheel of comment' – say something about her being – Oh don't you see that she has all the romance and poetry of bygone heroines, but with it she has the clear thinking bravery of 1929 girlhood. You know, that is what all this is leading us to

– sin will cease to be a nasty baster – there wont be a 'fallen woman' anymore than there are 'fallen men'. It is revolting to me that in a civilized world a woman's virtue rests entirely upon her hymen.

Excuse me I always get worked up over this. Wong[1] is roaming around demanding 'letter come now post, maybe no postman'.

So here goes,

L.

---

1.   Chinese servant who features in a number of letters to Chambers.

LETTERS

To Anne Johnston of Bobbs-Merrill
February 1929

Dear Miss Johnston
The respirator story is funnier in its origin than it is in the book, that is, it was funnier to other people but for *me* it was a painful faux pas of my youth.

My Dad and I were 'very thick' as the Scotch saying is. My mother had the upper hand about bringing up the rest of us, but my Dad got a chance to try all his theories of child raising on me, probably because my mother felt that nothing could make me more unsatisfactory than I was already. Anyway, Dad's sandal theory, his all-clothes-hung-from-the-shoulder theory, and his no-mystery-about-sex theory were all tried out on me. So I got a good start in life with an untrammelled waist-line, nice straight toes, and nice straight ideas on sex (as my Dad fondly believed). He very early read Darwin's *Origin of Species*, Heckel's *Riddle of the Universe*, and Mendel's *Law of Hybrids* to me. The latter he illustrated with a cage full of white rats. And so he was convinced that he had reared a child with complete knowledge of sex and no morbid curiosity about it. It's true that I had no curiosity, morbid or otherwise. You see, the rats being perfect gentlemen never did anything but rub whiskers when I was looking, so this, and Miss Clark's respirator solved the mystery of sex for me perfectly.

Time passed (as the movie subtitles say) and I was fourteen. My mother gave a marriage benefit (called in America a shower) for the organist who was about to be married. I was permitted to help 'pass the buns' (cookies, not donuts). The bride-to-be was radiant in a new silk dress, which excited the envy of one of the women, who said: 'Wait till you have a few bairns hanging onto your tails. You'll no be wearing silken gowns *then*, I'll warrant.' To which the giggling bride-to-be replied: 'Oh but I'm not going to have children.' Whereupon I suspended the bun passing to say gravely: 'Then you must wear a respirator like Miss Clark.'

The silence that followed this is the most vivid recollection of my life. I remember my Dad's face seen across the room – his life's work shot to hell, as it were. He called me out and questioned me: 'What did you mean about the respirator, lassie?' 'So she won't get a germ, Dad.' 'You're never thinking that that's the way to get a baby, are you?' 'Don't be silly, Dad. I've seen the rats doing it. I *know* the man has to have whiskers. Miss Clark is scared to get a baby from the butcher's whiskers. But she needn't be. She isn't fat enough. *I'm* not fat enough even. I've been sniffing at the groom for weeks but nothing's happened yet.'

You may imagine my Dad's terror. He could see me saying to the groom some morning: 'I'd like you to give me a baby this morning, if you're not too busy.'

Yours cordially,
LORNA MOON

LETTERS

To David Laurance Chambers.
Letter begun 29 April 1929, delayed for typing, sent 2 May 1929

Lawrence Dear

This is in answer to your wire of this morning. I remember all about the questionnaire of December. But let me go back to the beginning of this Journal thing and show you how these misunderstandings have come about:

1. During the first week in November 1928 I wrote you a long letter telling you how well I seemed to be, and that I thought writing, far from holding me back, really made me better. I had some extracts typed from my journal to prove it. In this letter I asked you to destroy the journal extracts immediately upon reading them. Miss Johnson answered this letter November tenth telling me you were away.

2. On November twenty-seventh I had a letter from you saying you had just returned and had received my letter of the eighteenth. But you said nothing about having received the earlier letter with the Journal extracts.

3. On December twelfth, 1928, your questionnaire arrived. I did not refer you for further publicity to Journal extracts as your telegram says. What I said was: 'The rest of the story you know from the journal' or 'have from the Journal' I did not at any time say, 'you may quote the exact entries in my journal.'[1] How could I? My journal extracts were by this time in my opinion destroyed according to my request.

I did not refuse you the right to tell the story of the journal, although I felt it to be unwise and said so. But, when I received the typed copy of my Journal extracts with a request that they be used in publicity, I was shocked. I wondered why you had not long ago destroyed them. Then thinking it over, I realized that since the letter came and was answered during your absence you probably never saw it, but saw only the Journal, and that the request in the letter had slipped the memory of Miss Johnson, which is not unnatural.

My answer about it was however most emphatic – too much so to be mistaken. When I wrote to you reasonably later, I showed you how I felt about people who give out extracts from their private journal to show how brave they were, and I told you how I thought the public would feel about it.

I added something about, 'this is not the time, perhaps later' meaning later when I am dead, or later when I am so well and so far removed from this condition, that there will be no question of seeming to ask for sympathy. Will you collect and destroy all copies of this damned thing for me? You see, I was sending them to you as a friend and you were receiving them as a publicity man, that is the rock we were wrecked on. And your angle is quite right, you probably thought I was Elinor Glyn's[2] illegitimate child, *hell* bent on publicity no matter how vulgar.

You may wonder where the difference lies in writing an article for Ray Long[3] admitting that I have T.B. and this other thing. But you will see the difference when you read the article.

Quite apart from making me seem the kind of creature I most loath, printing the extracts is damned unfair to me.

Suppose now, that there was created a beautiful statue, one so arresting that it won people for itself and they hailed the creator as a fine, a masterly sculptor. Some weeks later a newspaper man finds out that the sculptor had only one finger on his right hand. Immediately, the statue becomes 'the statue that was made with one finger.' All the dignity of that artist is gone. His fine piece of work is a freak show. People forget that it has merit or beauty quite apart from the 'one finger' thing. This is what would have happened to Dark Star. Indeed, out here on the coast, where well-meaning but misguided people are at work, Dark Star is 'a book written by a consumptive.'

MAY 2

All the afore written seems sort of insistent after your dear letter of this morning, and for a couple of dish-rags I'd tear it up and throw it away. But since it is written, we would better understand each other if I sent it, so I will.

Well, I rather guessed who made the slip up because a newspaper woman from San Jose who is a friend of Mary Rose[4] wrote me that 'Dark Star is a remarkable book for a sick woman to have written'. Only the fact that she wound up the letter asking me to help her to sell a family heirloom to a movie queen kept me from throwing chairs. But that last touch was too quaint for words. I had to laugh.

But will you connive and gum shoe around and pry Mary Rose loose from the copy of the extracts because she is, I *know*, going to think of me as 'a poor brave girl', no matter what befalls, and I shall have to come East and vamp her beau away from her before she will get over it, and too many beaux is what I'm suffering from now.

Tell me. Is the New Yorker trying to high hat me? I haven't even appeared on their list of books received yet, let alone be reviewed.[5]

LETTERS

The Saturday Review of Literature as you may have noticed made up nobly for their neglect by listing Dark Star first in their editorial in which they say that since they have only their own taste to guide them, and not being publishers have nothing to sell, and not being a Book-of-the-Month-Club with a broad audience to please, they will tell their readers of books which they have enjoyed. But that they will call none 'best'. And if they think a book is the best book of the century they will not call it so. Thereafter they proceed to mention six books which they have enjoyed and which they feel do not receive the acclaim that they deserve. They are in order: Dark Star, Six Mrs. Greens, (oh Lord, I haven't got the clipping) but one was The Further Poems of Emily Dickenson. Only six books were mentioned, and only two were fiction.

The Book of the Month also unlaces its heavy corsets and says a few kind words.

That outfit suffers from a complaint which were you a student of endocrinology I would explain to you.

Oh gosh, I'm tired.

All love,

LORNA

---

1. 'You know the rest of the story from having read the journal', letter to David Laurance Chambers, 24 December 1928.
2. Elinor Glyn: best-selling novelist whose idea of 'it' came to represent sex appeal in Hollywood.
3. Ray Long: editor of *Hearst's International Cosmopolitan*.
4 Mary Rose Himler, Dobbs-Merrill publicist.
5. *Dark Star* was not reviewed by *The New Yorker*.

To David Laurance Chambers
1 July 1929

Dear Laurence:

What could prove my devotion to you more completely than the fact that, on hearing the news of your illness, I proceeded to have haemorrhage upon haemorrhage. Not big but frequent. I'm disgusted, because I hadn't done this for a year and really thought that I was getting out of the woods. If I didn't have Macabre[1] to write I'd take the good old cyanide. I am really quite bored with this disease. I won't be ready for Spring with Macabre, because I can't slash things out, and I haven't really the strength I had last year at this time. Mr Curtis[2] says that if I got it ready by March you could still get it out in the Spring. If so, there is a chance that I can make it if my lungs give me a fair deal.

Right now I can't do anything because I must build up my lost gore and heal my leak a bit. It knocks my trip East, of course, and I had so hoped to see you. Gollancz is coming and wants me to meet him in New York in December, but the chance is slim.[3] My last examination found me not quite as well as two years ago. This doesn't mean that I'm going to check in on you, because I was really getting on fine last September, but started to slip in the winter. I'll pull up again.

My article which is out in September Cosmopolitan is bringing me a flood of letters. If you have any doubts of the interest which a T.B. novel would create they would fade after reading these.

The English criticisms on D.S. have been not at all bad (for *English* criticisms). You know how they are. Do you know a soft-bosomed yearning old bird called George Matthew Adams?[4] He is one of these only-God-can-make-a-tree men, well, the bastard thinks my book is 'a genuine work of art' (accent on the 'ine'). This has taken me down quite a bit. He came out here to see me – God what a bore! I can be Mrs Adams if I like – oh death where is thy sting! He says that Dark Star is: 'sweet clean an wholesome,' and I am ditto. Oh Laurence, shall it be the knife or the briny deep?

Write to me. Comfort me. I walk in a world of nit wits, or rather I lie in it and that is even worse.

You are the morning and the evening star, and things like that, if you know what I mean. And please don't get sick any more.

LORNA

1. *Macabre*: planned book, described in letter to Chambers (7 November 1928) as 'the story of a T.B. sanatorium told by an inmate.'
2. John Jay Curtis, president of Bobbs-Merrill Publishers.
3. The publisher, Victor Gollancz, was coming over from Britain.
4. George Matthew Adams: American writer of self-help books, including *You Can* (1913) and *Take It* (1917).

LORNA MOON'S
PUBLISHED WORK

NOVEL

Dark Star (Bobbs-Merrill Co., Indianapolis, 1929; Victor Gollancz,
London, 1929)
Dark Star, with an Introduction by David Toulmin (Gourdas House
Publishers, Aberdeen, 1980)

STORIES

'Silk Both Sides', *Century Magazine*, 103, December 1921, pp. 191–5
'Feckless Maggie Ann', *Century Magazine*, 103, April 1922,
pp. 877–86
'The Sinning of Jessie MacLean', *Century Magazine*, 104, July 1922,
pp. 385–93
'The Corp'', *Century Magazine*, 105, November 1922, pp. 91–7
'The Tattie Doolie', *Century Magazine*, 107, January 1924, pp. 448–61
'Wantin' a Hand', *Century Magazine*, 109, November 1924, pp. 15–18
'The Courtin' of Sally Ann', *Woman's Home Companion*, 52, October
1925, pp. 27–8
'The Funeral of Jimmy McBride', *Century Magazine*, 112, September
1926, pp. 526–31
Doorways in Drumorty (Bobbs-Merrill Co., Indianapolis, 1925). Collects
six stories listed above except 'Feckless Maggie Ann' and 'The Funeral
of Jimmy McBride'. Two stories added (the latter as 'The Funeral'),
to the British edition (Jonathan Cape, London, 1926)
Doorways in Drumorty, with an Introduction by David Toulmin
(Gourdas House Publishers, Aberdeen, 1981)
'The Wedding of the Wheat', *Hearst's International Cosmopolitan*,
February 1932, pp. 74–6, 79–80
Too Gay! [& Lipstick Lady] undated 32-page booklet published as a 6-
penny 'novel' (Clifford Lewis, Newcastle-under-Lyme, 1945)

POETRY

'Broken', *Woman's Home Companion*, 51, July 1924, p. 24

ARTICLES

'Flat on My Back', *Hearst's International Cosmopolitan*, September 1929, pp. 92–3, 135 (published in Britain in *Nash's Magazine*, 1929, as 'How It Feels to Be an Invalid')

FILMOGRAPHY

The Affairs of Anatol, dir. Cecil B. DeMille (Famous Players Lasky Paramount, 1921)
Don't Tell Everything, dir. Sam Wood (Famous Players Lasky Paramount, 1921)
Too Much Wife, dir. Thomas N. Heffron (Realert Paramount, 1922)
Her Husband's Trademark, dir. Sam Wood (Famous Players Lasky Paramount, 1922)
Upstage, dir. Monta Bell (MGM, 1926)
Women Love Diamonds, dir. Edmund Goulding (MGM, 1927)
Mr. Wu, dir. William Nigh (MGM, 1927)
After Midnight, dir. Monta Bell (MGM, 1927)
Love, dir. Edmund Goulding (MGM, 1927)
Min and Bill, dir. George Hill (MGM, 1930)

FURTHER READING

Anon., 'Lorna Moon', *Aberdeen Leopard Magazine* (February 1981), p. 15.

Anderson, C. and Christianson, A. (eds.), *Scottish Women's Fiction 1920s to 1960s: Journeys Into Being* (Tuckwell Press, East Linton, 2000).

Edwards, A., *The DeMilles: An American Family* (Collins, London, 1988).

Gifford, D. and McMillan, D., *A History of Scottish Women's Writing* (Edinburgh University Press, Edinburgh, 1997).

Hamilton, S. 'The Missing Years of the Exile of Drumorty', *Aberdeen Evening Express* (5 October, 1981).

Higham, C., *Cecil B. DeMille* (W.H. Allen, London & New York, 1974).

Marion, F., *Off With Their Heads! A Serio-Comic Tale of Hollywood* (The Macmillan Company, New York, 1972).

de Mille, Richard, *My Secret Mother: Lorna Moon* (Farrar, Straus and Giroux, New York, 1998).

Murray, I. (ed.), *Scottish Writers Talking* (Tuckwell Press, East Linton, 1995).

Norquay, G., 'Dark Star over Drumorty: The Writing of Lorna Moon', in Schwend, J. and Drescher, H.W. (ed.), *Studies in Scottish Fiction: Twentieth Century*, Scottish Studies 10 (Peter Lang, Frankfurt am Main, 1990), pp. 117–31.

Norquay, G., 'Wantin' Bodies: Female Sexuality and the Grotesque in the Fiction of Lorna Moon and Jessie Kesson', in Hagemann, S. (ed.), *Terranglian Territories: Proceedings of the Seventh International Conference of Region and Nation* (Peter Lang, Frankfurt am Main, 2000), pp. 349–59.

Riddoch, L., 'Lost-lost Moon', *Aberdeen Leopard Magazine* (May 1992), p. 12.

Shepherd, G., 'The Kailyard', Gifford, D. (ed.), in *History of Scottish Literature Vol. 3 The Nineteenth Century* (Aberdeen University Press, Aberdeen, 1988), pp. 309–18.

Toulmin, D., 'Moondust on Mormond Hill', *Aberdeen Leopard Magazine* (November 1980), pp. 23–4.
Waton, R., *The Literature of Scotland* (Macmillan, London, 1984).
Webster, J., *Grains of Truth* (B&W Publishing, Edinburgh, 1994).